Feasts for Twelve (or More)

Paul Rubinstein

FEASTS FOR TWELVE (OR MORE)

Macmillan Publishing Co., Inc.
NEW YORK

Macmillan Publishing Co., Inc.
866 Third Avenue, New York, N.Y. 10022
Collier-Macmillan Canada Ltd.
First Printing 1975
Printed in the United States of America

Library of Congress Cataloging in Publication Data

Rubinstein, Paul.
    Feasts for twelve (or more)

    Includes index.
    1. Cookery. I. Title.
TX820.R83   641.5'6   74-30482
ISBN 0-02-605790-5

For Jason and Kim—
may they always eat well.

1866852

Contents

Introduction

As the title indicates, this book is expressly intended to help the person who has twelve or more people to feed, either as an everyday occurrence or just when company is invited.

Standard cookbooks, with very few exceptions, contain recipes for four or six people. The exceptions tend to be recipes for fewer people rather than for more. This book is designed to save you time and avoid disasters of faulty measurement by putting between two covers a full selection of recipes in large quantity. When selecting your menu, it is most important that you carefully schedule your use of the oven and stove top. If the oven will be occupied by a large roast, you cannot also count on it to be available for other baking or roasting at the same time. On the stove top, you cannot expect to use two very large pots on adjoining burners—they won't fit.

Although the chances are that a household with a large family already has the necessary equipment, I feel that it is important to enumerate the "indispensables" for large-quantity cooking for the kitchen which only occasionally serves twelve or more at one time. You definitely do *not* need to have every pot and pan in giant restaurant size.

You will find following a list of items which you should try to own in the largest sizes consistent with the size of your oven and the space above your burners. It is particularly important to know the inside dimensions of your oven before buying any of the large pots or pans to be used in it.

I once made the mistake of buying a large lobster and clam steamer without measuring the space between the burners on my stove and the bottom of the overhanging upper oven. Result: I couldn't use the steamer on the top of the stove and was forced to buy an electric hotplate to use it separately.

Remember that such things as a large griddle or a fish poacher can be placed across two burners easily. I don't advise running out and getting this whole list at once. But when you choose a recipe that requires one of the pieces of equipment, then get a good one which is large enough and will last a long time. Eventually you will build up a collection that will meet your every large-quantity cooking need.

LARGE-SIZE EQUIPMENT

Tea kettle (6 qt.)
Roasting pan (14 × 18 inch)
Broiling pan (14 × 18 inch)
Stockpots (20 qt.: 5 gal. and 12 qt.: 3 gal.)
Double boiler (4 qt.)
Frying pan or skillet (12–14 inch)
Paella pan (16 inch)
Deep fryer (6 qt.)
Flat griddle (cast aluminum) (10 × 20 inch)
Fish poacher (24 inch)
Lobster and clam steamer (5 gal.)
Vegetable steamer (4 qt.)
Casseroles (heatproof glass, 4–6 qt.)
Assorted cooking and baking dishes (heatproof glass)
Carving board with well (24 inch)
Jelly roll pan (18 × 12 × 1 inch)
Cookie sheets (heavy-gauge aluminum, 18 × 14 inch)
Salad bowl (16 inch)
Colander (16 inch)
Dutch oven (8 qt.: 2 gal.)
Blender (with 1½ qt. jar)
Long-handled wooden spoons (12–16 inch)
Four-cup measure
Assorted strainers
Graters
Saucepans
Dessert molds

Coffee maker (32-cup electric, with spigot)
Assorted mixing bowls

If you have a standard-size refrigerator, you must learn some of the techniques for getting maximum usage of the space. For refrigerators with adjustable shelves, it is wise to buy from the manufacturer or dealer two or three extra shelves. These can be kept in storage, but when you have a dozen or more gelatins to cool, you can add to the capacity of the box by simply adding a shelf or two. This applies as well to platters of hors d'oeuvre, salads, and many other foods. You can also get temporary extra space in the refrigerator by pulling out the vegetable drawer and its partition, which should make possible enough space for a larger pot or container to be refrigerated.

Remember, too, that your freezer or freezing compartment can be emptied of its ice-cube trays and racks. The cubes can be stored in an insulated ice bucket while you are using the freezer space for a dessert or frozen food prepared in advance.

When it comes to buying food in large quantities, substantial savings are possible. Many cities have a wholesale market area where the prices are lower for bulk buying. In the country you can often go right to the source. It is well worth your while to explore this avenue. The greatest savings are probably available to you if you are willing to learn to cut large pieces of meat into their components for the kitchen. There is nothing terribly mysterious about how a butcher separates steaks, chops, loin roasts, rib roasts, etc., from a side of meat. Either get a detailed chart showing the cuts of beef, lamb, veal and pork; or just go spy on the local butcher and learn by observation.

Vegetables and fruits purchased by the basket, whole large fish, sacks of flour and sugar, sides of bacon, all these and more can yield big savings and make an occasional major shopping expedition pay off.

Finally, if this idea frightens you, remember you can always enlist a friend or two to go along and help. Afterwards divide up the loot when you get home.

The large-quantity savings principle applies to liquids as well as solids. You can buy wine, olive oil, vinegar, juices, milk and other beverages by the gallon without too much trouble. Cheese is frequently cheaper if bought by the "wheel" or unopened large box, and this is very easy food to divide up with your friends later. Chocolate, yeast and other baking ingredients can be found at bakery supply houses at much lower unit cost than at the grocery.

The important thing is to be inquisitive and not afraid to go across town into unfamiliar territory which could be teeming with bargains.

Once you are equipped and have found your local sources of bulk buying food, the remaining consideration is the serving of large numbers of people. Here I don't have any strong recommendations because of the enormous variety of possibilities. The formality, or lack of it, in serving will often determine what is required.

In general, the use of large serving platters which are a nuisance to carry and to wash can be avoided by filling each individual plate in the kitchen and serving it. Another approach is to collect large cooking utensils in decorative enamelware which can be brought to the dining room. These are not unattractive, and with these one is not required to transfer food from its cooking vessel to a serving dish. Finally, you can double your supply of standard-size serving dishes and fill two platters for each course to be served at the table.

The main thing, in my opinion, is the food and not the details of the service. If you plan carefully and pay close attention to each phase of preparation, you will be rewarded by the empty plates and happy countenances of those assembled.

Paul Rubinstein

Feasts for Twelve (or More)

1

Appetizers

Bacon-Wrapped Bread Sticks, Curry Dip

These hors d'oeuvre are particularly good as an accompaniment to the cocktail hour. Although I use the number 24 (two per person for twelve), you can obviously increase or decrease the number quite easily. The sticks can be prepared in advance, but for the best results they should be warmed up in the oven just before serving. Once you serve them I think you will find that the guests don't leave them lying around to get cold.

24 dry, packaged, 6-inch bread sticks
24 thin slices of hickory-smoked bacon
 2 cups mayonnaise
 2 tbsp. curry powder
 1 tbsp. Worcestershire sauce
 1 tsp. seasoned salt
 2 tsp. lemon juice

1. Preheat oven to 325°.
2. Wrap each bread stick in a spiral fashion with 1 slice of bacon, so that all except about 1 inch of the stick at one end is covered. There is no need to secure these with food picks because the bacon will stiffen in the cooking and stay on the stick by itself.

3. Arrange the wrapped bread sticks on the rack of a broiling pan. It is important to use a rack so that excess fat drips away.

4. Place the pan in the preheated oven and bake for about 20 minutes, or until the bacon is browned, but not burned.

5. If you plan to serve the sticks later, remove from oven and set aside. Just before serving, put the pan under the broiler and broil the sticks for about 60 seconds on each side, turning once. Then remove to platter and serve immediately.

6. Serve the dip in a bowl with the bread sticks. To prepare, mix together the mayonnaise, curry powder, Worcestershire sauce, salt and lemon juice. No implements are necessary because the exposed inch of each bread stick can be picked up with the fingers.

Cheddar Cheese Balls

This recipe will make about 100 cheese balls, each a little less than 1 inch in diameter.

⅜ *lb. butter (1½ sticks)*
2 *cups grated sharp Cheddar cheese (1 to 1½ lbs. cheese)*
3 *cups all-purpose flour*
2 *tsp. salt*
1 *tsp. freshly ground black pepper*
1 *tbsp. Worcestershire sauce*
1 *cup ground cornmeal*

1. Allow the butter to soften at room temperature. Using an electric mixer (or by hand with a wooden spoon) blend the cheese and butter together thoroughly.

2. While continuing to run the mixer, add the flour, a little at a time, until all the flour is blended into the mixture and it becomes quite stiff. Add the salt, pepper and Worcestershire sauce and mix in well.

3. Set up an "assembly line" for making the cheese balls.

First the bowl of cheese mixture, then a container such as a pie plate or dish containing the loose cornmeal, and finally jelly roll pans or cookie sheets, lightly buttered. Use a melon-ball cutter or a tablespoon measure to form the cheese balls. Spoon out an amount of the cheese mixture which will yield a ¾-inch ball, roll it between your palms quickly, roll it in the cornmeal, then place it on the cookie sheet or jelly roll pan. Continue this process until all the cheese balls are made.

4. Refrigerate the cheese balls for several hours until well chilled.

5. Before serving, preheat oven to 400°. Bake in the preheated oven for 10 minutes.

6. Serve piping hot with a food pick stuck in each ball.

Optional: Serve with a mustard or tomato-ketchup dip if you like.

Salami and Cream Cheese Rolls

There is an almost unlimited variety of salami to suit every taste. My particular favorite is the Genoa style, which is about 3 inches in diameter, with the meat a rich wine red in color mottled with little circles of white fat and an occasional peppercorn. For this recipe you can use almost any kind of salami, but you should avoid the very hard-textured ones, and also avoid those which are less than 2½ inches in diameter because they will be hard to roll. I recommend letting the butcher do the slicing on his machine.

8-inch length of salami, sliced very thin (less than
⅛-inch-thick slices)
2 *lbs. cream cheese*
½ *cup chopped fresh or frozen chives*
2 *tbsp. Worcestershire sauce*
2 *tsp. seasoned salt*
1 *tsp. freshly ground white pepper, or 6 drops of Tabasco*

(cont'd)

2 tbsp. lemon juice
½ cup sour cream
60 or 70 cocktail picks

1. Discard any little strings of outer skin that may be left clinging to the slices of salami.

2. Using either a potato masher or an electric mixer, cream together the cream cheese, chives, Worcestershire sauce, salt, pepper, lemon juice and sour cream.

3. To assemble the hors d'oeuvre, spoon 1 tablespoon of the cream cheese mixture onto each slice of salami, roll it into cylindrical or cornucopia shape, and fasten by transfixing with a cocktail pick. Set on serving platter.

4. This recipe should yield 60 to 70 pieces. Cover the filled platter with plastic film, tucked in around the edges, and refrigerate until shortly before serving.

Smoked Salmon Rolls

---

1 lb. cream cheese, softened
½ cup capers
1 tsp. lemon juice
1 lb. thin slices of smoked Nova Scotia or Scotch salmon
fresh black pepper in a pepper mill

1. Combine the cream cheese, capers and lemon juice in a mixing bowl and mix well.

2. Lay out the slices of salmon on a cutting board or wooden surface. Sprinkle them with a little pepper from the mill.

3. Using a flat spreader, spread the cream cheese mixture evenly over the slices of salmon.

4. Roll up each slice of salmon tightly, fix with a food pick if necessary, and place the rolls on a plate. Refrigerate them.

5. After 2 or 3 hours, when the salmon rolls are well chilled,

or just an hour or so before serving, remove them from the refrigerator.

6. Using a very sharp knife, slice the salmon rolls into ¼-inch round slices. Arrange on a platter and serve, providing food picks for easier handling.

Alternative: You can prepare the right number of toast squares or rounds and place 1 little slice of salmon roll on each to make canapés. Yield is about 80 pieces.

Chopped Herring Garnished with Hard-Cooked Egg Slices

There is an enormous variety of herrings and they are a favorite food of all the countries touching the North Sea and Atlantic habitats of the fish. For this recipe, you must begin with herring fillets from the delicatessen counter at the market. They are called Schmaltz Herring, and they have been marinated and cooked and are ready to eat. The Schmaltz is the gray-colored herring which is frequently found for sale in jars, either with or without sour cream and onions. If you have no delicatessen-style shopping facilities available, you will have to settle for the bottled herring, which is quite good, although due to some preservatives used in the bottling process, not quite as good as the fresher variety. This recipe is intended to be used as a cracker spread. Serve in a bowl with spreaders and crackers on the side, or as prespread canapés.

2 lbs. Schmaltz herring fillets
1 cup finely chopped onion
3 tbsp. white vinegar
2 tsp. freshly ground white pepper
4 hard-cooked eggs

1. Pass the herring fillets through the fine blade of a meat grinder into a mixing bowl.

2. Using a wooden spoon, blend in thoroughly the chopped onion, vinegar and pepper.

3. Peel the hard-cooked eggs and cut into thin round slices.

4. Arrange the mixture in a serving bowl, garnish with egg slices and serve with saltine crackers.

Optional: If you decide to serve prespread canapés, you may want to cook more eggs and serve 1 egg slice on each canapé.

Caviar Dip

2 *cups sour cream*
2 *tbsp. minced onion*
1 *tsp. lemon juice*
4 *oz. caviar, red or black*

1. Combine first three ingredients well.
2. Fold in the caviar gently, trying not to break the eggs.
3. Serve with rye toast rounds for the cocktail hour.

Onion Dip

2 *cups sour cream*
½ *cup finely minced onion*
1 *tbsp. chopped fresh parsley*
1 *tbsp. chopped fresh or frozen chives*
½ *tsp. seasoned salt*
¼ *tsp. freshly ground white pepper*
1 *pinch of cayenne pepper*

1. Combine all ingredients and mix well.
2. Serve with raw vegetable dippers for the cocktail hour.

Clam Dip

4 cups drained canned minced clams
12 oz. cream cheese
½ cup sour cream
3 tbsp. Worcestershire sauce
2 tbsp. lemon juice
2 tsp. seasoned salt
1 tbsp. Maggi liquid seasoning
1 tsp. freshly ground white pepper

1. Combine all the ingredients in a mixing bowl and mix thoroughly. Make sure the clams are well drained to avoid making the dip too liquid.

2. Serve in a decorative bowl surrounded by crackers, chips or raw vegetables such as carrot sticks and cauliflower florets. This dip goes particularly well with toasted corn chips or taco chips. For the cocktail hour.

Stuffed Celery

2 heads of celery
8 oz. cream cheese
4 oz. Danish Blue cheese or Roquefort cheese
¼ lb. butter (1 stick), softened
1 tbsp. chopped fresh dill
½ tsp. salt
paprika (for decoration)

1. Separate the celery ribs from the heads, wash and trim off leaves. Cut the ribs into 2-inch lengths. Put the celery pieces in cold water in a bowl with a few ice cubes and refrigerate until shortly before serving time.

2. Cream the remaining ingredients except paprika together thoroughly, making sure that the blue cheese is well distributed.

3. Drain the celery pieces on a paper towel.

4. Using either a spreader or a pastry bag, fill the cavities of the celery pieces with the mixture and arrange on a platter. Sprinkle the tops with a little paprika and serve.

Artichoke Bottoms Stuffed with Sour Cream and Red Caviar

This recipe is a bit time-consuming and I advise doing it a day in advance if you can. The long part is removing the bits of artichoke meat from the leaves to add to the stuffing before discarding the leaves. If you pass up this thrifty gesture and use only the bottoms of the artichokes you can do the whole thing much faster.

12 *small to medium-size fresh artichokes*
2 *garlic cloves, peeled and chopped*
¼ *cup olive oil*
1 *bay leaf*
1 *tsp. cracked black pepper*
3 *cups sour cream*
8 *oz. red caviar (substitute black beluga caviar if you're rich)*
1 *tbsp. lemon juice*
1 *tsp. seasoned salt*
½ *tsp. freshly ground white pepper*
1 *tbsp. Worcestershire sauce*

1. Cut off the stems of the artichokes (if necessary) so that the vegetables will stand up straight on flat bottoms. Be careful not to cut away any of the bottom itself. Trim the sharp points off the ends of the leaves with shears.

2. Use a large deep pot with a cover; pour water into it to such a depth that the level of liquid just touches the bottom of a steamer platform which will be inserted in the water. (*Note:* the steamer platform is a perforated metal platform which stands on 3 or 4 adjustable legs. The edges of the platform are made of folding leaves which expand or contract to fit the size of various pots.)

3. Add the chopped garlic, olive oil, bay leaf and black pepper to the water. Insert the steamer platform, and arrange the artichokes on the platform. If your pot is not large enough to do all twelve at once, do this operation in two shifts, adding a little water before the second shift if too much has boiled away.

4. Bring the water to a boil and cover the pot. Time 20 minutes of steaming time. After 20 minutes, reach in with tongs and pull one leaf from an artichoke. If it comes off with a gentle pull, the artichokes are done. If it resists enough so that you are lifting the artichoke off the platform without separating the leaf, allow 5 more minutes of cooking time and try again. When done, remove the artichokes from the pot with tongs and set them out on a counter to cool.

5. While the artichokes are cooling, mix the sour cream, red caviar, lemon juice, seasoned salt, white pepper and Worcestershire sauce in a mixing bowl.

6. Pull out all the leaves from the cooled artichokes; with a small knife carefully remove the choke from the bottoms. Here is the point where, if you are thrifty, you can remove, with a knife, the bits of artichoke meat clinging to the leaves, and add the bits to the sour cream mixture. If you don't plan to do this, discard the leaves.

7. Fill each artichoke bottom with enough of the sour cream mixture so that the filling forms a mound. Arrange the

artichokes on a serving platter and refrigerate until serving time.

8. Serve the artichokes on a lettuce leaf on individual plates as a first course.

Marinated Mushrooms

2 *cups olive oil*
1½ *cups strained fresh lemon juice*
1 *bay leaf*
1 *tbsp. black peppercorns*
1 *large celery rib, sliced*
2 *tbsp. salt*
1 *tsp. dried thyme*
1 *tsp. ground coriander*
½ *cup white vinegar*
1 *large onion, peeled and sliced very thin*
6 *quarts water*
2 *lbs. medium-size to small fresh mushrooms*
(50 to 70 pieces)

1. Into a large stockpot put all the ingredients listed except the mushrooms themselves.

2. With a damp cloth, carefully clean the mushrooms, one by one, removing bits of dirt or discoloration. Be careful not to separate the stems from the caps, but if it happens by accident, do not discard the stems. (I simply feel they are more attractive whole.)

3. Put all the mushrooms into the liquid, and bring to a boil. Stand by with a timer when the boil is near. When the liquid boils, time for 10 minutes.

4. While the mushrooms are boiling, prepare a large earthenware or pottery crock or bowl. Pour the hot mixture and mushrooms into this crock when the 10 minutes are up.

5. Allow the mushrooms to cool at room temperature for

about 3 hours, then refrigerate for another hour or two before serving.

6. To serve, arrange the mushrooms on a platter with a cocktail pick stuck in each one. Or serve them in small bowls, four or five per person, with a little of the sliced onion and some of the liquid, as a first course at the table.

Cold Stuffed Mushrooms

48 medium-size fresh mushrooms, about 2 lbs.
1 tbsp. olive oil
3 tbsp. butter
½ cup chopped shallots
1½ lbs. fresh chicken livers
½ cup heavy cream
1 tsp. salt
3 hard-cooked eggs, peeled and chopped fine
¼ cup sherry
¼ lb. butter (1 stick), softened

1. Wash the mushrooms with damp paper towels. Remove the stems, and set the caps aside.

2. Chop the stems fine and sauté them gently in a heavy skillet in the oil and 3 tablespoons butter along with the chopped shallots until the shallots are transparent but not browned. Remove the shallots and chopped mushroom stems from the pan with a slotted spoon and reserve.

3. In the same butter, sauté the chicken livers until they are browned on all sides but still faintly pink in the center. Test by cutting one through.

4. Pass the cooked chicken livers through the finest blade of a meat grinder or through a food mill.

5. Combine the chicken livers, shallots, chopped stems, heavy cream, salt, chopped eggs, sherry and softened butter in a

bowl and mix well. Run this mixture through a blender. This may take several shifts; take care not to overfill the blender jar. Gather the blended liver mixture in one bowl and chill until the consistency is fairly stiff (2 or 3 hours minimum).

6. To assemble, stuff the mushroom caps with the liver mixture, arrange on a platter, and keep refrigerated until shortly before serving.

Alternative: Use Onion Dip (p. 6) as a filling for the mushroom caps.

Hot Stuffed Mushrooms

  6 *tbsp. butter*
  2 *tbsp. olive oil*
 ½ *cup dry white wine*
  1 *tsp. salt*
  1 *tsp. freshly ground black pepper*
48 *medium-size fresh mushrooms, about 2 lbs.*
  1 *lb. cream cheese*
  2 *cups grated Parmesan cheese*
  1 *cup finely chopped onions*
  1 *tsp. seasoned salt*

1. Melt the butter over low heat in a large saucepan which will hold all the mushroom caps. Add the olive oil, wine, salt and pepper.

2. Clean the mushrooms; remove the stems and reserve them for another use. Place the mushroom caps in the pan with the liquid from step 1.

3. Cover the pan and cook over medium heat for 15 minutes, turning the mushrooms several times so that they are all coated with the cooking liquid.

4. When done remove from heat, remove the mushrooms and set them on paper towels to drain.

5. In a mixing bowl cream together the cream cheese, Parmesan, chopped onions and seasoned salt until well blended.

6. Turn on broiler.

7. Stuff each mushroom cap with a spoonful of the cheese and onion mixture.

8. Arrange the stuffed mushrooms in a broiling pan, set under broiler at the maximum possible distance from the heat. Broil until the top of the cheese stuffing is just beginning to brown. Serve hot.

Tomatoes Stuffed with Tuna

---

   12 *medium-size tomatoes*
    3 *tbsp. red-wine vinegar*
 1½ *tsp. salt*
   ¾ *tsp. freshly ground black pepper*
    2 *cans (8 oz. each) tuna packed in oil, or one 16-oz. can*
   ½ *cup mayonnaise*
   ¼ *lb. butter (1 stick), softened*
    2 *tsp. lemon juice*
    3 *hard-cooked eggs*

1. Using a serrated tomato knife, cut about one third off the tops of the tomatoes. Scoop out the insides with a spoon, leaving a fairly firm shell. Season the insides of the shells with a mixture of the vinegar, 1 teaspoon of the salt and ½ teaspoon of the pepper; let stand while you prepare the filling.

2. In a mixing bowl blend together the tuna, with the oil from the cans, the mayonnaise, butter, lemon juice and remaining salt and pepper. Make sure this filling is well mixed.

3. Peel the eggs and push them through a medium-coarse sieve with a wooden spoon.

4. Drain the vinegar seasoning out of the tomato shells, then stuff them with the tuna filling.

5. Sprinkle the tops with the sieved eggs and serve chilled.

Cold Shrimps with Sour Cream and Horseradish Dip

For this recipe I recommend fresh shrimps which have not been cooked. Most stores that sell cooked shrimps charge an excessive price just for having cleaned and cooked them. Avoid this by doing it yourself. For appetizers or hors d'oeuvre portions I am using 3 pounds, which should yield about 20 shrimps to the pound, or 60 altogether. This provides 5 shrimps per person for 12 people. You can increase the proportions if you wish.

FOR THE SHRIMPS:

3 lbs. medium-size fresh shrimps
1 large stalk of fresh dill
1 lemon, sliced
1 tbsp. salt
1 tbsp. cracked pepper
1 tbsp. dried onion chips or flakes
1 tbsp. dried parsley flakes, or 2 tbsp. chopped fresh parsley

1. Peel and devein the shrimps, leaving in place the last section of shell at the tail, then wash the peeled shrimps thoroughly under cold running water. It is best to wash each shrimp separately.

2. Using a large stockpot, bring 6 quarts of water to a boil. Just as the water is starting to boil, add the dill stalk, sliced lemon, salt, pepper, onion chips and parsley flakes.

3. As the water comes to a rolling boil, quickly slip the cleaned shrimps into it, being careful not to splash boiling water on yourself. Tongs or a slotted spoon are recommended.

4. Stand by with your kitchen timer at the ready. When the water comes back to a boil after adding the shrimps, set the timer for 5 minutes.

5. After 5 minutes, turn off heat and immediately drain the shrimps in a colander. Refrigerate them until shortly before serving time.

1 *quart sour cream*
2 *tsp. seasoned salt*
1 *tbsp. lemon juice*
4 *tbsp. freshly grated horseradish root, or 6 tbsp. bottled white horseradish drained of excess liquid*

1. Combine all the ingredients in a bowl and mix well.
2. Transfer to serving bowl or bowls and serve as a dip with the shrimps. You can stick a food pick into each shrimp to facilitate dipping, or simply arrange them, with the tail sections up, on a platter around a bowl of dip.

Grilled Shrimps with Garlic Butter Sauce

The best and easiest way to prepare this appetizer is to use an outdoor-type charcoal grill. If this facility is available to you, you can grill the shrimps and get them served almost as fast as you can lay them down on the grill, turn them once and pick them up again. If, however, you must cope with indoor cooking in a normal kitchen, then you need a special piece of equipment which has many uses and is well worth the investment. This piece of equipment is a cast-iron griddle with raised ridges and a gutter running all around the edges, which is large enough to fit over two burners on a normal stove. I cannot name several manufacturers of this item, but mine is made by Le Creuset, a well-known French manufacturer of all kinds of kitchenware, including the familiar bright-orange enameled cast-iron pots and pans. At this writing, the grill costs under twenty dollars. Besides using the grill in this recipe, it can be used for grilling all meats (steaks, chops, hamburgers, etc.), fish and shellfish. The big advantage is that the heat comes from below, and the fat drips down between the ridges, into the gutter, and into a corner well which can be drained during the cooking with an ordinary basting bulb.

¾ lb. butter (3 sticks)
4 garlic cloves, peeled and crushed
2 tsp. seasoned salt
3 lbs. medium-size fresh shrimps (about 60 pieces) (the same weight of jumbo-size shrimps will yield about 50 pieces)
fresh black pepper in a pepper mill

1. Melt the butter in a saucepan over medium-low heat. Do not allow the butter to turn brown. When it is melted, add the crushed garlic and the seasoned salt, and keep warm over very low heat while you are preparing the shrimps. The purpose of this is to flavor the butter with the taste of the garlic.

2. Peel and devein the shrimps and wash under cold running water, then dry them on paper towels.

3. Heat the grill. If you are using charcoal, make sure the coals have burned out and that you have red glowing coals covered with white ash. Brush the grill with a little olive oil. For the indoor grill, heat it until a drop of water sizzles immediately on contact.

4. Transfer the hot garlic butter to a large bowl or shallow dish. Put all of the shrimps into the butter and pat them down so that they are all covered.

5. Put a large serving platter into the oven and set the heat at 200°, or "keep warm" temperature.

6. With long tongs, quickly place the shrimps on the grill. As soon as the grill is filled, grind a little pepper from the mill over the shrimps, then turn over the first shrimp placed, then continue turning in the same order until they are all turned. Sprinkle with pepper again, then starting with the first shrimp, remove the shrimp to the hot platter.

7. When all the shrimps are cooked, strain the remaining butter from the bowl through a piece of cheesecloth, reheat for a minute or two, and serve as a sauce for dipping. Provide cocktail picks or small forks with the platter of shrimps.

Lobster Cocktail

This recipe will be greeted by your guests with great enthusiasm, but perhaps your budget will be a little cooler about it. If lobster is too expensive or unavailable, you can substitute equivalent amounts of cooked shrimps, crab meat, cooked scallops, abalone meat or a mixture of two or three of the alternates. The most important element is freshness of the seafood, and it is better to offer something freshly prepared than a superior category from a can.

    3 live Maine lobsters, 1¾ to 2 lbs. each
1½ cups mayonnaise
    2 tbsp. grated fresh horseradish
    ½ cup tomato ketchup
    1 tsp. dry mustard
    1 tsp. freshly ground white pepper
    1 tsp. dried tarragon
    1 tbsp. sherry
    1 small head of iceberg lettuce
    3 tomatoes, cut into 8 wedges each, for a total of 24 wedges
    1 green pepper, cored, seeded and cut into julienne

1. Steam the lobsters according to the instructions for Steamed Live Lobsters on page 117 in the chapter on fish and seafood.

2. Refrigerate the cooked lobsters and allow them to chill before cutting them open.

3. In a mixing bowl, combine the mayonnaise, horseradish, ketchup, mustard, pepper, tarragon and sherry.

4. Split the chilled, cooked lobsters into halves with a large chef's knife or cleaver. Remove the tail meat carefully, and take out the veins. Cut the 6 tail halves again into halves and set them aside. Remove all the remaining meat from the claws and other sections and cut this into chunks. Divide the sauce into halves,

and add the chunks of meat to one half.

5. Wash the lettuce and place 1 or 2 leaves into each of 12 cocktail glasses or bowls. Arrange 2 tomato wedges in each glass.

6. Divide the chunks of lobster in the sauce equally among the 12 glasses. Add 1 large piece of the tail meat to each glass. Pour remaining sauce over the large pieces, and finally sprinkle each cocktail with some of the green pepper. The cocktails should be kept cold until serving time.

Crab Legs with Mustard Sauce

The ideal type of crab to use for this recipe is the Alaskan Snow Crab, whose legs or claws are about 2 inches in length. The legs can be cracked open so that most of the meat is exposed, and the leg can be handled by the extremity of the claw with the fingers. Lacking these, you can use Dungeness crab from the Pacific coast, stone crab from Florida or Alaskan King crab, although the latter's pieces tend to be larger and the meat adheres more tightly to the interior of the shell. In any case, this is a very attractive appetizer requiring very little cooking but much care in arranging for service.

48 crab legs, cooked
3 cups mayonnaise
1 cup Dijon mustard
4 lemons, cut into wedges

1. With sharp poultry shears or kitchen scissors, cut away enough shell from each crab leg so that most of the meat is exposed, but so there is enough shell left so that the leg can be picked up easily with the fingers.

2. Mix the mayonnaise and the mustard well and transfer to a serving bowl.

3. Prepare a large round platter with a bed of crushed ice.

Place the bowl of mustard sauce in the center and surround it with crab legs interspersed with lemon wedges. You might want to provide some lobster picks or small forks for those who need them.

Chinese Barbecued Spareribs

If you like dining in Chinese restaurants you have probably wondered how they manage to make spareribs taste so good. There is no deep mystery about it. If you follow a series of important steps, the spareribs are unlikely to disappoint you. The one rule is not to try to make this recipe in a hurry.

FOR THE MARINADE:

2 *garlic cloves*
2 *cups soy sauce (I recommend* Japanese *soy sauce because it is less salty than the Chinese)*
½ *cup sweet sherry or Madeira wine*
2 *tbsp. sugar*
2 *tbsp. honey*

Optional: 2 tbsp. hoisin sauce (this is a standard Chinese condiment available where Chinese products are sold)

1. Peel the garlic cloves and crush through a press.
2. Combine with all the remaining ingredients and mix well.
3. Pour half the marinade into each of 2 shallow roasting pans or large casseroles which will accommodate the spareribs.

FOR THE SPARERIBS:

2 *racks of spareribs, about 3 lbs. each*

1. With a small sharp knife trim any excess fat and gristle from the ribs. Cut between the ribs, about three quarters of the way through.
2. Place each rack in one of the pans containing the marinade and baste well, especially between the ribs.

3. Allow the ribs to marinate for about 3 hours, turning them over once every 30 minutes or so, and basting occasionally.
4. During the last 30 minutes of marinating, preheat the oven to 350°.
5. Remove the ribs from the marinade but do not discard the liquid—it will be used for basting.
6. Place each rack of ribs on a metal rack in a roasting pan containing about 1 inch of water, and put in preheated oven. Roast for 1½ hours, basting with the marinade, and turning the ribs over every 20 minutes. For the last 5 minutes of roasting time, turn the oven up to 500° to crisp the ribs.
7. If your oven is not big enough to do both racks at the same time, you can do it in two shifts. Just make sure you don't marinate the second shift too long, and reheat the first shift before serving.
8. To serve, remove from oven, cut the ribs apart, and serve hot, in the Chinese style, with hot mustard and duck sauce, but you can use barbecue sauce or even ketchup if you prefer.

Deviled Egg Variations

This recipe, using 24 eggs, yields 48 pieces, each consisting of a half egg stuffed with filling. There are recipes for three different fillings, each in sufficient quantity to stuff one third of the eggs. Naturally you can vary the quantities, omitting one or two of the variations. For an extra touch of visual appeal, you can cut the hard-cooked eggs into halves the short way, across the "waist" of the egg. Then slice off the tip of each half, about ⅛ inch, making a little rounded "cap," which can be reserved and placed on top of the stuffing later. Slicing off the cap creates a flat surface on the bottom so that each egg half will stand up without rolling over. For further effect, you can use a wavy-bladed knife to halve the egg, thus creating scalloped edges.

24 eggs
1 tbsp. salt

1. Allow the eggs to reach room temperature before cooking.

2. Add the salt to about 4 quarts of water in a large pot, then lower the eggs into the water. Turn heat to high and allow the eggs to boil for at least 8 minutes. Time from when water starts to boil.

3. When eggs are cooked, run cold water into the pot in the sink until the temperature gradually drops low enough so that you can handle the eggs. Refrigerate them until they are well chilled.

4. Peel the eggs and cut into halves, either the decorative way described above or the long way, making oval-shaped halves.

5. Arrange 3 medium-size mixing bowls on the counter. Carefully remove the hard-cooked yolks from the whites without tearing the whites. Place 8 yolks (16 halves) in each of the 3 bowls.

CURRY FILLING:

8 hard-cooked yolks
½ cup mayonnaise
¼ tsp. salt
1 tbsp. curry powder

ONION FILLING:

8 hard-cooked yolks
½ cup mayonnaise
¼ tsp. salt
2 tbsp. finely chopped onion, softened over low heat in butter until transparent, then patted dry on paper towels

HAM FILLING:

8 hard-cooked yolks
½ cup mayonnaise

(cont'd)

¼ *tsp. salt*
½ *cup ground cooked ham*

6. Blend the ingredients in each bowl well with a wire whisk or wooden spoon. The resulting texture should be fairly stiff, not too runny. Or use a hand-held electric mixer for this operation, making sure to clean the mixers between bowls.

7. Using either a pastry bag with a narrow nozzle or only a spoon, stuff 16 egg halves with one of the fillings, and fill the rest with the others. If you used the decorative method, top the filling with the little white "cap."

8. Arrange the eggs on a platter, alternating the flavors, garnish with parsley sprigs, and serve.

Eggs in Aspic with Variations

One of the most appealing and delicious appetizers is the egg in aspic. The various combinations of garnishes and accompanying ingredients are limited only by your imagination. The most important parts of the preparation are first, making a clear and tasty broth, clarified to a beautiful luster, and second, making sure that the eggs are cooked to the exact point desired. My personal preference here is using coddled eggs (*oeufs mollets*), with a hard white and a runny yolk. If you prefer, you can make them hard-cooked or poached. Poaching eggs properly is much more difficult than cooking them in the shells, and poached eggs require trimming.

FOR THE BROTH:

8 cups (2 quarts) chicken broth, beef broth, fish stock or clam broth, canned or homemade

Note: The choice of broth depends on what kind of garnishes you intend to use. Chicken broth will go well with cooked chicken or turkey meat; beef broth with any vegetables, red meat or ham; fish stock or clam broth with any kind of seafood.

> 1 egg white
> salt and pepper (amounts of salt and pepper depend on
> how seasoned the broth is)
> Maggi liquid seasoning
> 4 envelopes unflavored gelatin

1. Have ready 2 clean, enamelware saucepans for the broth. You will be straining the broth at least twice.

2. Strain the broth through muslin or cheesecloth into a saucepan. Bring it to a simmer, reduce heat, and with a shallow spoon skim off as much as possible of the fat and any impurities that rise to the surface.

3. Add the egg white to the broth and stir it vigorously with a whisk until it breaks up. Turn off the burner.

4. The egg white will draw to itself most of the remaining impurities in the broth. Skim off as much as possible, then strain broth, again through cheesecloth, into the other saucepan.

5. Dip out about ½ cup of the broth and add the gelatin. Make sure all the gelatin has dissolved, then return the broth with gelatin to the rest of the broth and bring it to a simmer again. Season to your taste with salt, pepper and Maggi seasoning.

6. If at this point the broth is not perfectly transparent, strain it again through clean cheesecloth into a clean empty saucepan. Set aside to cool at room temperature. Do *not* refrigerate.

THE EGGS:

> 12 eggs
> 1 tbsp. salt

1. Place the eggs in a saucepan with the salt. Add cold water to cover by ½ inch. Bring to a boil. Time them exactly 3 minutes from beginning of boiling. At that point immediately remove from heat and place under the cold water tap to cool gradually. The cold water should run into the hot, overflowing into the sink as the eggs cool.

2. Refrigerate the eggs and allow them to chill.

3. When chilled, very carefully peel the eggs, leaving them whole. They are now ready for the final assembly.

THE GARNISHES:

3 cups julienne of white meat of chicken or turkey, cooked ham, roast beef; or lump crab meat, sliced cooked shrimps, flakes of cooked fillet of flounder or bass; or diced cooked vegetables such as carrots, peas, mushrooms, etc.

THE ASSEMBLY:

1. Set out 12 heatproof glass cups, or molds of about 1 cup capacity, on a tray which will fit onto one shelf of your refrigerator. (This is an occasion to use one of the extra refrigerator shelves suggested in the Introduction.)

2. Spoon about 1 tablespoon of the broth into each mold; place the tray of molds in the refrigerator until the aspic jells. This should take only a few minutes.

3. Take out the tray and place in each mold a small amount of the garnish you have chosen, enough to make a layer not more than ¼ inch thick. Place 1 peeled egg in the center of each mold and add broth to barely cover the egg. Return the tray to the refrigerator and allow to jell.

4. Repeat the operation, adding the rest of the garnish, or a different garnish, and filling the molds to the top with broth. Refrigerate again until just before serving time.

5. To serve, dip a sharp knife into hot water, then run it around inside the edges of the molds, one by one. Unmold each egg in aspic onto a serving platter or individual plate.

6. For added decoration, after filling the molds pour whatever broth is left into a flat shallow pan such as a jelly-roll pan with sides. Refrigerate the pan at the same time as the molds. At serving time, remove the pan from the refrigerator and with a knife score the gelatin in crisscross lines, creating little squares. This will yield several large spoonfuls of little aspic cubes which can be used on the platter or on the individual serving plates as decoration.

7. You can serve mayonnaise as an accompaniment with the eggs in aspic, especially if you have used a seafood or chicken garnish.

CHAPTER 2

Soups

All the soup recipes in this chapter are calculated to produce twelve 1-cup portions, or a total of 3 quarts. However, because of the many variables involved in preparing soups, such as evaporation during long simmering, size of vegetables and other ingredients, loss of volume after certain straining operations, it is difficult to be as precise with quantity as in other foods. One solution I can offer is reliable and simple. Take a 5- or 6-quart stockpot which you will be using regularly for soup preparation, and fill it with a measured 3 quarts of water. Set the pot on a level surface; with some sharp instrument make a little scratch right at the water level on the side opposite the handle. This scratch can be your reference mark to be sure that during the cooking you do not allow too much loss of volume. If by any chance you are using a glass stockpot, then make the scratch on the *outside* of the glass.

As you probably know, the finest French chefs are famous for always having a stockpot bubbling on the back of the stove, providing a ready source of tasty broth for soups and sauces. Naturally this is most desirable, but at the same time highly unlikely in most American kitchens. There are dozens of excellent cookbooks containing recipes for preparing such broths, and I will not attempt to duplicate them here. In my recipes, use homemade stock if you have it, but I find that the canned beef broth, chicken broth, clam juice, etc., are quite satisfactory and will allow you to make excellent soups without using the classic French method.

Beef, Barley and Mushroom Soup

3½ *quarts water*
¾ *cup medium pearled barley*
2 *tsp. salt*
1 *package, about 2 oz., European dried mushrooms*
¼ *lb. fresh mushrooms*
4 *tbsp. butter*
2 *cups diced leftover cooked beef (from a roast, steak, brisket or any other lean cut of beef)*
6 *cups condensed beef broth or consommé, or about 2 quarts homemade beef stock*
½ *tsp. freshly ground black pepper*
1 *tbsp. Maggi liquid seasoning (optional)*

1. Bring 2 quarts of the water to a boil in a saucepan. Add the barley and 1 teaspoon salt to the boiling water, reduce heat to a simmer, cover, and cook for 1 hour, stirring occasionally.

2. When done, pour out the contents of the pan into a colander and allow the barley to drain while proceeding with the next steps.

3. Place the dried mushrooms in a 1-cup heatproof measure, pour boiling water from the kettle over them to fill the cup, and let stand.

4. Wash, drain, then thinly slice the fresh mushrooms.

5. Melt the butter in a skillet over medium heat, then add the sliced mushrooms. Sauté them, turning frequently, for about 5 minutes, then remove from the skillet with a slotted spoon and lay them out on paper towels to drain. Reserve the remaining butter in the skillet.

6. Turn up the heat under the skillet and add the diced

cooked beef. Brown it on all sides for about 2 minutes, remove from heat, and spoon the meat onto paper towels to drain off fat.

7. Remove the dried mushrooms from the soaking water, reserving the water, and chop mushrooms very fine on a board.

8. In your large stockpot combine the cooked barley, chopped mushrooms, sautéed sliced mushrooms, diced beef, condensed beef broth, 1½ quarts of water (if you are using homemade beef stock, use only about 1 quart of water), the mushroom soaking liquid, pepper, remaining teaspoon of salt and Maggi liquid seasoning.

9. Bring the soup to a simmer, cover, and cook for about 1 hour. Keep hot until serving time.

Beef and Vegetable Soup

In this recipe you can substitute canned or frozen vegetables for any fresh vegetables that are not available. I recommend using fresh vegetables wherever possible.

4 tbsp. butter
½ cup chopped peeled carrot
1 cup chopped onions
1 cup thinly sliced celery
1 cup thinly sliced leeks (make sure you wash them well before slicing)
1 cup diced leftover cooked beef
1 cup diced peeled tomatoes
1 cup diced peeled potatoes
½ cup shelled fresh green peas or corn kernels
4 cups condensed beef broth or consommé
4 cups water
1 tsp. salt

¼ tsp. freshly ground black pepper
2 tbsp. chopped fresh parsley

1. Melt the butter in a cast-iron skillet, add the carrot, onions, celery and leeks to the skillet, and sauté over medium heat, turning frequently, for 5 minutes.

2. Remove from skillet with a slotted spoon and set aside. Add the cubed beef to the skillet and brown over high heat for about 2 minutes. Remove from heat, and place meat on paper towels to drain off fat.

3. In your large stockpot, combine the vegetables and meat from steps 1 and 2, then add the tomatoes, potatoes, peas, beef broth, water, salt, pepper and parsley. Bring to a simmer, cover, and cook for 1 hour. Keep hot until serving time.

Beet Borsch

2½ quarts water
12 medium-size fresh beets, each about 2 inches in diameter
1 cup finely chopped onions
2 cups shredded cabbage
2 tbsp. vinegar
6 cups condensed beef broth or consommé
1 tsp. salt
¼ tsp. black pepper

1. Using a large pot, first put in 1 quart of the water, then a steamer platform, then the beets, with their tops trimmed off and their skins scrubbed. Cover the beets and steam for about 1 hour, or until a knife inserted in a beet goes in without much pressure.

2. When done, remove the beets with tongs and set aside to cool. Remove steamer platform, then strain the remaining liquid through a cheesecloth and reserve it.

3. When beets are cool, peel them, then run them through

the coarse blade of a grater or food mill.

4. Combine the grated beets, chopped onions, shredded cabbage, beet liquid, vinegar, beef broth, 1½ quarts water, salt and pepper in a stockpot. Cover and cook at a simmer for 45 minutes. Serve hot.

Optional: In summer this soup can be served cold. After cooking is completed, refrigerate until chilled. Serve in bowls with a generous spoonful of sour cream added to each bowl just before serving. You can also add about 2 cups of peeled and chopped cucumbers to the soup before serving.

Chicken Soup with Rice

2 *whole small chickens, about 2½ lbs. each*
2 *large onions, sliced*
2 *celery ribs, cut into about 6 pieces*
4 *whole carrots, peeled*
1 *tsp. salt*
½ *tsp. freshly ground white pepper*
6 *chicken bouillon cubes*
1 *bay leaf*
2 *tbsp. chopped fresh parsley*
2 *tsp. Maggi liquid seasoning*
3 *cups cooked white rice (see recipe for Plain Steamed Rice, p. 90)*

1. In a large deep stockpot place the chickens, including giblets and necks, the sliced onions, celery, carrots, salt and pepper. Add cold water to cover the chickens by about 2 inches.

2. Turn on heat and bring to a simmer. Simmer for at least 1½ hours, or until the chicken meat is tender and will easily separate from the bones.

3. Skim the impurities and fat from the surface of the liquid.

4. Using a slotted spoon or tongs, remove the pieces of

onion, celery and carrots from the broth, rub them through a coarse sieve, and reserve the resulting purée.

5. Carefully remove the chickens from the liquid. Place them on a cutting board and allow them to cool until they can be handled. Using a small sharp knife, remove the skin, then all the meat from the bones. Add the meat to the vegetable purée.

6. Strain the remaining cooking liquid, then return it to the stockpot. Add to it the vegetable purée, the chicken meat, the bouillon cubes, bay leaf, parsley and Maggi seasoning.

7. Add the cooked rice and check to see that you are up to the 12-cup mark. If not, add a little water up to the mark.

8. Bring the soup once again to a simmer; taste for correct seasoning, adding a little more salt and pepper if needed. Serve hot, using a ladle to assure equal portions of rice and chicken meat.

New England Clam Chowder

1½ *quarts shucked hard-shell clams (Littlenecks)*
3 *cups bottled clam juice*
3 *cups water*
4 *slices of bacon*
1½ *cups finely chopped onions*
2 *tbsp. butter*
3 *tbsp. flour*
4 *large potatoes, peeled and cubed*
1 *bay leaf*
6 *cups hot milk (not boiling)*

1. Wash the clams in cold running water. Soak them in a mixture of the clam juice and water for about 1 hour.

2. Drain the clams, and strain all the liquid through cheesecloth. Set aside 1 cup of the clams separately, and chop them very fine.

3. In a large stockpot cook the bacon over low heat until most of the fat is rendered. Remove pieces of lean bacon, then add the chopped onions, chopped clams and butter to the pot. Cook gently until onions are transparent and butter is melted but not brown.

4. Stir in the flour and make a paste.

5. Stir in the reserved strained clam liquid, a little at a time, and blend well while heating.

6. Add the cubed raw potatoes and the bay leaf. Simmer for about 15 minutes, or until the potatoes are cooked but still firm. Remove bay leaf.

7. Add the hot milk and remaining clams, and heat well. Taste for possible adding of some salt. The saltiness of the clam juice may not require any. Serve hot.

Fish Chowder

The most important element in the success of this recipe is the freshness of the fish. You can use any combination of fresh ocean fish such as cod, bass, red snapper, halibut, sea perch, pompano, flounder, bluefish or others.

> 8 *lbs. assorted fresh ocean fish, cleaned, but with heads and tails left on*
> 6 *large onions, peeled and sliced*
> 6 *large carrots, peeled and cut into 1-inch pieces*
> 6 *celery ribs, washed and cut into large slices*
> 1 *tbsp. salt*
> 10 *whole black peppercorns*
> 1 *bay leaf*
> ¼ *cup white vinegar*
> 2 *tbsp. lemon juice*
> 4 *quarts water*
> 2 *cups dry white wine*

6 large potatoes, peeled and cubed
2 cups milk

1. Remove heads and tails from the fish, save them. Fillet the fish and save the bones. Set the fillets aside.

2. Place the heads, tails, bones, onions, carrots, celery, salt, peppercorns, bay leaf, vinegar and lemon juice in a large stockpot with the water. Bring to a boil and simmer, uncovered, for 45 minutes to 1 hour, until the carrots are fairly tender and the fish still clinging to the heads and tails is falling off the bones.

3. Strain the broth through a fine sieve, wash out the stockpot, and return the strained broth to the pot. Fish out the pieces of carrot, wash them under cold water to remove any little bones or debris, and return them to the pot. Do the same for the pieces of celery and onion.

4. Cut the uncooked fish fillets into 1-inch chunks and place them in the pot; add white wine and cubed potatoes.

5. Bring the broth to a simmer and cook, uncovered, until the potato cubes are tender and the fish chunks are cooked but not falling apart. Add the milk, and heat again, but do not boil.

6. This recipe probably will yield 12 servings, allowing a little more than 1 cup per person.

Oyster Stew

¼ lb. butter (1 stick)
2 tbsp. finely minced onion
1 cup finely minced celery
6 dozen shucked fresh oysters, with their juice
2 quarts milk
1 pint heavy cream
½ cup sherry
4 tbsp. Worcestershire sauce
½ tsp. paprika

(cont'd)

1 tsp. salt

12 slices of French bread, toasted and buttered

Note: Great care must be exercised not to burn this stew, a possibility because of the high proportion of milk. I recommend using a large, enamelware pot set on an asbestos pad over the burner.

1. Melt the butter over medium heat in the soup pot, then add the onion and celery, and cook gently without allowing the onion to color, for about 3 minutes.

2. Reduce heat, and add the oysters and their juice, milk and cream. Cook over low heat for 10 to 15 minutes, until the stew is hot but not boiling and the oysters float to the surface.

3. Stir in the sherry, Worcestershire sauce, paprika and salt, and cook for another 2 minutes.

4. Serve in large soup dishes, carefully counting out 6 oysters for each portion and floating 1 slice of the toasted bread in each dish.

Egg-Drop Soup

This is a good way to add body to a clear soup and make it more nourishing. The recipe is for *chicken* egg-drop soup, but the same technique can be used with a beef or fish stock as well, changing some of the seasonings.

3 quarts chicken broth or consommé

2 tbsp. chopped parsley

6 eggs

¾ cup freshly grated Parmesan cheese

1 tsp. salt

¼ tsp. freshly ground black pepper

1. Bring the broth to a simmer in a large pot.

2. Add the parsley to the soup.

3. In a mixing bowl, beat the eggs until the yolks and whites are combined.

4. Turn off heat under the soup.

5. From a height of about 6 inches above the surface of the soup, holding the bowl of beaten eggs in one hand and a wire whisk in the other, pour the eggs into the soup, a little at a time, stirring briskly with the whisk the whole time. The eggs should cook on contact with the hot broth and form into little threads. If this does not happen immediately, heat the soup a little, but not to a rolling boil.

6. Add the Parmesan, salt and pepper, and stir well. Serve soup hot.

Minestrone

---

2 lbs. dried kidney beans
7 quarts water
3 tsp. salt
1 cup chopped celery
2 cups chopped onions
1 garlic clove, peeled and crushed through a press
2 large carrots, peeled and sliced
2 cups (one 1-lb. can) Italian plum tomatoes
½ cup olive oil
1 lb. spaghettini (very thin spaghetti)
1 cup grated Parmesan cheese

1. Soak the beans in cold water to cover for several hours or overnight. Drain before beginning preparation of the soup.

2. In a large stockpot place the drained beans, 4 quarts of the water and 2 teaspoons salt. Bring to a boil, reduce heat, cover, and cook at a steady boil for 1 hour.

3. Add the celery, onions, garlic, carrots, tomatoes and olive oil, and cook covered at a simmer for another hour.

4. Break the spaghettini into 1½-inch pieces. Bring remaining 3 quarts water to a boil in a separate saucepan with remaining 1 teaspoon salt, drop in the spaghettini, and boil for exactly 8 minutes. Drain immediately and add to the main soup pot. Mix well.

5. Serve the soup hot, with grated Parmesan on the side.

Black Bean Soup

3 cups dried black beans
4 cups condensed beef broth or consommé
8 cups water
1 ham bone, preferably with some meat still clinging to it
4 strips of bacon
1 cup finely chopped onions
1 cup finely chopped celery
1 garlic clove, peeled and minced
1 bay leaf
1 tbsp. lemon juice
2 tsp. salt
½ tsp. freshly ground black pepper
3 tbsp. butter
2 tbsp. arrowroot
¾ cup sherry

1. Wash the dried beans in cold running water.

2. Soak them in a mixture of the beef broth and water for 3 hours in a stockpot.

3. Add the ham bone and bacon strips, cover, and simmer over medium heat for 2 hours. You may have to add some water to get back to the 12-cup mark during this cooking. (See remarks at beginning of chapter.)

4. After the 2 hours in step 3, add the onions, celery, garlic,

bay leaf, lemon juice, salt and pepper, and simmer for 45 minutes more.

5. Remove the ham bone and rub the soup through a coarse sieve. Chill in refrigerator until fat hardens on surface.

6. Remove fat when cold, then return soup to stockpot and heat.

7. Melt the butter in a small pan, and stir in the arrowroot until a paste is formed. Spoon in about 1 cup of the soup from the main pot, blend well, then return the arrowroot mixture to the soup. Stir well, and continue cooking. Add the sherry to the soup.

8. Bring the soup to a simmer and serve hot.

Split-Pea Soup with Ham

---

3 cups dried split peas
1 ham bone, with plenty of meat still on it
1 large onion, chopped fine
3 celery ribs, chopped fine
3 large carrots, chopped
1 bay leaf
1 tsp. salt

1. Wash the split peas, then soak them in enough cold water to cover them by 1 inch for at least 3 hours or overnight.

2. Add to the peas enough water so that you have about 3½ quarts. Add the ham bone, cover, and cook in a large soup pot over medium heat for 3 hours.

3. Add the onion, celery, carrots, bay leaf and salt, and simmer slowly for 45 minutes more.

4. Remove the ham bone, and rub the soup through a sieve. After the bone has cooled, cut off all the meat (which should be falling away from the bone). Discard gristle and pieces of fat,

and return small pieces of lean meat to the soup.

5. At this point, either skim the fat off the top of the soup or refrigerate it and let the fat harden on top, then remove it.

6. Reheat the soup and serve hot with croutons. (See recipe p. 52.)

Lentil Soup

4 cups dried lentils
8 strips of bacon
3 quarts chicken consommé or broth
3 large carrots, peeled and sliced
2 medium-size onions, peeled and quartered
1 bay leaf
3 tbsp. chopped fresh parsley
1 tsp. salt
½ tsp. freshly ground black pepper
1 tbsp. Maggi liquid seasoning

1. Wash the lentils in warm water and drain.

2. In your large stockpot assemble the lentils, bacon strips, consommé, carrots, onions, bay leaf, parsley, salt, pepper and Maggi.

3. Bring the soup to a boil, skim off any impurities, and cook at a simmer for 45 minutes, stirring occasionally to prevent burning on the bottom.

4. Remove the bay leaf, then strain the soup through a coarse sieve, rubbing the lentils and vegetables through the sieve with a wooden spoon.

5. Return the soup to the pot, heat again, and serve hot. You can dilute the purée with a little extra consommé if it is too thick, and you can boil it down a little if it is too thin.

Cream of Asparagus Soup

If you were preparing a small quantity of thrs soup, it would be best to use a double boiler. If you have a double boiler big enough to hold 3 quarts of soup without danger of spilling, fine! But since this is not likely to be found in the average kitchen, you will have to replace the double boiler with your own invention. I recommend using a large stockpot, with an asbestos mat placed between the burner and the bottom of the pot. Also, once the cream is mixed in, stir frequently to avoid burning on the bottom.

> 3 lbs. fresh green asparagus
> 2½ quarts chicken broth or consommé
> ½ cup minced onion
> ¼ lb. butter (1 stick)
> ½ cup flour
> 1 cup heavy cream
> 1 tsp. salt
> ½ tsp. freshly ground white pepper

1. Wash the asparagus in cold running water. Cut off the tips and place them in a saucepan with enough water to cover them by 1 inch. Add a pinch of salt and simmer them over medium heat for 8 to 10 minutes, until they are just tender. When they are done, remove from heat, pour off the water (holding the cover over the saucepan), and set aside the cooked tips for later.

2. Examine the stalks of asparagus. If the thick ends are very rough and fibrous, cut off about ½ inch and discard. Cut up the usable portion of the stalks into 1-inch pieces and put them in your large stockpot. Add the chicken broth and the onion and simmer over medium heat for about 45 minutes, until the stalks are tender enough to rub through a sieve. You can test for this easily by fishing out one piece and feeling it.

3. Pass the broth through a sieve, pushing through the pieces of asparagus and onion with a wooden spoon, and return the purée and broth to the stockpot.

4. In a separate small saucepan melt the butter, not allowing it to brown, then stir in the flour to make a paste. Let the paste cook, stirring frequently, for about 2 minutes.

5. Stir the heavy cream into the paste, a little at a time, mixing well until you have a heavy smooth cream with no loose bits of flour paste.

6. Add the cream to the stockpot, stir in well, then add the reserved asparagus tips. Place the asbestos pad under the pot, and warm the whole soup over low heat. Do not allow it to boil because that will curdle the cream. Stir in the salt and pepper while the soup is heating. If you do not plan to serve the soup immediately, I suggest using an electric hot tray on a medium setting to keep it hot. This cannot get hot enough to boil, but will maintain the desired temperature.

Onion Soup

¼ lb. butter (1 stick)
8 large onions, 3 inches in diameter
2 tbsp. flour
3 quarts beef broth or consommé
2 tsp. salt
1 tsp. freshly ground black pepper
12 rounds of crusty French bread
    butter to spread the bread slices
½ cup freshly grated Parmesan cheese (Please, don't use
    the bottled kind!)
½ tsp. paprika

1. In a large stockpot melt the ¼ pound butter. While it is melting, peel the onions and slice very thin.

Note: This is a perfect opportunity to try out that slicer attachment on your food-processing machine.

2. Sauté the sliced onions in the butter until they are transparent and just beginning to color, but are not deeply browned.

3. Add the flour, stir it in, and cook for another 2 minutes.

4. Add the consommé to the pot, bring it to a simmer, and cook covered for 20 minutes. Season with the salt and pepper. The onions should now be very soft.

5. Spread the slices of French bread with butter and sprinkle them with the Parmesan cheese and a little paprika for decoration. Toast them under the broiler until the cheese starts to brown. Serve the soup hot in earthenware bowls and float 1 slice of the toasted bread in each bowl.

Cream of Mushroom Soup

Please refer to my remarks at the beginning of the recipe for Cream of Asparagus Soup (p. 39), about how to avoid burning a cream soup.

> 1½ lbs. fresh mushrooms
>   6 tbsp. plus ¼ lb. butter
> 2½ quarts chicken broth or consommé
>   1 cup chopped onions
>   ½ cup flour
>   1 cup heavy cream
>   1 tsp. salt
>   ½ tsp. freshly ground white pepper
>   2 tbsp. Worcestershire sauce
>   ½ cup sherry

1. Wash the fresh mushrooms and pat dry. Slice them into ⅛-inch slices without separating the caps from the stems.

2. Melt 6 tablespoons of the butter in a large stockpot. Add the mushrooms and sauté them for about 5 minutes, turning fre-

quently so that all are exposed about equally to the heat.

3. Add the chicken broth to the pot, then the chopped onions. Cover, and simmer over medium heat for about 30 minutes, until the onions are very tender.

4. Strain the soup, reserving the liquid; transfer the mushrooms and onions to a food mill or coarse sieve. Pass the vegetables through the mill, or sieve by rubbing with a wooden spoon, then return to the broth, off the heat.

5. In a separate small saucepan melt remaining ¼ pound butter, not allowing it to brown. Stir in the flour to make a paste, and cook the paste for about 2 minutes, stirring frequently. Add the heavy cream, a little at a time, until you have a smooth heavy cream sauce.

6. Stir the cream sauce into the main stockpot, and add the salt, pepper, Worcestershire sauce and sherry. Put an asbestos mat under the pot. Turn on low heat and warm the soup slowly to almost, but *not* the boiling point. Keep hot on an electric hot tray until serving time.

Shrimp Bisque

    4 lbs. fresh shrimps
    6 quarts water
    1 medium-size onion, peeled and sliced
    2 garlic cloves, peeled and halved
    1 bay leaf
    4 celery ribs, cut into 3-inch pieces
    3 tsp. salt
    ¼ lb. butter (1 stick)
    ½ cup finely minced onion
    ½ cup finely minced celery
    2 quarts milk
    1 pint cream
    4 egg yolks

½ tsp. paprika
½ cup sherry
2 tbsp. chopped fresh parsley

1. Peel and devein the fresh shrimps and wash them under cold running water.

2. Bring the water to a boil in a large stockpot. Drop the cleaned shrimps into the boiling water, along with the *sliced* onion, garlic, bay leaf, celery and 2 teaspoons salt. Boil for 5 minutes.

3. Turn off heat and remove shrimps from the water. Run them through the coarse blade of a meat grinder.

4. Place an asbestos pad over a burner on the stove and put your soup pot on it. Melt the butter over medium heat, add the *minced* onion and celery, and cook for about 2 minutes, not allowing the onion to brown.

5. Add the ground shrimps, milk and cream, and cook over low heat. Be careful not to allow the bisque to boil at any time.

6. While the soup is cooking, in a separate bowl beat the egg yolks. Using a ladle, spoon about 1 cup of the warm soup over the egg yolks and beat well with a wire whisk. When the soup is just about hot enough to serve, pour the egg-yolk mixture into the main pot and stir well. Do not allow boiling after this point!

7. Add the remaining teaspoon of salt, the paprika, sherry and parsley, and cook for another 2 minutes. Serve hot.

Optional: For decorative purposes, you may hold out from the grinder 1 or 2 shrimps per person, slice them lengthwise into halves, and add them to the soup just before serving.

Cheddar Cheese Soup

This is a marvelous rich, hot soup for a cold night. If you serve it, I suggest you avoid planning anything very heavy in the same meal. The soup goes very well with fresh French bread or garlic bread.

> 6 tbsp. butter
> 1 cup finely chopped onions
> 4 tbsp. flour
> 3 quarts milk, hot but not quite boiling
> 1½ lbs. Cheddar cheese, sharp rather than mild, grated
> 2 tbsp. Worcestershire sauce
> 1 tbsp. Maggi liquid seasoning
> 2 tsp. seasoned salt
> 1 tsp. freshly ground black pepper
> 1 cup Madeira wine
> 20 oz. canned, whole stewed tomatoes (you need at least 6 whole tomatoes)

1. Using your large stockpot, melt the butter over medium heat and simmer the chopped onions in it, without allowing them to brown, for about 3 minutes or until they are transparent.

2. Add the flour to the butter and onions, and stir into a paste. Cook for about 1 minute, stirring quickly with a wooden spoon. Turn off heat while you get the milk ready.

3. Bring the milk almost to a boil in a separate saucepan (one with a pouring lip is ideal).

4. Add the hot milk to the main pot, a little at a time, stirring and blending well over medium heat until all the milk is added.

5. Add the cheese, Worcestershire sauce, Maggi liquid, salt, pepper and wine. Keep cooking over medium to low heat until the cheese is completely melted and well blended.

6. When the soup is almost ready, open the can of tomatoes and heat them in their liquid in a small saucepan for just a few minutes, long enough to warm them but not make them very hot.

7. With a slotted spoon or tongs, remove the tomatoes from the pan onto a cutting board. Quickly slice them into halves and put ½ tomato in each of 12 soup bowls.

8. Add the soup to the bowls, ladling it carefully to avoid covering the tomatoes. Serve immediately.

Tomato Soup with Rice

4 cups chopped, peeled and seeded fresh tomatoes or
   equivalent amount canned, stewed tomatoes without
   liquid
1 cup finely chopped celery
½ cup finely chopped onion
1 cup water
¼ lb. butter (1 stick)
½ cup flour
4 tbsp. tomato paste
6 cups milk
1 tsp. salt
¼ tsp. freshly ground white pepper
2 cups cooked white rice (see recipe for Plain Steamed
   Rice, p. 90)

1. The best way to peel a fresh tomato is to dip it into boiling water for about 15 seconds, then peel immediately with a small sharp paring knife. Prepare tomatoes, and combine them with the chopped celery and onion and 1 cup of water in a large soup pot. Bring to a simmer over medium heat and cook, covered, for 20 minutes.

2. While the tomatoes are cooking, melt the butter in a separate saucepan over medium low heat, not allowing it to color. Stir in the flour to make a smooth paste. Cook the paste for about 3 minutes, stirring frequently.

3. Stir the tomato paste into the flour and butter roux. Add the milk, a little at a time, stirring constantly to produce a smooth texture. When it is all added, cook for 10 minutes, not allowing it to come to a boil.

4. Remove the tomatoes from heat and allow them to cool for a minute or two. Stir the cream sauce into the tomatoes, a little at a time, until well blended.

5. Season with the salt and pepper, add the cooked rice, and heat again to just under the boiling point. Serve hot.

Note: If after adding the rice the soup seems too thick, add a little tomato juice, water or milk to dilute it to the desired consistency.

Sorrel Soup

Sorrel, also sometimes called "sour grass," and in French, *oseille,* can be found both fresh and preserved as a purée in jars. This leafy herb is handled much like spinach in the kitchen, but it has a delicate, tart taste which provides a refreshing difference. It is often seasoned with some sugar and combined with sweet cream because otherwise unrelieved the taste might be a little too sour. Although you are not likely to find sorrel at the supermarket, a knowledgeable fruit and vegetable dealer should be able to find it for you. If you seek the preserved variety, look at your local gourmet shop.

> 4 lbs. fresh sorrel, or 4 pints preserved purée of sorrel
> 4 quarts water
> ¼ lb. butter (1 stick)
> 6 tbsp. flour
> 6 cups chicken broth or consommé
> 1 tsp. salt
> 1 tbsp. granulated sugar
> 4 eggs
> 6 cups heavy cream

1. If you are using preserved sorrel, disregard these steps and go right on to step 3. Wash the fresh sorrel thoroughly under cold running water several times, making sure to remove all dirt.

Put the washed sorrel in a large pot, add 4 quarts of water, cover, and cook over medium high heat for 30 minutes. Drain the sorrel and allow it to cool.

2. Run the sorrel through a blender, adding enough water to make sure the blender functions properly. This will take several shifts. When this step is done, put the purée back in a sieve and press out most of the water. Now you have the fresh equivalent of the preserved sorrel in jars.

3. In your soup pot melt the butter over medium heat without allowing it to color. Stir in the flour with a wooden spoon and mix into a smooth paste. Let the paste cook, stirring frequently, for about 3 minutes.

4. Add the chicken broth, a little at a time, mixing well. When all the broth is mixed in, you should have a smooth, fairly thick soup.

5. Add the purée of sorrel (either from step 2 or from the jars) to the soup, and add the salt and sugar. Cook over low heat for about 20 minutes, barely allowing the soup to simmer slightly at the edges.

6. While the soup is cooking, beat the eggs in a mixing bowl, add the cream to the eggs, and beat again until well blended.

7. Add the cream and egg mixture to the soup, a little at a time, until all of it has been blended in. Be careful not to allow the soup to boil at any time after the cream is added because this could curdle the cream and scramble the eggs.

8. When the soup is hot but not boiling, taste it. It may need a little more sugar or salt, depending on the acidity of the sorrel and the salt content of the chicken broth used. Serve hot.

Cold Greek Lemon Soup

½ cup uncooked rice
1 tbsp. salt
3 quarts chicken broth

(cont'd)

6 *eggs*
½ *cup lemon juice*
1 *tsp. white pepper*
2 *tbsp. granulated sugar*
2 *lemons, sliced paper-thin*

1. Boil the rice with the salt in the chicken broth for 15 minutes.

2. Remove the pot from heat and set aside.

3. In a mixing bowl, using an electric mixer, beat the eggs until well blended and frothy, then beat in lemon juice, pepper and sugar.

4. With a ladle dip up about 3 cups of broth from the pot, and beat into the egg mixture, 1 ladleful at a time.

5. Pour beaten egg mixture back into main pot, stir well with a wire whisk, and refrigerate.

6. When chilled, serve in individual bowls garnished with thin lemon slices. This soup is very attractive served in glass soup bowls set in beds of crushed ice.

Gazpacho Soup

The gazpacho soup is not only a delicious cold soup for the summer, but also a very attractive dish; it requires a little extra effort for arranging. The garnishes are traditionally spooned into the soup individually by each person being served; these should be passed after everyone has a bowl of soup before him.

FOR THE SOUP:
2 *large cucumbers, peeled and seeded*
2 *medium-size onions, peeled and chopped roughly*
2 *garlic cloves, peeled and quartered*
8 *ripe tomatoes, peeled, quartered and seeded*
2 *green peppers, quartered, cored and seeded*
1 *tender celery rib, cut into 1-inch pieces*

½ cup olive oil
3 cups tomato juice
3 cups cold water
1 tsp. salt
¼ tsp. freshly ground white pepper
3 drops of Tabasco
1 tsp. Worcestershire sauce

1. Unless you have a giant blender, you will have to do this in stages. Arrange all the solids in one big bowl and all the liquids in separate containers conveniently around your blender. Run all the ingredients except the last four through the blender. For each run, combine some of the solids and some of each of the liquids, not filling the blender jar more than two thirds full.

2. When the soup is blended, stir in the salt, pepper, Tabasco and Worcestershire sauce and refrigerate to chill.

FOR THE GARNISHES:

2 cucumbers, peeled, seeded and chopped
1 medium-size onion, peeled and chopped fine
1 green pepper, cored, seeded and chopped fine
3 firm tomatoes, chopped into ½-inch pieces
2 hard-cooked eggs, rubbed through a sieve
1½ cups small dry croutons

1. Arrange the garnishes, each in its own bowl, with a teaspoon for serving, on a tray.

2. Pass the tray of garnishes at the table after serving the soup.

Vichyssoise

This soup is very well known by name but often misunderstood. In the first place, the name is pronounced Vee-she-

SWAHZ. It is *not* correct French pronunciation to leave the final "s" silent. Secondly, the soup is delicious both hot and cold, although more commonly served cold in the United States. Thirdly, I have never tasted a decent canned vichyssoise. I think that some of the preservatives and starches used in the canned versions give the soup a gelatinous quality which ruins the taste and texture. Vichyssoise should be made only from the freshest ingredients. This applies even to the chopped chives you sprinkle just before serving. The frozen ones simply will not do.

> 6 *medium-size to large leeks (if you've never seen one, it looks like a giant scallion)*
> 8 *medium-size potatoes*
> 6 *tbsp. butter*
> 2 *quarts chicken broth or consommé*
> 1 *quart milk*
> 1 *pint heavy cream*
> 1 *tsp. salt*
> ¼ *tsp. freshly ground white pepper*
> ½ *cup chopped fresh chives*

1. Cut off the green parts of the leeks and discard them. Wash the white parts several times under cold running water, making sure you remove all bits of dirt.

2. Chop the white parts of the leeks very fine. Peel the potatoes. Slice them paper-thin; the best way is to use the slicing blade of your grater.

3. Melt the butter in your soup pot, add the chopped leeks, and simmer over low heat for 15 minutes.

4. Add the sliced potatoes and the chicken broth, cover, and cook gently for 20 minutes.

5. When the potatoes are very tender, pass the whole mixture through a fine sieve or run in shifts through a blender; then return to the soup pot.

6. Add the milk, cream, salt and pepper, and bring to a gentle simmer; do not allow it to boil! Taste and add more salt and pepper if taste is too bland.

7. To serve hot, ladle the soup into bowls, sprinkle a teaspoon of chopped chives on top of each portion, and serve.

8. To serve cold, refrigerate the soup until chilled. Serve in cups set in beds of crushed ice, and sprinkle on the chopped fresh chives at the last minute before serving.

Jellied Madrilène

6 large ripe tomatoes
3 quarts clear chicken consommé
1½ cups tomato juice
⅛ tsp. cayenne pepper
6 envelopes unflavored gelatin
1 cup sour cream
¼ cup chopped fresh chives
lemon wedges

1. Run the tomatoes, cut into rough pieces, through a blender. You should have about 2½ cups of tomato purée. If it is less due to the size of the tomatoes, add some more tomatoes.

2. Combine the chicken consommé, tomato purée, tomato juice, cayenne and the gelatin, dissolved in about 1 cup of water, in a large stockpot. Cover and simmer gently over medium heat for 30 minutes, not allowing the mixture to boil.

3. Strain through a cheesecloth into a large bowl. Set up 12 soup cups or bowls on a tray and fill them with the soup. Place the tray of filled bowls in the refrigerator to allow madrilène to jell.

4. At serving time, top each portion with a generous tablespoon of sour cream, and sprinkle some chopped chives over the cream. Serve cold, garnished with lemon wedges.

Croutons

Croutons are a marvelous addition to many soups. To my taste they go best with thick cream soups and do not belong in cold soups or in clear soups. It is well worth the trouble of preparing them because what passes for packaged croutons is dry and tasteless.

> 1 loaf of crusty French or Italian bread
> ¼ lb. butter (1 stick)
> 1 tbsp. olive oil
> 1 garlic clove, peeled and minced fine

1. Using a serrated bread knife, cut the bread, crusts and all into ½-inch cubes.
2. Using a large black cast-iron skillet, melt the butter with the olive oil.
3. Add the minced garlic to the sizzling butter and stir it around. Put enough bread cubes in the pan to make one layer. With a spatula, turn the cubes every 10 seconds until they are golden brown on all sides. Remove them promptly to a bowl lined with paper towels to absorb the fat. Then start again with another layer of bread cubes. You may have to add a little butter from time to time, depending on the amount of croutons you are preparing and how absorbent the bread is.

Dumplings

For adding to any hot clear soup.

> 4 tbsp. butter, softened
> 4 eggs
> ¾ cup sifted flour
> ¼ tsp. salt

1. Using an electric mixer, beat the softened butter, then beat in the eggs, one at a time.

2. Turn the mixer down to the slowest speed and add the sifted flour, a little at a time. Then add the salt.

3. Bring the clear soup to a simmer; using a teaspoon, spoon the dumpling mixture into the simmering soup, 1 spoonful at a time. Cover and cook for about 5 minutes, then serve. The dumplings should not sit and soak in the soup too long before serving because they tend to fall apart.

Matzo Balls

These are the traditional Jewish dumplings made from unleavened matzo meal to add to chicken soup. They are excellent in any season and can be used in any clear soup.

4 tbsp. softened butter or chicken fat
4 eggs
1 cup matzo meal
2 tbsp. chopped fresh parsley
2 tsp. salt
¼ cup chicken broth or other broth
3 quarts water

1. Beat the softened butter with the eggs, then blend in matzo meal, chopped parsley and salt.

2. Pour the ¼ cup of broth over the batter, and refrigerate, covered, until the batter chills.

3. To cook, bring the water to a boil in a large pot. Form balls from the batter, about 1½ to 2 inches in diameter, and drop them into the boiling water. Reduce heat to maintain a simmer, cover, and cook for 30 minutes. Remove pot from heat, and remove matzo balls from water with a slotted spoon. Keep them at room temperature until shortly before serving soup.

4. To serve, bring soup to a simmer, add the matzo balls to

the soup, and simmer for 4 or 5 minutes, or long enough to heat the matzo balls through. Serve immediately. This recipe should make 12 large matzo balls, or more smaller ones.

Wonton Soup

3 dozen wontons (see recipe for Wontons, p. 78, or use frozen wontons)
4 quarts boiling water
3 quarts chicken broth or consommé
4 scallions, including green part, minced
1 cup slivers or julienne of roast pork
1 tbsp. soy sauce (use the Japanese, which is less salty than the Chinese)
1 tsp. salt

1. Drop the wontons into the boiling water and cook until they float, about 5 minutes. Remove from water and keep warm until soup is completed.

2. Bring the chicken broth to a boil in your soup pot.

3. Just before serving, add the wontons to the boiling soup, drop in the minced scallions and roast pork, stir in the soy sauce, and add salt.

4. Serve immediately, being careful that each bowl gets some of all the different ingredients.

3

Eggs,
Pasta,
Crêpes,
Quiches,
and Rice

Eggs en Cocotte

One of the best ways to serve hot eggs to as many as 12 people is *en cocotte*. A cocotte is a round pottery dish about 3½ inches in diameter, 1¾ inches deep, with a capacity of about 8 fluid ounces (1 cup). It will easily hold 2 eggs, or 1 egg with other ingredients such as sauces, meat, vegetables, etc. The cooking method is very simple. Butter the inside of the cocotte with softened butter, break the egg(s) into it, and set the cocotte in a pan which contains hot water about 1 inch deep; cook on top of the stove over medium heat for 3 minutes without allowing the water to boil, then transfer the whole thing—pan, water, cocotte—into a preheated 325° oven; cover the cocotte with a piece of foil or a cookie sheet, and bake for 4 minutes. The result is a cooked egg with the white firm and the yolk soft, which will stay warm in the cocotte for several minutes, but it should be served as promptly as possible.

The eggs *en cocotte* and the poached eggs described in these recipes will provide a portion of 1 egg per person. If your containers are large enough, you can make the same recipes using 2 eggs per person without changing anything else in the recipes.

Eggs en Cocotte with Chicken Cream Sauce

    4 cups ground cooked chicken
    2 tbsp. chopped parsley
    ½ cup heavy cream
      softened butter for buttering cocottes
    12 eggs
    4 tbsp. butter
    ½ cup chicken broth
    2 tbsp. lemon juice
      pepper mill with white peppercorns

1. In a mixing bowl combine the cooked chicken, parsley and heavy cream.

2. Butter the bottoms and sides of the cocottes with the softened butter.

3. Divide the chicken mixture equally among the 12 cocottes.

4. Break 1 egg into each, on top of the chicken mixture.

5. Melt the 4 tbsp. butter, mix with the chicken broth and lemon juice, and keep this mixture warm. Preheat oven to 325°.

6. Set the filled cocottes in a pan of hot water, and cook on top of the stove over medium heat for 3 minutes, not allowing the water to boil. Cover the cocottes with a piece of aluminum

foil or a cookie sheet, transfer pan to oven, and bake for 4 to 5 minutes, until whites are firm and yolks still soft.

7. Remove the pan from the oven. Divide the warm butter, broth and lemon juice mixture equally over the tops of the 12 cocottes, top with a turn of white pepper from the mill, and serve hot.

Eggs en Cocotte in Tomato Sauce

> 4 cups chopped, peeled and seeded fresh tomatoes (about 8 small or 4 large tomatoes)
> 2 tbsp. tomato paste
> 1 tsp. salt
> 2 tbsp. chopped fresh parsley
> ½ cup heavy cream
> softened butter for buttering cocottes
> 12 eggs
> pepper mill with white peppercorns

1. To peel the fresh tomatoes, dip each one into boiling water for about 15 seconds. The peel should come off easily with a small paring knife. Cut the tomato into halves or quarters and scoop out the seeds with your finger. Allow excess juice to run off because this sauce should not be too watery.

2. Put the chopped fresh tomatoes, tomato paste, salt and parsley in saucepan, bring to a simmer, and cook over medium heat for about 10 minutes, until tomatoes are reduced to a mass. Turn off heat; stir in heavy cream until well blended.

3. Divide the tomato sauce evenly among the 12 cocottes. Break 1 egg into each dish.

4. Preheat oven to 325°.

5. Set the cocottes in a pan of hot water, and cook on top of the stove over medium heat for 3 minutes, not allowing the water to boil. Cover the cocottes with a piece of aluminum foil or a cookie sheet, transfer pan to oven, and bake for 4 to 5 min-

utes, until whites are firm and yolks still soft.

6. Remove from oven, grind one turn of white pepper from the mill on each egg, and serve hot.

Eggs Florentine

Use a heatproof glass dish, 9 by 14 inches and 1½ inches deep. Or use 2 smaller ovenproof dishes if you prefer. For poaching the eggs, I recommend using a 6-receptacle egg poacher. Poaching the eggs individually in hot water would take too long and would guarantee that the first ones cooked would be ice cold by the time you finished.

> 3 lbs. fresh spinach
> 2 quarts water
> ¼ lb. butter (1 stick)
> ½ cup finely minced onion
> 4 tbsp. flour
> 2 cups heavy cream at room temperature
> 1 tbsp. lemon juice
> 2 tsp. sugar
> 1 tsp. salt
> ¼ tsp. freshly ground black pepper
> softened butter for poaching cups
> 12 eggs
> 1 cup grated Parmesan cheese

1. Wash the spinach under cold running water, breaking off and discarding any thick ribs. Wash several times to make sure all sand or dirt is removed.

2. Bring the water to a rapid boil in a large pot. Drop the washed spinach into the water, reduce the heat, and simmer for 15 or 20 minutes, until the spinach is tender. Younger spinach takes less time, older spinach takes longer. When done, drain the spinach, discarding the water.

3. Chop the cooked spinach medium fine, using any kind of chopper, or even a blender. If you use a blender, be careful to let the spinach cool first, and to reserve some of the cooking liquid for blending, which then may be drained off afterwards.

4. Preheat oven to 325°.

5. Melt the ¼ pound butter in a large skillet, add the chopped onion and sauté for 2 or 3 minutes until onion is softened but not browned. Stir in the flour and make a paste, then cook the paste for about 3 minutes, stirring frequently and not allowing it to brown.

6. Add 1 cup of the cream, a little at a time, stirring to make a smooth sauce. Stir in the lemon juice, sugar, salt and pepper.

7. Add the chopped cooked spinach to the sauce, stir together, and cook over low heat for 3 or 4 minutes. The texture should be fairly smooth but not liquid. The spinach should hold together in a mass on a spoon. If it is too liquid, let it cook a little longer.

8. When the creamed spinach is ready, transfer it to the baking dish, spreading it in a smooth even layer on the bottom. With a cup or glass, make 12 indentations in the surface of the spinach, evenly spaced, to receive the eggs.

9. Butter the poaching cups of your egg poacher. Most such implements have 6 cups and you will have to repeat the process. Open 1 egg into each cup, place the rack of the poacher over simmering water, cover, and cook for about 5 minutes. The whites of the eggs should be just firm enough to allow removal from the poacher without breaking apart. The yolks should be quite soft.

10. Remove the eggs from the poacher and slip them directly into the indentations prepared in the spinach.

11. When all 12 eggs are in place, spoon the other cup of heavy cream carefully over the eggs, making sure they all get well moistened with it and that it is spread as evenly as possible over the whole dish.

12. Spoon the grated cheese as evenly as possible over the entire surface.

13. Cover the top of the baking dish with a sheet of aluminum foil or a cookie sheet and bake in the preheated oven for 5 or 6 minutes. Remove from the oven and finish off by placing the dish under the broiler for a few seconds, just long enough to brown the top of the sauce slightly. Serve hot.

Poached Eggs in Cream Sauce over Asparagus Tips

I recommend serving this dish in individual ramekins or small bowls. The ramekins should be warmed so that when the portions are assembled they are not chilled before service. The poached eggs should be prepared as in the recipe for Eggs Florentine (p. 58) in this recipe and in the following recipes for poached eggs with various sauces. All the other ingredients and sauces should be finished and piping hot before poaching the eggs.

> 6 *dozen asparagus spears*
> 4 *tbsp. butter*
> 4 *tbsp. flour*
> 1 *cup chicken broth or consommé*
> ½ *cup milk*
> ½ *cup heavy cream*
> ½ *tsp. salt*
> ¼ *tsp. freshly ground white pepper*
> *butter for buttering poacher cups*
> 12 *eggs*

1. Wash the asparagus well, then steam, standing the spears up on their thick ends in an asparagus steamer, for about 15 minutes, or until the tips are tender but not falling apart. See recipe for Steamed Asparagus (p. 203).

2. Cut off about 1½ inches of the tips of the cooked asparagus and put the tips in a covered dish on top of the stove to keep
warm.

3. Dice the rest of the stalks into pieces no more than ¼
inch in size.

4. In a saucepan melt the butter, stir in the flour to make a
paste, and let the paste cook, stirring frequently, over medium
heat for about 3 minutes without allowing it to brown.

5. Stir in the chicken broth, a little at a time, making a
smooth sauce. In the same manner, stir in the milk, then the cream.
Do not allow the sauce to boil. Add the diced asparagus stalks,
salt and pepper, and keep hot over low heat, stirring occasionally.

6. Butter the poacher cups and poach the eggs so that the
whites are firm and the yolks still soft.

7. As the first batch of 6 eggs is poaching, arrange 6 of the
asparagus tips in each of the first 6 warmed ramekins. Slip the
hot poached egg onto the tips, then spoon the cream sauce over
the egg. Repeat this process until all 12 ramekins are filled.

8. Serve quickly. If necessary during this process, you can
place the filled ramekins in a warming oven set at about 200° for
just a few minutes while you are completing the assembly, but not
too long because it might overcook the eggs.

Optional: Double the quantity of eggs and serve 2 eggs in
each ramekin.

Poached Eggs in Curry Sauce

This recipe can be served in individual ramekins like the
previous one, or all 12 eggs can be arranged on a warmed platter,
with the curry sauce spooned over them, and the platter can be
taken in for service at the table. In the latter case, the plates at
the table should be warmed.

    4 tbsp. butter
½ cup finely minced onion
    3 tbsp. curry powder
    4 tbsp. flour
    1 cup chicken broth or consommé
    1 cup milk
½ cup heavy cream
    2 tbsp. sherry
    2 tbsp. Maggi liquid seasoning
    1 tbsp. lemon juice
    2 tsp. sugar
½ tsp. salt
    butter for buttering poacher cups
    12 eggs

1. Melt 4 tablespoons butter in a saucepan, add the minced onion, and cook over medium heat for several minutes, until onion is tender but not brown.

2. Add the curry powder, stir well, and cook with the onion for about 1 minute. Add the flour and mix into a paste. Cook the paste for about 3 minutes, stirring frequently.

3. Add the chicken broth, a little at a time, stirring well and making sure that all the lumps are smoothed down into the sauce. When the broth is added, start adding the milk in the same manner, and finally the cream. Do not allow the sauce to boil, but keep hot just under the boiling point.

4. Add the sherry, Maggi liquid, lemon juice, sugar and salt, and keep warm while the eggs are being prepared.

5. Poach the eggs in the poacher as in the previous recipe, slipping them onto the warmed platter or into individual warmed ramekins.

6. As soon as the eggs are all done, spoon the sauce over the eggs and serve quickly.

Optional: To make this dish more substantial, you can serve it with steamed rice. Arrange the rice in a mound in the center of the platter surrounded by the sauced eggs, or serve separately.

Poached Eggs with Mornay Sauce

The best way to serve this recipe is to put all the eggs on a large warmed heatproof platter, cover them with the sauce, and bring the platter to the table. This makes it possible to put the platter under the broiler for a few seconds before serving to brown the top of the sauce just slightly, which makes it attractive to the eye and tasty.

¼ *lb. butter (1 stick)*
4 *tbsp. flour*
1 *cup milk*
1 *cup heavy cream*
1 *cup chicken broth or consommé*
½ *cup grated Swiss cheese*
½ *cup grated Parmesan cheese*
1 *tsp. salt*
¼ *tsp. freshly ground black pepper*
   butter for buttering poacher cups
12 *eggs*

1. In a saucepan melt 4 tablespoons of the butter, stir in the flour, and cook for about 3 minutes without allowing the paste to brown.

2. Add, a little at a time, first the milk, then the cream, stirring continually and making a smooth sauce. Do not allow the sauce to boil.

3. Stir in the chicken broth, the two grated cheeses and remaining 4 tablespoons butter, and remove from heat. Off heat, stir in the salt and pepper.

4. Poach the eggs in your poacher as in the previous recipes. Transfer the hot poached eggs directly to a warmed platter.

5. Spoon the Mornay sauce over the eggs, put the platter under the broiler for a few seconds until the top of the sauce browns slightly, then serve immediately. You can follow this same

procedure using individual ramekins, but it is a little bit more difficult to handle.

Poached Eggs with Red Wine and Mushroom Sauce

4 tbsp. butter
3 cups finely chopped fresh mushrooms
½ cup finely chopped shallots
2 tbsp. flour
2 cups red wine
½ tsp. salt
¼ tsp. freshly ground black pepper
  softened butter for buttering poacher cups
12 eggs

1. In a saucepan melt the butter over low heat. Add the chopped mushrooms and shallots, and cook very slowly for about 10 minutes, not allowing the mushrooms and shallots to brown. Stir frequently.

2. Add the flour, mix in well, and cook over low heat for 3 minutes.

3. Add the wine, a little at a time, mixing thoroughly to produce a smooth sauce, but not pasty or thick. If the sauce is too thick add a little more wine or a little beef broth. Season with the salt and pepper, and keep hot while poaching the eggs.

4. Poach the eggs as in the previous recipes, and transfer them immediately to a warm platter or to warmed individual ramekins.

5. Spoon the sauce over the eggs and serve immediately.

Optional: Because this sauce is thinner than the ones in the previous poached-egg recipes, you may serve the poached eggs on individual buttered rounds of toast. The toast will soak up some of the wine sauce under the egg and will be delicious.

Scrambled Eggs with Crab Meat

For this recipe you need a large warmed platter ready to receive the finished eggs, a large fairly deep enamelware skillet or a well-seasoned cast-iron skillet, and a medium-size saucepan for the sauce and crab-meat preparation.

¼ *lb. butter (1 stick)*
½ *cup finely minced scallions, both green and white parts*
2 *tbsp. flour*
1 *cup clam juice*
½ *cup sherry*
1 *tbsp. chopped fresh parsley*
½ *tsp. salt*
¼ *tsp. freshly ground white pepper*
3 *cups cooked crab meat (you can substitute cooked lobster or diced cooked shrimps)*
12 *eggs*
½ *cup half and half (½ cream, ½ milk)*

1. In the saucepan melt 4 tablespoons of the butter, add the minced scallions, and simmer them for about 1 minute. Stir in the flour and mix well to make a loose paste. Cook for about 3 minutes, stirring frequently.

2. Add the clam juice, a little at a time, then the sherry, and stir into a smooth sauce. If the sauce is too thick, add a little milk. Add the chopped parsley, salt, pepper and cooked crab meat, and keep hot without allowing to boil.

3. In a large mixing bowl, combine the eggs and the half and half. Beat them together with a wire whisk or a fork.

4. Place the warm platter in a spot near at hand so that when the eggs are cooked you can immediately dump them onto the platter.

5. Melt the other 4 tablespoons butter in the skillet. Set the heat under the skillet at medium high. Pour the egg mixture into the skillet. Let it cook for a few seconds until the eggs harden

slightly and curl just a little at the edges of the skillet. With a fork or spatula turn the eggs, bringing the solidified portions up and letting the still liquid portions reach the surface of the skillet.

6. After 1 to 1½ minutes, when the eggs are partially cooked but still very loose and liquid in the center, spoon the crab-meat sauce into the center of the eggs. Do this as quickly as possible without splashing or spilling. Turn the eggs again quickly, but don't allow the pieces of crab meat to fry on the surface of the skillet.

7. When the eggs are almost cooked, but still fairly loose, slip them onto the warm platter and serve as soon as possible. Remember, the eggs continue to cook even after being removed from the pan. If they look perfect to you *before* you remove them from the pan, they will be overdone and too dry by the time they reach the table. So, force yourself to remove them when they don't look quite done yet! You will be rewarded.

Scrambled Eggs with Chives or Shallots

6 tbsp. butter
24 eggs
1 cup half and half (½ milk, ½ cream)
½ cup chopped fresh chives or fresh shallots
½ tsp. freshly ground black pepper
1 tsp. salt

1. Melt the butter in a large skillet. If you don't have a large enough skillet to hold all the eggs, you can use a saucepan, as wide-mouthed as possible. I do not recommend doing this in two shifts in a smaller pan.

2. Mix all the other ingredients in a mixing bowl with a whisk, then gently pour the mixture into the skillet.

3. Let the egg mixture lie in the skillet with the heat at medium high until the edges solidify and begin to curl just a

little. With a fork or spatula turn the eggs, exposing the more liquid portions to the heat and bringing the cooked portions to the top. Repeat this process until the eggs are almost all cooked, but they are still fairly loose in the center.

4. Quickly transfer them to a warmed platter and serve immediately. Remember, the eggs continue to cook for some seconds after removal from heat, so they will turn out just right.

Variation:

WESTERN SCRAMBLED EGGS:

Replace the chives in the preceding recipe with 1 cup of mixed minced green pepper, bits of ham or bacon and chopped onions and chopped pimientos (red sweet peppers).

Shirred Eggs Périgord

Shirred eggs are similar to eggs *en cocotte*, except that they are baked in the oven at 350° without first being cooked on top of the stove, and also without using a pan of water. This recipe provides 2 eggs per person, and the shallow ramekins or shirred-egg dishes used should be large enough to hold 2 eggs sunny side up, with a leeway in depth of at least ½ inch.

softened butter for buttering ramekins
4 *tbsp. butter*
1 *tbsp. flour*
½ *cup finely minced black truffles*
1½ *cups dry red wine*
½ *tsp. salt*
¼ *tsp. freshly ground black pepper*
24 *eggs*

1. Butter the 12 ramekins with the softened butter and arrange handily for inserting in oven. Preheat oven to 350°.

2. In a saucepan melt the 4 tablespoons of butter, stir in the flour, make a loose paste, and cook over medium to low heat for about 3 minutes. The paste may be permitted to brown just slightly.

3. Stir in the minced truffles, then the wine, a little at a time, until it is all mixed in and a smooth, fairly liquid sauce results. Season with the salt and pepper and cook for about 5 minutes to reduce the sauce by about one third.

4. Place a spoonful of sauce in each buttered ramekin, then break 2 eggs into each one.

5. Put all the ramekins in the preheated oven and cover with aluminum foil or 1 or 2 cookie sheets. Set the timer for 5 minutes.

6. After 5 minutes, without removing the ramekins from the oven, uncover them, and spoon the remainder of the sauce onto the eggs, dividing it equally. Replace the covers and bake for 3 to 5 minutes more. The eggs are ready when the whites are firm and the yolks still soft.

7. When ready, remove them from the oven and serve immediately. The eggs will continue to cook in the hot ramekins for a minute or two, so do not be afraid if when you take them out of the oven, the centers still seem too soft. If you wait too long I can guarantee they'll be overdone.

Welsh Rarebit (Rabbit)

4 tbsp. butter
2 cups milk
2 lbs. aged Cheddar cheese, grated
2 cups beer
2 eggs
1 tbsp. Worcestershire sauce
1 tsp. Maggi liquid seasoning

½ *tsp. paprika*
12 *rounds of crusty French bread, toasted*

1. In a saucepan melt the butter over medium heat, then add the milk. When the milk is hot but not boiling, add the grated cheese and stir until it is all melted.

2. Add the beer and bring almost to the boil again.

3. Beat the eggs in a small bowl, then stir them into the hot cheese mixture with a whisk. Add the Worcestershire sauce, Maggi and paprika, and stir well.

4. Serve hot, spooned over the toast.

Homemade Egg Noodles

Here is a staple food which is not only much easier to make than most people think, but also surprisingly inexpensive to make at home. If you were to compare the cost of the ingredients in this recipe with the price of an equivalent amount of ready noodles in a package at the supermarket, you would be pleasantly surprised.

3 *eggs*
2 *tbsp. cold water*
1 *tsp. salt*
2 *tsp. olive oil*
3 *cups all-purpose flour*

1. Beat the eggs with the water, salt and oil in a small bowl. Beat only enough to combine the ingredients, but not to a froth.

2. In a large mixing bowl mix the flour and the egg mixture with your hands until it will hold together in a large ball.

3. Knead the dough thoroughly on a floured board. (*Note:* If you happen to own one of those magnificent all-purpose powered kitchen appliances with all kinds of attachments, now is the time to use the *dough hook*.)

4. When the dough is smooth and has a slightly elastic quality and all the loose bits have been incorporated, cover it with a damp (not wet) towel and let it stand at room temperature for about 1 hour.

5. Divide the dough into 3 or 4 portions, depending on the size of your board. Roll out each portion with a floured rolling pin into a very thin sheet. Let the sheets dry for 30 minutes, but do not let them get brittle.

6. Roll each sheet up loosely, leaving about 1 inch of space in the center. With a small, sharp knife, cut the dough into strips of whatever width pleases you. You can now cook the noodles immediately, or you can store them in a covered container for future use. They will keep indefinitely.

7. To cook, drop the noodles into several quarts of rapidly boiling water with 1 teaspoon salt and 2 tablespoons olive oil, wait until the water returns to the boil, and time them for 8 minutes. Drain in a colander and serve hot.

Variation:

GREEN NOODLES:

To make green noodles, simply cook enough fresh spinach so that you have ½ cup of very finely chopped cooked spinach after squeezing out all the moisture. Add the spinach to the liquid ingredients beaten together in step 1. You can also add 2 or 3 drops of green vegetable food coloring.

Homemade Lasagne

For this recipe you will need a baking dish 9 by 14 inches, or 2 smaller ones.

> *1 recipe Homemade Egg Noodles (p. 69), cut into 1-inch strips*
> *4 tbsp. butter*

6 tbsp. flour
1½ tsp. salt
1½ cups milk
1 cup minced onions
½ cup olive oil
½ cup minced celery
½ lb. ground beef
2 cups chopped fresh mushrooms
½ lb. Italian sausages, peeled and chopped
½ cup tomato paste
2 cups beef broth or consommé
½ cup Madeira wine or sherry
¼ tsp. freshly ground black pepper
2 tbsp. chopped parsley
¾ cup melted butter
3 cups grated Parmesan cheese

1. Cook the noodles in rapidly boiling water according to the directions in the recipe. Drain them in a colander and set aside for assembling lasagne.

2. Preheat oven to 350°.

3. Melt 4 tablespoons butter in a saucepan, then stir 4 tablespoons flour into it and make a smooth paste. Stir in 1 teaspoon of the salt. Let the paste cook over medium heat for 3 minutes, stirring frequently, without allowing it to brown.

4. Add the milk, a little at a time, to make a smooth sauce. Do not allow the white sauce to boil, but cook it for 3 more minutes. Remove from heat and set aside.

5. Cook the onions in the olive oil in a skillet over medium heat until they are translucent but not browned. Add the celery and cook for another 2 minutes.

6. Add the beef, mushrooms and sausages to the onions and cook a little longer, until the beef begins to brown. Stir in the tomato paste.

7. Combine the beef broth, wine and remaining 2 tablespoons flour in a bowl, making sure all the flour has dissolved

and no lumps are left. Add this mixture to the meat sauce. Season with ½ teaspoon salt, the pepper and parsley, and simmer for a few minutes until the sauce thickens.

8. Assemble the lasagne in the baking dish: First a little melted butter on the bottom, then a layer of the noodles, then a layer of the meat sauce, a layer of white sauce, a layer of Parmesan cheese, then more melted butter. Repeat the process. Allocate your ingredients so that the top layer is grated cheese with melted butter poured over it.

9. Bake in the preheated oven for 30 minutes, until the mixture is hot throughout and the top has browned in spots. Serve hot.

Note: This dish is delicious reheated; it may be refrigerated overnight and cooked the next day, provided you let it warm up to room temperature before putting it in the preheated oven.

Linguine with Red Clam Sauce

1 tbsp. olive oil
½ cup chopped onion
3 cups stewed tomatoes (if you like a canned brand that contains other vegetables such as celery or onions, use it)
1 cup tomato paste
½ tsp. salt
¼ tsp. pepper
1 cup plus 4 quarts water
3 cups clam juice (count the liquid from the canned minced clams below as part of this item)
1 tsp. dried oregano
3 cups canned minced clams
4 tbsp. butter
½ cup chopped fresh parsley
1 recipe Homemade Egg Noodles (p. 69), cut into ⅛-inch strips

1. In a large saucepan heat the olive oil and simmer the onion in it over medium heat for 3 or 4 minutes, until onion is transparent but not browned.

2. Add the stewed tomatoes, tomato paste, salt, pepper and about 1 cup of water. Turn up heat and bring to a simmer, then reduce heat and simmer for 15 minutes.

3. Add the clam juice, oregano, minced clams, butter and parsley, bring to a simmer, and keep hot until ready to serve.

4. Cook the noodles (linguine) in 4 quarts of boiling water for 8 minutes. Drain, and serve hot with the clam sauce poured over them in the serving dish.

Note: Do *not* serve grated Parmesan cheese with this dish; it doesn't go well at all.

Spaghetti Carbonara

For this recipe you will have to buy packaged spaghetti. I do not recommend trying to make spaghetti at home because, although the dough is the same as the other noodle dough in this book, the shape is different. Spaghetti are round and are made by a machine which extrudes the dough through round holes to form them. This equipment is too expensive and not worth the trouble of handling in a home kitchen. I strongly advise buying an imported brand of Italian spaghetti and not an American brand. The reason is that American-made packaged spaghetti tends to be too white and soft, and does not have the *al dente* quality of the Italian.

> 4 *quarts water*
> ¼ *lb. butter (1 stick)*
> 4 *cups sliced boiled ham, cut into ¼-inch-wide strips*
> 2 *cups heavy cream*
> 1 *lb. spaghetti*
> 6 *egg yolks*

(cont'd)

½ *tsp. salt*
¼ *tsp. freshly ground black pepper*

1. Have 4 quarts of water in a large pot at the boiling point, ready to cook the spaghetti, on top of the stove. This dish should be served as soon as it's ready, so the timing should be coordinated.

2. In a large skillet or saucepan melt the butter and add to it the ham and all but ½ cup of the cream. Cook over medium heat for 8 to 10 minutes without boiling.

3. At this point, plunge the spaghetti into the boiling water and set the timer for 8 minutes after the water comes back to the boil.

4. While the spaghetti is cooking, blend the egg yolks with the remaining cream in a mixing bowl and beat a little with a wire whisk (not enough to whip the cream). Add salt and pepper.

5. Reduce heat under the ham, and stir the egg-yolk mixture into the saucepan, a little at a time, until it is all incorporated. Allow it to heat through but do not boil.

6. When the spaghetti is ready, drain it in a colander and transfer to a serving dish. Pour the ham and cream sauce over it, toss, and serve hot.

Optional: Serve with grated Parmesan cheese.

Homemade Ravioli

Anything I said in favor of making your own egg noodles at home goes double for ravioli. In the case of ravioli, you can't buy it at the supermarket in packages; you may be able to find it in the frozen foods section, but it won't compare with homemade. In the recipe below, first I give you the basic assembly instructions, then a choice of fillings. I have found that it is easier to make a larger quantity of ravioli squares which are fairly small, with about 1 teaspoon of filling in each, than to try to make large squares.

1 recipe Homemade Egg Noodles (p. 69), not cut into strips
4 cups filling (see various recipes following)
  melted butter
1 cup grated Parmesan cheese

1. Roll out the noodle dough into either 2 or 4 very thin sheets, depending on the size of your work area. Each *pair* of sheets must be equal in size because one will cover the other eventually.

2. With a teaspoon spoon the filling onto one of the sheets in little mounds, 1½ to 2 inches apart, in even rows.

3. With the second sheet of dough carefully cover the bottom sheet. One easy way is to roll it loosely onto a rolling pin, then slowly reverse it onto the lower sheet. Once the top sheet is placed, don't try to move it around any more, because you might mess up the mounds of filling. With your fingers, press down firmly around each mound of filling so that the two sheets stick together.

4. Using a sharp knife or a circular pizza cutter, cut through the dough forming the ravioli squares. The ravioli are now ready to cook in boiling water for about 10 minutes. If you want to wait, put the squares into a bowl and cover with a damp towel until ready to cook.

5. Serve the cooked ravioli with melted butter and grated Parmesan cheese, or with a light tomato or meat sauce.

Cheese Filling for Ravioli

2 cups ricotta cheese
¾ cup grated Parmesan cheese
¾ cup grated Romano cheese
½ cup heavy cream
2 tbsp. chopped fresh parsley
¼ tsp. freshly ground black pepper

1. Cream the cheeses together with the heavy cream, making a thick, pastelike mixture.

2. Blend in the parsley and the pepper. Filling is now ready for use.

Meat Filling for Ravioli

½ cup minced onion
1 garlic clove, peeled and minced
¼ cup olive oil
1 lb. ground beef
½ cup cracker crumbs, bread crumbs or matzo meal
½ cup heavy cream
1 cup finely chopped cooked spinach
2 tbsp. chopped fresh parsley
½ tsp. salt
¼ tsp. freshly ground black pepper

1. In a skillet sauté the onion and garlic in the oil over medium heat for 3 or 4 minutes, until the onion is soft but not browned.

2. Add the ground beef, turn up heat, and toss the meat with the onion for a minute or two until the meat is slightly browned. Remove from heat and transfer to a mixing bowl.

3. Add all the remaining ingredients to the mixing bowl, and blend well. Filling is now ready for use.

Chicken Filling for Ravioli

Follow the instructions in the recipe for Meat Filling for Ravioli (preceding recipe), substituting 1 pound ground raw boned chicken breasts for the ground beef.

Homemade Tortellini

Tortellini are similar to ravioli, but they contain about half the amount of noodle dough because instead of being a "sandwich" of two sheets of dough, the tortellini have 1 square of dough which is *folded* over the mound of filling. Also, tortellini are cooked in chicken broth; they can be either drained and served as a pasta dish, or can be served in the broth as a soup garnish.

1 recipe Homemade Egg Noodles (p. 69), not cut into strips
3 cups ground cooked chicken meat
2 cups ricotta cheese
½ cup grated Parmesan cheese
4 eggs
½ tsp. salt
¼ tsp. freshly ground white pepper
2 tbsp. chopped fresh parsley
3 quarts chicken broth or consommé

1. Roll out the noodle dough into thin sheets, and cut into 2- to 2½-inch squares.

2. Mix together the chicken meat, cheeses, eggs, salt, pepper and parsley in a bowl. You can do this at slow speed with an electric mixer. If the filling seems a little too dry, add a little water so that a teaspoonful of the filling will hold together in a mass on the spoon.

3. To assemble the tortellini, place 1 teaspoon of filling on each square of dough, fold it over, and press the edges together; moisten fingers if necessary.

4. Cook the tortellini in boiling chicken broth for about 15 minutes, until tender but not falling apart. Fish one out after 12 minutes and check for consistency.

5. Serve hot in the broth, or drained of the broth. Sprinkle on a little Parmesan cheese at the table if desired.

Wontons

These filled noodles can be found in the standard Chinese soup in almost every Chinese restaurant. They have a resemblance to tortellini and ravioli, but they are different. They are not only served boiled in soups, but can be deep-fried, pan-fried or steamed and served with various sauces or dips.

WONTON DOUGH:

2 cups all-purpose flour
1 tsp. salt
1 egg

1. Sift the flour and salt into a bowl.

2. Beat the egg separately in a little bowl, add it to the flour. Blend into a dough with your hands. If the dough is too dry, sprinkle a little water on it as you knead it. Knead until the dough is smooth and shiny.

3. Refrigerate the dough and let it rest for about 1 hour.

4. On a floured board, roll out the dough to a paper-thin sheet, as thin as possible without tearing. If your work surface is small, divide the dough into halves before you start.

5. Sprinkle a little flour on top of the dough and spread it with your hand to make the surface of the dough fairly dry. With a sharp knife cut the dough into 2-inch squares. The wonton dough is now ready for the filling.

WONTON FILLING:

This filling is essentially a mixture of shredded meat and vegetables, mostly meat. It is loose, not sticky, and will be firmly pinched into the dough envelopes.

3 cups shredded cooked meat (chicken, beef or pork)
1 cup shredded celery, leeks or onions, or any combination of the three
2 tbsp. soy sauce (use the Japanese, not the Chinese kind)
1 egg, beaten in a small bowl

Crab-Meat Filling for Crêpes

4 tbsp. butter
4 tbsp. flour
2 cups clam juice
1 cup heavy cream
3 tbsp. tomato paste
½ tsp. salt
¼ tsp. freshly ground white pepper
3 cups cooked crab meat

1. In a saucepan melt the butter, add the flour, and stir into a paste. Cook the paste over medium heat for about 3 minutes, not allowing it to brown and stirring frequently.

2. Add the clam juice, a little at a time, stirring into a smooth sauce. Stir in the cream and the rest of the ingredients, not allowing the sauce to boil. Cook under boiling point for about 5 minutes and turn off heat.

3. Preheat the oven to 350°.

4. Butter 1 large or 2 small baking dishes. Stuff the crêpes, arrange in baking dishes, and bake for 20 minutes according to the instructions in the recipe for Creamed Chicken Filling.

Russian Blini

These are delicate pancakes made with a yeast batter which is light and quite different from other pancake batters. To make it possible to serve the blini while they are hot to a dozen people it is necessary to preheat your oven to about 200°, place in it an ovenproof serving platter of some kind which has a cover, and put the blini into the platter in the oven as they come off the griddle. This recipe makes 4 dozen blini, or about four per person for 12 people.

1. Combine the meat, vegetables and soy sauce in a bowl, mixing well. The filling will be loose.

2. Take 1 square at a time of the wonton dough. Put 1 teaspoon of filling in the center of the square.

3. Dip your fingers in the beaten egg, then fold the dough into a triangle over the filling, moistening the inside edges with the fingers dipped in egg and pressing the edges together.

4. Bring two points of the triangle together and press them together firmly with the fingers dipped into egg. The wontons are now ready for cooking.

5. You can cook them for the soup as directed in the recipe for Wonton Soup (p. 54). You can fry them in hot oil in a skillet after boiling, until they are browned on both sides, and serve them hot with Chinese plum sauce and hot mustard. You can deep-fry them after boiling and draining until they are browned and serve them as in the preceding suggestion. You can steam them on a steaming platform over boiling water, covered, for about 20 minutes until tender.

Stuffed Crêpes

In case you are not familiar with thin French crêpes, a word or two of description may be necessary. Crêpes are thin pancakes, made in a 9-inch crêpe pan, and each takes only a minute or two to prepare. Although they may be served hot directly after frying, it would be difficult to do this for many people. However, these crêpes are very versatile. They can be prepared in quantity, stuffed with various fillings and reheated either in a baking dish in the oven, or in a frying pan on top of the stove. If they are to be reheated in a frying pan, the best system is to fry them only on one side the first time. The cooked side of the crêpe then is on the inside when the crêpe is rolled up around its filling. The outside has not yet been cooked, and when it is re-fried it is therefore not burned or overdone.

There are two different fillings for these crêpes, one

chicken and one crab meat. However, the possible fillings for the crêpes are limited only by your imagination and could fill a book all by themselves. Here are a few suggestions for other fillings you can make: curried shrimps, sautéed chicken livers, tomatoes in cheese sauce, sour cream and caviar; for dessert, various jams and jellies with a powdered sugar topping.

Crêpes

1 tbsp. liquid vegetable shortening or cooking oil
3 cups all-purpose flour
1 tsp. salt
8 eggs
4 cups milk
¼ lb. butter (1 stick), softened, for cooking

1. Combine all the ingredients except the butter in a bowl, using an egg beater or electric mixer, until the crêpe batter is smooth without lumps.

2. Heat a shallow-lipped 9-inch crêpe pan or frying pan over medium heat. Melt about 1 teaspoon butter in the pan. As soon as it has melted, but not browned, pour about 4 tablespoons of the batter into the pan, and give the pan a quick turn, making sure that the batter thinly covers the whole surface of the pan. If there is not quite enough, add a little batter right away. If there is too much, quickly pour off the excess batter before it hardens.

3. With a long, flat-bladed spatula, turn the crêpe over when the edges begin to brown. You will find this is quite easy to do with one flipping motion. If you intend to stuff the crêpes and reheat them in a frying pan later, remove the crêpes to a waiting dish at this point instead of cooking them on the second side. If not, cook them on the second side for about 30 seconds, then remove to a dish.

4. You can simply make a stack of the finished crêpes and store them, covered with plastic wrap, until ready for stuffing.

5. This recipe should produce about 36 [...]
for 12 people.

Creamed Chicken Filling for Crê[pes]

4 tbsp. butter
4 tbsp. flour
2 cups chicken broth or consommé
1 cup heavy cream
2 tbsp. chopped chives
2 tsp. Maggi liquid seasoning
½ tsp. salt
¼ tsp. freshly ground white pepper
3 cups diced cooked chicken meat

1. In a saucepan melt the butter, add the flour, and [...] a paste. Cook the paste over medium heat for about 3 [...] stirring frequently and not allowing it to brown.

2. Add the chicken broth, a little at a time, stirring [...] smooth sauce. Stir in the cream, then the rest of the ingred[...] not allowing the sauce to boil. Cook under the boiling poin[...] about 5 minutes and turn off heat.

3. Preheat oven to 350°.

4. Butter 1 large or 2 small baking dishes. Stuff the crêp[...] place about 3 tablespoons of filling in the center of each crêp[...] roll the crêpe, folding in the ends, and place in the buttered bak[...] ing dish. Arrange crêpes next to each other in the dish. If you use[...] a deep dish, arrange the crêpes for the second layer in the oppo-site direction from the first layer for easier removal after baking.

5. Bake the stuffed crêpes for 15 to 20 minutes.

6. Remove from oven and serve hot. There is no need for a sauce because the filling is moist enough by itself, but if you have filling left over you may warm it and serve it in a gravy boat as a supplement.

Blini are served with melted butter in a small cup for each person and bowls of sour cream and red or black caviar, and sometimes some chopped herring (see recipe for Chopped Herring, p. 5). You can even serve a small quantity of minced onion. I do not indicate quantities for the garnishes because you can serve them in serving bowls if you prefer.

4 cups milk
1 cake compressed fresh yeast, or 1½ envelopes active dry yeast
6 cups all-purpose flour
3 tbsp. sugar
6 eggs
¼ lb. butter (1 stick), softened
1 tsp. salt
butter for baking blini

1. In a saucepan heat the milk to just below the boiling point, then remove from heat and allow to cool until it is lukewarm (80° to 90° for fresh yeast, 105° to 115° for dry yeast).

2. Pour about ½ cup of the warm milk into a bowl, and dissolve the yeast thoroughly in this milk. When dissolved, return it to the rest of the milk.

3. Sift 3 cups of the flour into the milk and add the sugar. Mix well until the milk and flour are well blended. Pour into a large deep bowl, cover with a towel, and set in a warm place to rise. The batter should be allowed to rise undisturbed for about 2 hours.

4. Separate the eggs. Beat the yolks with the softened butter, then sift into this mixture the remaining 3 cups flour and add the salt. Mix this well to combine the flour and egg yolks, then combine it with the first mixture that has risen.

5. Cover and allow to rise again for about 2 hours, until the batter has doubled in volume.

6. Beat the egg whites until they form stiff peaks, then fold them carefully into the risen batter.

7. Heat a flat griddle over medium heat and butter it

lightly. It is not necessary to use a lot of butter in the cooking because the batter already has a high butter content. Pour the batter so as to form round cakes 2 inches in diameter, as many as will fit on the griddle, without touching each other. Bake on the first side until bubbles start to pop on top and the blini are a light brown on the baked side (lift one with a spatula to check color). Then turn them and cook long enough on the second side to produce the same medium brown color.

8. Remove immediately to the warm platter or dish in the oven and continue until all the batter has been used. Serve hot, with garnishes described above.

Quiches

Before launching into the following recipes, a word of explanation is in order. To prepare a quiche, you first must make a partially baked pastry shell. The filling is then poured in and the quiche is baked for about 30 minutes. The shape of the pastry shell is not important, but the size, or aggregate size, is quite important when you are planning to feed 12 people. Here are the options: you need 2 round shells of 8-inch diameter, or 1 round shell of 12-inch diameter, or 1 square shell with 10-inch sides, or 1 rectangular shell 9 by 12 inches. You can find flan rings in all these sizes and many more. The flan ring or square is placed flat on a cookie sheet, thus creating the form into which the pastry dough is fitted. If you wish, you can even use 12 individual-size shells for separate portions. In any case, the amount of dough given in the recipe for the pastry shell is about the same and will fill whatever shape and size form you choose.

PARTIALLY BAKED PASTRY SHELL
FOR QUICHE RECIPES:

  3 cups all-purpose flour
¼ lb. unsalted butter (1 stick)

Crab-Meat Filling for Crêpes

4 tbsp. butter
4 tbsp. flour
2 cups clam juice
1 cup heavy cream
3 tbsp. tomato paste
½ tsp. salt
¼ tsp. freshly ground white pepper
3 cups cooked crab meat

1. In a saucepan melt the butter, add the flour, and stir into a paste. Cook the paste over medium heat for about 3 minutes, not allowing it to brown and stirring frequently.

2. Add the clam juice, a little at a time, stirring into a smooth sauce. Stir in the cream and the rest of the ingredients, not allowing the sauce to boil. Cook under boiling point for about 5 minutes and turn off heat.

3. Preheat the oven to 350°.

4. Butter 1 large or 2 small baking dishes. Stuff the crêpes, arrange in baking dishes, and bake for 20 minutes according to the instructions in the recipe for Creamed Chicken Filling.

Russian Blini

These are delicate pancakes made with a yeast batter which is light and quite different from other pancake batters. To make it possible to serve the blini while they are hot to a dozen people it is necessary to preheat your oven to about 200°, place in it an ovenproof serving platter of some kind which has a cover, and put the blini into the platter in the oven as they come off the griddle. This recipe makes 4 dozen blini, or about four per person for 12 people.

5. This recipe should produce about 36 crêpes, or three each for 12 people.

Creamed Chicken Filling for Crêpes

4 tbsp. butter
4 tbsp. flour
2 cups chicken broth or consommé
1 cup heavy cream
2 tbsp. chopped chives
2 tsp. Maggi liquid seasoning
½ tsp. salt
¼ tsp. freshly ground white pepper
3 cups diced cooked chicken meat

1. In a saucepan melt the butter, add the flour, and stir into a paste. Cook the paste over medium heat for about 3 minutes, stirring frequently and not allowing it to brown.

2. Add the chicken broth, a little at a time, stirring into a smooth sauce. Stir in the cream, then the rest of the ingredients, not allowing the sauce to boil. Cook under the boiling point for about 5 minutes and turn off heat.

3. Preheat oven to 350°.

4. Butter 1 large or 2 small baking dishes. Stuff the crêpes: place about 3 tablespoons of filling in the center of each crêpe, roll the crêpe, folding in the ends, and place in the buttered baking dish. Arrange crêpes next to each other in the dish. If you use a deep dish, arrange the crêpes for the second layer in the opposite direction from the first layer for easier removal after baking.

5. Bake the stuffed crêpes for 15 to 20 minutes.

6. Remove from oven and serve hot. There is no need for a sauce because the filling is moist enough by itself, but if you have filling left over you may warm it and serve it in a gravy boat as a supplement.

---

chicken and one crab meat. However, the possible fillings for the crêpes are limited only by your imagination and could fill a book all by themselves. Here are a few suggestions for other fillings you can make: curried shrimps, sautéed chicken livers, tomatoes in cheese sauce, sour cream and caviar; for dessert, various jams and jellies with a powdered sugar topping.

Crêpes

1 tbsp. liquid vegetable shortening or cooking oil
3 cups all-purpose flour
1 tsp. salt
8 eggs
4 cups milk
¼ lb. butter (1 stick), softened, for cooking

1. Combine all the ingredients except the butter in a bowl, using an egg beater or electric mixer, until the crêpe batter is smooth without lumps.

2. Heat a shallow-lipped 9-inch crêpe pan or frying pan over medium heat. Melt about 1 teaspoon butter in the pan. As soon as it has melted, but not browned, pour about 4 tablespoons of the batter into the pan, and give the pan a quick turn, making sure that the batter thinly covers the whole surface of the pan. If there is not quite enough, add a little batter right away. If there is too much, quickly pour off the excess batter before it hardens.

3. With a long, flat-bladed spatula, turn the crêpe over when the edges begin to brown. You will find this is quite easy to do with one flipping motion. If you intend to stuff the crêpes and reheat them in a frying pan later, remove the crêpes to a waiting dish at this point instead of cooking them on the second side. If not, cook them on the second side for about 30 seconds, then remove to a dish.

4. You can simply make a stack of the finished crêpes and store them, covered with plastic wrap, until ready for stuffing.

1. Combine the meat, vegetables and soy sauce in a bowl, mixing well. The filling will be loose.

2. Take 1 square at a time of the wonton dough. Put 1 teaspoon of filling in the center of the square.

3. Dip your fingers in the beaten egg, then fold the dough into a triangle over the filling, moistening the inside edges with the fingers dipped in egg and pressing the edges together.

4. Bring two points of the triangle together and press them together firmly with the fingers dipped into egg. The wontons are now ready for cooking.

5. You can cook them for the soup as directed in the recipe for Wonton Soup (p. 54). You can fry them in hot oil in a skillet after boiling, until they are browned on both sides, and serve them hot with Chinese plum sauce and hot mustard. You can deep-fry them after boiling and draining until they are browned and serve them as in the preceding suggestion. You can steam them on a steaming platform over boiling water, covered, for about 20 minutes until tender.

Stuffed Crêpes

In case you are not familiar with thin French crêpes, a word or two of description may be necessary. Crêpes are thin pancakes, made in a 9-inch crêpe pan, and each takes only a minute or two to prepare. Although they may be served hot directly after frying, it would be difficult to do this for many people. However, these crêpes are very versatile. They can be prepared in quantity, stuffed with various fillings and reheated either in a baking dish in the oven, or in a frying pan on top of the stove. If they are to be reheated in a frying pan, the best system is to fry them only on one side the first time. The cooked side of the crêpe then is on the inside when the crêpe is rolled up around its filling. The outside has not yet been cooked, and when it is re-fried it is therefore not burned or overdone.

There are two different fillings for these crêpes, one

¼ lb. *hydrogenated vegetable shortening*
½ tsp. *salt*
 1 tsp. *sugar*
½ cup *ice water*

1. Sift the flour into a mixing bowl. Make sure the butter and shortening are well chilled before using.

2. Cut the butter, then the shortening, into small pieces into the flour, then add the salt and sugar.

3. Mix the ingredients together with your hands, then add the ice water and gather the dough into a ball. Flour a pastry board lightly and put the ball of dough on it. With the heel of your hand, mash the dough down, a little at a time, to blend the ingredients thoroughly.

4. Scrape up the dough, roll it into a ball again, wrap it in foil, and refrigerate until it chills through and is fairly hard.

5. On a floured board, roll out the chilled dough to a size 2 inches larger all around than the flan ring or form you plan to use. Do not worry if you can't do this exactly, because you can always make patches later.

6. Preheat oven to 400°.

7. Butter the inside of the flan ring and the surface of the cookie sheet. Lay the rolled-out dough in the buttered form; with your fingers press it into the corners and against the sides. Excess dough can be rolled out again and used to patch places that need it by moistening one side with a little water, sticking it on, and smoothing down by hand.

8. Score the edges of the pastry with a fork to make a decorative pattern. Prick the bottom of the pastry with a fork every inch or so all over the area.

9. Butter the bottom of a slightly smaller pie pan, or other pan, and set it on the pastry to prevent the bottom puffing up. Or you may butter one side of a sheet of foil, fit it, buttered side down, into the pastry shell and weight it with some dried beans or with marbles.

10. Bake the pastry in the preheated oven for 10 minutes.

(cont'd)

Remove from oven, remove weight, prick the bottom again if necessary, and bake again for 6 to 8 minutes, until the surface of the pastry is just beginning to brown. Remove from oven, do *not* remove flan ring, and set aside to await the filling.

Ham Quiche

> 1 or 2 partially baked pastry shells
> 1½ cups diced cooked ham, or ¼-inch-wide strips cut from ham slices
> 6 eggs
> 3 cups heavy cream
> 1 tsp. salt
> ¼ tsp. paprika

1. Spread a layer of the diced or sliced ham over the bottom of the pastry shell, using all the ham.

2. Using an egg beater or electric mixer, combine the eggs, cream, salt and paprika in a mixing bowl.

3. Preheat oven to 375°.

4. Pour the egg and cream mixture into the pastry shell.

5. Bake for 40 minutes, until the surface of the quiche has puffed up and browned in spots. Do not worry if after opening the oven the quiche deflates. The main thing is to test it for doneness by inserting a cake-testing needle in the center. If it comes out clean the quiche is ready. If not, bake for another 5 or 10 minutes, watching that the top doesn't get too brown, and test again. You do not want the center to be liquid.

6. To serve, slip off the outside flan ring, then slide the quiche off the cookie sheet onto a serving platter. Use a knife to cut the portions and some sort of spatula or cake server to lift the pieces onto plates.

Tomato and Bacon Quiche

½ lb. sliced bacon
1 or 2 partially baked pastry shells
2 tbsp. butter
2 cups chopped, peeled and seeded fresh tomatoes
1 garlic clove, minced
4 tbsp. tomato paste
1¼ tsp. salt
⅛ tsp. freshly ground black pepper
6 eggs
3 cups heavy cream
¼ tsp. paprika

1. Bring a quart of water to a boil in a saucepan. Cut the bacon slices into 1-inch lengths, drop them into the boiling water, and boil for 3 minutes. Remove from water and drain.

2. Sauté the bacon in a skillet just long enough to brown slightly. Drain the bacon on paper towels, and arrange in a layer on the bottom of the pastry shell.

3. In a saucepan melt the butter, add the fresh tomatoes, garlic, tomato paste, ¼ teaspoon salt and the pepper. Simmer for about 10 minutes, so that the liquid cooks off and the tomatoes form into a mass. Remove from heat, let the tomato mixture cool for a few minutes, then spread it over the bacon in the pastry shell.

4. Beat together the eggs, cream, 1 teaspoon salt and the paprika with an egg beater or electric mixer until well blended.

5. Preheat oven to 400°.

6. Pour egg mixture into the pastry shell over the tomato layer. Bake for 40 minutes in the preheated oven, until the surface has puffed and browned. Test for doneness with a cake needle as in the previous recipe.

7. Remove flan ring and transfer quiche from the cookie sheet to the serving platter. Serve hot.

Pizza

This delicious Italian invention is often consumed in restaurants or "pizza parlors." But it can be made at home with relative ease, and the ingredients are not particularly expensive. If you do not have a 15-inch-diameter round metal pizza pan, you can use a jelly-roll pan (rectangular), or even several metal pie dishes. The recipe for the crust here will make 2 15-inch-round pizzas, or 2 rectangular pizzas 10 by 18 inches or 12 by 15 inches.

PIZZA CRUST:

½ *oz. compressed fresh yeast, or 1 envelope active dry yeast*

1 *tsp. plus ¼ cup sugar*

½ *cup lukewarm water (80° to 90° for fresh yeast, 105° to 115° for dry yeast)*

5 *tbsp. vegetable shortening*

¾ *cup water*

1 *tsp. salt*

1 *egg*

5 *cups all-purpose flour*

1. Dissolve the yeast and 1 teaspoon sugar in the lukewarm water. Make sure all the granules are dissolved if you use dry yeast.

2. Melt the shortening over low heat and add to it ¾ cup water, ¼ cup sugar and the salt. Remove from heat after sugar is dissolved, then add the water with the dissolved yeast and beat in the egg.

3. Put the liquid in a bowl; add the flour, 1 cup at a time, mixing it with your hands into a dough. Knead the dough by hand on a floured board until it is smooth, or use the dough hook of an electric mixer.

4. Put the ball of dough into a bowl, cover with a towel,

and let stand in a warm place for 1½ hours until the dough doubles in bulk.

5. Divide the dough into 2 equal parts. Roll out each part to a thickness of about ¼ inch. Each half should be sufficient for a 15-inch-diameter pizza pan. Form the dough into desired shape, put into oiled pan, and refrigerate until ready to bake.

PIZZA FILLING:

1 cup finely chopped onions
½ cup olive oil
4 cups canned stewed tomatoes, drained of their liquid
1 cup tomato paste
1 tsp. salt
½ tsp. freshly ground black pepper
1 lb. mozzarella cheese, thinly sliced

1. Preheat oven to 400°.

2. Cook the onions in the olive oil over medium heat for 5 minutes, until onions are soft but not browned.

3. Add tomatoes, tomato paste, salt and pepper. Continue to cook at a simmer for several minutes until the shape of the tomatoes is lost and the sauce will hold together in a mass on a spoon.

4. Turn off heat and allow sauce to cool.

5. Spread tomato sauce over prepared unbaked pizza crusts. Arrange slices of mozzarella cheese over the surface of the sauce.

6. Bake in the preheated oven for 30 to 40 minutes, until the edges of the crust are browned and crisp. Serve hot.

Note: If the baking time seems long, remember that in a "pizza parlor" the pizzas have been baked once, and are only reheated in the oven for 5 minutes before you are served. Also, they have special ovens which distribute the heat more efficiently for baking pizzas than your home oven can do.

Optional: This pizza filling is just the basic tomato and cheese variety. You can add with the cheese sliced Italian sausages, sliced cooked mushrooms, anchovies, red peppers or any other additional ingredients you like before baking.

Plain Steamed Rice

3 cups uncooked rice
6 cups water
4 tbsp. butter
1 tsp. salt

1. In a large enamelware pot which has a tight-fitting cover, bring all the ingredients to a boil, uncovered.

2. When the water begins to boil, reduce heat to medium low, cover, and cook for 15 minutes.

3. At this point, all the liquid should have been absorbed and the rice should be perfect. If there is still some fluid at the bottom, cook for another 2 or 3 minutes, being careful not to allow the rice to burn. This recipe yields 6 to 8 cups of cooked rice.

4. If you are not ready to serve immediately, you can place the pot, covered, on an electric hot tray, or on an asbestos pad over a burner of the stove set at low, to keep the rice hot until serving time.

5. If you wish to impart a particular taste to the rice in the preparation, you can substitute chicken or beef broth for the water in the recipe.

6. To reheat cooked rice which has been refrigerated or stored, put about 2 inches of water into a large saucepan. Set a steamer platform on its legs in the water, then spoon the rice onto the platform. Bring the water to a boil, cover the pan, and allow it to steam for 10 minutes. This will restore moisture and heat to the rice without breaking down the grains, which would happen if you reboiled it.

Rice with Mushrooms

    1 lb. fresh mushrooms
    4 tbsp. butter
    ½ cup white wine or sherry
    ¼ tsp. freshly ground black pepper
    1 recipe Plain Steamed Rice (p. 90), made with beef consommé

    1. Wash the mushrooms, pat dry, then chop them medium fine.

    2. In a saucepan melt the butter; add the mushrooms, wine and pepper and simmer, stirring occasionally, over medium heat for 15 minutes.

    3. Prepare the rice according to the instructions in the recipe, using beef consommé instead of water as the liquid.

    4. Add the contents of the saucepan with the mushrooms in wine to the pot of rice, toss well, and serve piping hot.

Saffron Rice

    1 tbsp. saffron
    1 recipe Plain Steamed Rice (p. 90), made with chicken broth

    1. Follow the instructions for the plain steamed rice, using chicken broth instead of water.

    2. When the broth first comes to a boil, stir in the saffron, making sure it is well distributed throughout.

    3. The rest of the instructions remain the same.

4

Fish
and
Shellfish

Although breading and frying fish is a perfectly acceptable cooking method which often yields excellent results, it is not by any means the only way to prepare fish. Also, one disadvantage of this method is that it tends to make all fish taste the same, that is, they taste of the breading and the cooking oil.

I'm for variety and for preservation of the taste. If you try some of the recipes in this chapter you will discover that poached and baked fish are often superior to the fried version.

There is one classic cooking instruction often given in recipe books which I think is wrong. I do not believe that fish should be cooked until it "flakes easily." If it does flake easily, it is definitely overdone. The only test of doneness of a fish, especially a large fish, is to push a fork, as the fish is cooking, into the thickest part of the flesh until the fork touches the spine. Tilt the fork so that you can see into the aperture it has made, to see if the color of the flesh is the same from the outside all the way down to the bone. If the flesh closer to the bone has a texture and color different from the flesh close to the skin, then the fish is not yet cooked. If the color and texture are the same all the way through, the fish is ready. Since fish come in different sizes and thicknesses, the timings given in the recipes here are approximate and must be combined with this test to determine whether the fish is ready.

When you are poaching fish or making sauces, you often need a fish stock, or *fumet*. A fish stock is made by cooking bones, heads, tails and trimmings from the fish with some parsley, onions, white wine and water for an hour or so, and then straining. You can also use shells and heads of shellfish for this purpose. If you do not have the time or the materials to do this, the best easy substitute is bottled clam juice, but keep in mind that clam juice is saltier than fish stock and therefore less salt should be used in the sauce or poaching liquid made with it.

Baked Stuffed Striped Bass

Striped bass is one of the finest fish to be found in North American waters. They come in all sizes, from 1 or 2 pounds up. To serve 12 people you will need one 10-pound or two 5-pound fish. If you have a large enough baking pan, the larger fish will do. If not, the smaller ones, side by side in a baking pan, will be easier to handle if less spectacular to serve.

¼ lb. butter (1 stick)
½ cup chopped celery
½ cup chopped onion
1 tsp. dried dillweed
½ tsp. salt
¼ tsp. freshly ground white pepper
4 cups dry bread crumbs
¼ cup water
1 striped bass (10 lbs.) or 2 (5 lbs.), cleaned, with heads and tails left on
1 lemon

(cont'd)

½ cup melted butter for buttering baking pan and basting fish

4 strips of bacon

1. Preheat oven to 350°.

2. In a skillet melt the ¼ pound butter. Cook the celery and onion in it over medium heat until they are soft but not browned, about 10 minutes. Add the dillweed, salt and pepper. Stir in the bread crumbs and mix well. If the stuffing is too dry and crumbly, sprinkle some or all of the water onto the mixture until the stuffing holds together.

3. Wash the bass under cold running water. Cut the lemon into halves, squeeze the juice into the cavity, and rub the inside and outside of the fish with the lemon halves as you squeeze. Dry the cavity of the fish with a paper towel.

4. Stuff the cavity with the stuffing and secure the flaps with food picks or small skewers. It may be necessary to stick the picks or skewers through both sides of the fish near the bottom, then tie them with string to hold the stuffing in.

5. Use some of the melted butter to grease the baking pan, and reserve the rest.

6. Place the fish in the baking pan and lay the strips of bacon across the fish.

7. Bake in the preheated oven for 45 minutes to 1 hour, test for doneness according to the instructions on page 92, and basting occasionally with the remaining melted butter. When the bacon has shriveled up substantially, remove it and discard it.

8. To serve, carefully remove the fish from the pan with two spatulas, making sure the skin on the bottom is unstuck before you lift the fish. Remove the skewers and string before serving. Pour the pan juices over the fish on the platter.

Poached Cod with Dill Sauce

6 tbsp. butter
½ cup chopped shallots
6 lbs. fillets of cod
2 cups clam juice or fish stock
2 cups milk
2 tbsp. flour
2 tbsp. chopped fresh dill, or 1 tbsp. dried dillweed
2 tsp. lemon juice

1. In a large saucepan melt 2 tablespoons of the butter and add the chopped shallots. Cook them gently over low heat until they are soft.

2. Wash the fillets of cod and cut into portion-size pieces. Arrange the fillets in the saucepan on top of the shallots, then pour over them the clam juice and the milk. Cover the pan and cook over medium heat for about 10 minutes, or until done, using test for doneness described on page 92.

3. While the cod fillets are cooking, melt remaining 4 tablespoons butter in a small saucepan. Add the flour, stir into a paste, add the dill and the lemon juice, and cook the paste over medium heat for about 3 minutes without allowing it to brown. Turn off heat.

4. When the fish is ready, turn off the heat under the poaching pan. Turn the heat on again under the dill mixture. With a ladle spoon the poaching liquid into the dill paste, a little at a time, stirring constantly over medium heat, until you have a smooth sauce of the right texture, not too thick and viscous, not too runny. You may not need to use all the liquid.

5. Carefully transfer the cooked fish to a warm platter, spoon the dill sauce over, and serve hot.

Poached Haddock with Egg Sauce

3 quarts fish stock or clam juice
6 lbs. fillets of haddock
12 hard-cooked eggs
1½ cups melted butter
2 tbsp. chopped fresh parsley
1 tbsp. Maggi liquid seasoning
½ tsp. seasoned salt
¼ tsp. freshly ground white pepper

1. Use either a regular fish poaching pan with removable platform on the bottom or any large deep saucepan lined with cheesecloth of sufficient length so that the ends can be grasped and the fish fillets removed from the pan after poaching without breaking them.

2. Bring the fish stock or clam juice to a boil in the poaching pan, then reduce to a simmer. Lower the platform or cheesecloth containing the haddock fillets into the liquid, cover, and cook for about 10 minutes until fish is done. Be sure to test for doneness before removing.

3. While the fish is poaching, peel and chop fine the hard-cooked eggs.

4. In the top part of a double boiler over simmering water, combine the eggs, melted butter, parsley, Maggi, seasoned salt and pepper. Heat through, mixing occasionally.

5. When done, remove the fish from the broth carefully, arrange on a warm platter, and serve hot with the egg sauce.

Grilled Herring with Parsley Butter Sauce

1 cup bread crumbs
1½ tsp. salt

¾ tsp. freshly ground black pepper
12 fresh herrings, about 1 lb. each, cleaned with heads
   removed
½ cup olive oil
1 cup melted butter
2 tbsp. chopped fresh parsley
2 tbsp. lemon juice

1. Mix the bread crumbs, 1 teaspoon salt and ½ teaspoon pepper together and put the mixture in a shallow dish handy to the stove.

2. Wash and dry the herrings.

3. Heat a flat grill with raised ridges fitting over two burners of the stove, or preheat the broiler.

4. Brush the fish, one at a time, with the oil, then roll in the bread-crumb mixture.

5. Grill on the surface grill, or broil in the broiler, for 3 or 4 minutes on each side. Test for doneness according to the instructions on page 92.

6. Combine the melted butter with the chopped parsley, lemon juice and remaining salt and pepper in a saucepan. Heat, and serve as a sauce for the grilled herring.

Marinated Grilled Salmon Steaks

---

12 center-cut fresh salmon steaks, ¾ inch to 1 inch thick
1 cup chopped shallots
1 large carrot, sliced thin
2 celery ribs, sliced thin
1 garlic clove, minced
½ tsp. dried thyme
½ tsp. dried rosemary
1 bay leaf
1 tsp. black peppercorns

(cont'd)

½ *cup chopped fresh parsley*
½ *tsp. seasoned salt*
  2 *cups dry white wine*
  1 *cup white vinegar*
  1 *cup olive oil*

1. Arrange the salmon steaks in 1 or 2 rectangular baking dishes with the edges of the steaks touching. The dishes should be deep enough so that you can pour liquid over the steaks to cover.

2. Combine all the remaining ingredients in a saucepan, and bring to a simmer over medium heat. Cover and simmer for 5 minutes. Remove from heat and allow the marinade to cool.

3. Pour enough of the cooled marinade over the salmon steaks to cover them. Marinate in the refrigerator for at least 4 hours, or overnight, turning once about halfway through the time.

4. Heat a stove-top ridged grill over high heat, or preheat over broiler. The olive oil content of the marinade should be sufficient to prevent sticking, but you can brush both sides of the steaks with olive oil after removing them from the marinade if you wish to make sure.

5. Grill or broil the salmon steaks for about 5 minutes on each side, not more, with high heat. Baste them with the remaining marinade while cooking, but turn them only once.

6. Serve hot with 1 last spoonful of the marinade over each slice just before serving.

Poached Whole Salmon in Aspic

1 *salmon, 8 to 10 lbs., cleaned, with the head and tail left on*
3 *cups chopped onions*
3 *cups chopped celery*
4 *large carrots, peeled and diced*

2 quarts fish stock or clam juice
2 cups white wine
2 cups water
1 tbsp. black peppercorns
2 tbsp. soy sauce
3 envelopes unflavored gelatin
2 egg whites
3 hard-cooked eggs, sliced
   paper-thin slices of cucumber (optional)

1. In a large fish poacher with a platform for lifting out the fish, poach the salmon with the onions, celery, carrots, fish stock, wine, water, peppercorns and soy sauce. Bring the liquid to a simmer, cover the poacher, and cook for about 45 minutes. Check the salmon for doneness according to the instructions on page 92 because the exact cooking time depends on size and the test is the only way to be sure.

2. Remove the salmon from the liquid by carefully lifting out the platform, and set it aside to cool.

3. Strain the cooking liquid through a cheesecloth and discard the bits of vegetable and peppercorns. Dissolve the gelatin separately in 1 cup of the liquid. When it is fully dissolved, return it to the rest of the liquid.

4. Put the liquid into a clean saucepan and bring it to a simmer, not a boil. Stir in the egg whites, and simmer the stock, covered, without boiling for 15 minutes.

5. Remove from heat and allow the stock to cool to room temperature about 1 hour.

6. While the stock is cooling, carefully remove the skin from the salmon without breaking up the flesh of the fish. Refrigerate the skinned cooked salmon.

7. Skim the impurities from the top of the cooled stock, then strain it through cheesecloth again. The egg whites should have attracted all the particles in the stock and you should now have a very clear liquid.

8. Refrigerate the strained stock. You will have to watch

the stock carefully while it is refrigerated. You want the stock to become a viscous liquid, but you do not want to chill it long enough to jell firm. Stir the stock frequently; when it is thickened enough to coat a metal spoon, but will still pour (like honey), it is ready to take out of the refrigerator.

9. Slip the whole salmon onto a serving platter. Spoon the aspic (jelled stock) over the salmon until it is completely coated. Arrange the hard-cooked egg slices over the fish in a decorative manner.

Optional: Alternate overlapping slices of egg and paper-thin cucumber slices.

10. Refrigerate the salmon to allow the first coat of aspic to jell. Coat the decorated fish again with another layer of the aspic, making sure the aspic is at the right thickness. Refrigerate the coated salmon until serving time. Wipe any excess aspic off the platter.

11. If there is any aspic left, pour it into a flat jelly-roll pan and refrigerate. When it hardens, cut it into small cubes with a knife and surround the salmon on the platter with aspic cubes for decoration. Serve cold with mayonnaise.

Poached Whole Salmon with Sauces

1. Poach an 8- to 12-pound salmon according to the instructions in step 1 for Poached Whole Salmon in Aspic (p. 98).

2. Prepare egg sauce according to steps 3 and 4 for Poached Haddock with Egg Sauce (p. 96). *Or* prepare dill sauce according to steps 3 and 4 for Poached Cod with Dill Sauce (p. 95). *Or* serve the hot poached salmon with melted butter and lemon wedges.

Salmon Mousse

3 envelopes unflavored gelatin
1½ cups fish stock or clam juice
4 cups flaked cooked salmon (see poached salmon recipe, p. 98, or use canned salmon)
¾ cup mayonnaise
¾ cup heavy cream
2 tbsp. lemon juice
2 tsp. salt
1 tsp. freshly ground white pepper
olive oil for molds
2 bunches of watercress

1. Soften the gelatin in the fish stock or clam juice, then bring it to a simmer (not a boil) in a small saucepan to melt the gelatin. When the gelatin is melted, remove from heat and allow the liquid to cool at room temperature.

2. Pass the salmon meat through a sieve or run it through the fine blade of a food mill.

3. In a mixing bowl combine the salmon, the gelatin and stock, mayonnaise, heavy cream, lemon juice, salt and pepper, and mix well.

4. Put a little olive oil on a piece of paper towel and oil the inside of an 8-cup decorative metal mold or two 4-cup molds.

5. Turn the salmon mixture into the mold(s), and refrigerate for several hours or overnight until set.

6. To serve, unmold the mousse onto a cold platter, garnish with the watercress, and serve. You may want to serve some additional mayonnaise as a sauce.

Optional: Refer to the procedures in the recipe for Poached Whole Salmon in Aspic (p. 98) for coating with aspic. You can do the same thing with the unmolded salmon mousse and coat it with aspic for extra decoration.

Fried Smelts with Tartare Sauce

2 cups mayonnaise
2 tbsp. chopped fresh parsley
3 tbsp. chopped gherkin pickles
2 tbsp. chopped green olives
1 tsp. lemon juice
½ tsp. seasoned salt
¼ tsp. freshly ground white pepper
   olive oil for frying
3 dozen fresh smelts, cleaned, with heads and tails left on
2 cups flour

1. Combine the mayonnaise, parsley, pickles, olives, lemon juice, salt and pepper in a mixing bowl and blend well. Transfer to sauce dish for serving at the table.

2. Heat a large flat griddle or 2 large skillets and add oil for frying.

3. Wash the smelts, dry them quickly, roll them in flour, and fry them on the hot griddle for about 3 minutes on each side until they are golden brown. Turn only once to avoid breaking up the fish.

4. Remove them as they are done to a hot platter and serve hot, 3 smelts per person, with the tartare sauce.

Poached Fillets of Sole in Mornay Sauce

¼ lb. butter (1 stick)
½ cup flour
3 cups milk
1½ cups heavy cream
1 tsp. salt
¼ tsp. freshly ground white pepper

2 egg yolks
1 cup grated Parmesan cheese
12 large fillets of sole
3 cups dry white wine
½ cup grated Swiss cheese

1. Melt the butter in a medium-size saucepan over low heat. Add the flour, stir into a paste, and cook the paste for 3 minutes, stirring constantly and not allowing it to brown.

2. Stir in the milk, a little at a time, stirring constantly into a smooth sauce. Bring the sauce almost to a boil, then remove from heat. Stir in 1 cup of heavy cream and the salt and pepper and set aside.

3. Beat the egg yolks into remaining ½ cup of heavy cream, then add the mixture to the sauce. Stir in the grated Parmesan, and return to heat. Heat just enough to melt the cheese without boiling, then remove from heat and set aside.

4. Using a large skillet, and doing only two or three at a time, simmer the fillets of sole in the wine for about 10 minutes. Very carefully, using a spatula, transfer the cooked fillets to a buttered baking dish.

5. When they are all in, mix the remaining wine into the prepared sauce and pour the sauce over the fish. Sprinkle the surface of the sauce with the grated Swiss cheese. Put the dish under the broiler for a few minutes until the surface of the sauce browns in spots, and serve hot.

Cold Trout in Aspic

12 trout, 8 to 9 inches long, cleaned, with heads and tails
    left on
2 cups dry white wine
2 cups clam juice or fish stock
1 bay leaf

(cont'd)

1 tsp. dried thyme
½ cup chopped onion
½ cup diced carrot
1 envelope unflavored gelatin
1 egg white

1. Preheat oven to 325°.

2. Arrange the trout in a large baking dish or in 2 smaller ones.

3. Combine the wine, clam juice, bay leaf, thyme, onion and carrot in a bowl, and mix. Pour the liquid over the fish, and bake in preheated oven for 30 minutes, testing the fish for doneness according to the instructions on page 92.

4. Carefully transfer the fish from the baking pan to a large platter and allow them to cool.

5. Strain the cooking liquid through cheesecloth. Soften the gelatin in ½ cup of the liquid and add it to the rest. Bring the liquid to a simmer in a small saucepan. Stir in the egg white, simmer for 2 more minutes, then remove from heat and allow to cool to room temperature. Strain again through cheesecloth and refrigerate.

6. While the aspic is in the refrigerator, monitor it often. You want the aspic to become fairly thickened but not fully jelled. It is ready when it will coat a metal spoon but still run with the consistency of honey.

7. Coat the trout in the platter with the aspic, refrigerate the platter, and allow the aspic to jell firm. Then remove from refrigerator, and coat it again. Keep in refrigerator until time to serve.

8. If you have aspic left over, pour it into a flat jelly-roll pan and let it chill until jelled. Cut it into small cubes with a knife and surround the trout on the platter with aspic cubes for decoration.

Sautéed Trout with Almonds

¼ lb. butter (1 stick)
12 trout, 8 to 9 inches long, cleaned, with heads and tails
      left on
      flour for dusting trout
  1 cup sliced blanched almonds
  1 tsp. salt
½ cup white wine

1. Divide the butter equally between 2 skillets and melt.

2. Dust the trout with flour so that they have a light coating.

3. Sauté the trout in the butter over medium heat until golden brown on both sides, turning once.

4. As the trout are done (you can't do them all at once) remove them to a warm platter and continue until finished.

5. Pour all the cooking butter from one skillet into the other, add the almonds and salt to the skillet, and simmer until the almonds are slightly browned. Add the wine, and simmer for 2 minutes or more to reduce volume by about one third.

6. Pour the hot sauce over the trout in the platter and serve immediately.

Sashimi (Japanese-style raw fish)

Admittedly, this dish may not appeal to everyone because of the well-known aversion of some people to any kind of uncooked meat or fish. Before turning the page, however, consider the fact that if you have ever had a piece of smoked salmon, it was smoked raw, not cooked. The same applies to prosciutto (Italian smoked ham). So perhaps you don't object to raw food quite as much as you thought. *Sashimi* must be prepared with the freshest possible fish. Do not attempt to make it with frozen fish or any fish whose recent history is impossible to verify. You must use an extremely sharp knife, preferably specially sharpened for the occasion, and cut the fish into very thin slices, cutting away all skin.

> 3 lbs. fillets of very fresh fish such as tuna, bass, halibut, snapper and trout (a variety is recommended both for taste and for appearance)
>
> 1 head of iceberg lettuce
>
> 2 cups shredded carrots
>
> 24 tbsp. soy sauce (2 tbsp. per person served in individual cups)
>
> 3 tbsp. Japanese powdered horseradish mixed with water to form a paste

1. Wash the fish fillets in ice-cold water and pat them dry with paper towels.

2. Slice them with a very sharp knife at an angle into very thin slices. Discard any bits of skin which cling to the edges.

3. Arrange a bed of iceberg lettuce on a large platter. Arrange the slices of fish in an attractive pattern, and garnish with the shredded carrots. *Or*, arrange the slices of fish on individual plates on a leaf of lettuce, giving each person an equal selection of the different kinds of fish. Serve with the soy sauce for dipping and a teaspoon of the horseradish per person.

Deep-Fried Fish Croquettes

> 4 cups leftover cooked fish or canned fish (you can use one kind or more)
>
> 2 cups leftover mashed potatoes
>
> 1 tbsp. chopped fresh parsley
>
> ½ tsp. salt
>
> ¼ tsp. white pepper
>
> 3 tbsp. butter

6 tbsp. plus 1 cup flour
2 cups milk
   oil for deep frying
3 eggs, beaten with 3 tbsp. milk
2 cups bread crumbs or cornmeal

1. Make sure all bones and skin have been removed from the fish. Combine the fish, mashed potatoes, parsley, salt and pepper in a mixing bowl and cream them together.

2. In a saucepan melt the butter, add 6 tablespoons flour to make a paste, and stir over medium heat for 3 minutes, not allowing it to brown.

3. Add the 2 cups of milk, a little at a time, forming a smooth thick sauce. Cook the sauce for 3 or 4 minutes, until smooth and very thick.

4. Add the sauce to the fish mixture in the bowl and blend well. Refrigerate the bowl for at least 1 hour to chill thoroughly.

5. Pour enough oil into a cast-iron skillet to reach a depth of about ¼ inch. Heat, controlling this very carefully; do not let the oil get hot enough to smoke.

6. Form the fish mixture into balls, about 4 tablespoons of the mixture for each. Dust the ball with flour, dip into the beaten egg mixture, then roll in the bread crumbs or cornmeal.

7. Carefully put the croquettes into the oil with a slotted spoon and fry to a golden brown color, turning once. Be careful not to splash the oil while turning. During the process of cooking you may have to add oil to the pan from time to time.

8. As the croquettes are done, remove them to a warm platter lined with paper towels to drain the oil. Keep warm until they are all done.

9. Serve hot.

Optional: The croquettes can be served with a tomato sauce, a tartare sauce, or any egg sauce such as hollandaise.

Fish Stew

Sometimes I am in the mood for fish, but I can't pin down in my mind exactly what kind. This recipe gives you an excuse to go to a fish market and pick out several kinds of fish—whatever looks especially good and fresh or is recommended by the fishmonger.

> 5 to 6 lbs. assorted fish (cod, halibut, bass, flounder, salmon, etc.; you can also use shrimps, clams or lobster if desired)
> ½ cup olive oil
> 1½ cups chopped onions
> 1 cup chopped green peppers
> 2 garlic cloves, peeled and minced
> 6 cups clam juice or fish stock
> 2 cups canned stewed tomatoes
> ¾ cup tomato paste
> 2 tbsp. chopped fresh parsley
> 1 bay leaf
> 1 tsp. seasoned salt

1. Cut the fish into 1- to 2-inch chunks, cutting right through the bone. Clean and devein any shrimps, scrub the clams and cut the lobster into chunks with a cleaver, shells and all.

2. Heat the oil in a large saucepan or stockpot. Add the onions, peppers and garlic, and simmer over low heat for 8 to 10 minutes until onions are soft and garlic has cooked. Be careful not to burn.

3. Add the clam juice, tomatoes, tomato paste, parsley, bay leaf and salt, and heat to a simmer over medium heat.

4. When the liquid is simmering, add the chunks of fish and seafood, starting with the heavier varieties and leaving the smallest and most delicate kinds of fish for last. Simmer until the clams open and the fish is done, using the test for doneness (described on p. 92) on a large chunk.

5. Serve in large soup plates; this goes beautifully with fresh hot garlic bread.

Steamed Clams with Butter

This is a marvelously informal dish which makes an enjoyable meal accompanied by French fried potatoes, coleslaw and cold beer. Use steamer clams, the soft, long-necked clams for ideal results, but any other clams can be used. It is best to use a large clam steamer, which is a two-story vessel with holes in the upper level which allow the steam from the water boiling in the lower vessel to rise and cook the clams. If the clam steamer is too big for your stove, you will have to use a separate electric hotplate or an outdoor heat source such as a barbecue grill.

    3 quarts water
    2 garlic cloves, peeled
 ½ cup white wine
    1 tbsp. black peppercorns
   12 quarts fresh steamer clams
    1 quart bottled clam juice
    2 cups melted butter

1. In the lower vessel of a clam steamer, put about 3 quarts of water, the garlic cut into several pieces, the wine and the peppercorns. Turn on heat and bring to a boil.

2. While the water is heating, scrub the clams under cold running water with a stiff brush, getting off as much of the sand as possible. Use a small sharp knife to remove any bits of seaweed caught in the shells.

3. When the water begins to give off steam, put the washed clams in the upper vessel of the steamer, cover, and steam the clams until they open, about 30 minutes.

4. Serve immediately in a large basket lined with towels. Discard any clam that did not open in the steaming. Provide each

person with a small fork, a small cup of melted butter, and a cup of hot clam juice to wash the clams in. To provide the hot clam juice, mix the bottled clam juice with the cooking liquid, *strained*, bring to a boil, and serve.

Mussels Marinière

  12 quarts fresh mussels in their shells
   3 quarts water
   2 garlic cloves, peeled
   1 bay leaf
   1 tbsp. black peppercorns
   1 pint heavy cream
   3 tbsp. chopped fresh or frozen chives
   1 tsp. seasoned salt

1. Scrub the mussels under fresh cold running water. With a sharp knife, remove any "beards" of seaweed clinging between the shells.

2. Bring the 3 quarts of water to a boil in the lower level of a clam steamer. As the water is heating, add the garlic cloves, cut into quarters, the bay leaf and the peppercorns.

3. When steam begins to rise from the water, place the scrubbed mussels in the upper vessel of the steamer, cover, and steam for 20 to 30 minutes. During the steaming, rearrange the mussels by shaking the vessel or by using tongs to move bottom mussels toward top and vice versa. When all the shells are open, the mussels are ready. Lift off the upper vessel and set it aside.

4. Strain the cooking liquid remaining in the lower vessel through cheesecloth at least once; this will remove the bay leaf, peppercorns and garlic. If the broth seems at all sandy, strain it again to remove all sand, or pour it from one pan to another after the sand has settled on the bottom and leave the last few spoonfuls with the sand behind.

5. Boil down the broth in a saucepan over high heat until it is reduced to no more than 1½ quarts. Turn off heat and allow it to cool for 2 minutes. Add the cream, chives and salt. Heat again over a low heat until hot but not boiling.

6. Remove and discard any mussel which did not open during the steaming.

7. Serve the mussels in large soup plates, with 1 or 2 ladles of the creamed broth poured over them. There should be enough for 2 helpings per person.

Mussels Provençale

12 quarts fresh mussels in their shells
3 quarts water
2 garlic cloves, peeled
1 bay leaf
1 tbsp. black peppercorns
2 tbsp. butter
2 tbsp. finely minced garlic
1 cup tomato paste
2 cups canned stewed tomatoes

1. Follow the instructions for steps 1 through 4 in the recipe for Mussels Marinière (preceding recipe).

2. Boil down the broth in a saucepan over high heat until it is reduced to no more than 1½ quarts.

3. In a small separate saucepan melt the butter and simmer the minced garlic in it for several minutes until it is softened but not browned. Add the butter and garlic to the broth.

4. Add the tomato paste and the stewed tomatoes to the broth, bring to a boil, reduce heat, and stir well until the stewed tomatoes are broken up thoroughly.

5. Serve the mussels in large soup plates, discarding any that didn't open in the steaming. Pour 1 or 2 ladles of the tomato broth over the mussels in each plate and serve hot.

Fried Oysters

Admittedly, the elegant way to eat oysters is on the half shell, served on a bed of crushed ice, and of course, quite raw. In Europe, the good restaurants don't even include the traditional little cup of tomato sauce in the middle of the plate which Americans seem to require; all you get is a wedge of lemon and perhaps some horseradish if you request it. Serving raw oysters does not require a recipe, but besides that, many people simply do not like the texture, which is rather slippery. I have known people who become quite nauseated at the mention of a raw oyster, to say nothing of the sight of one. These same people, however, will cheerfully attack a platter of fried or stewed oysters with gusto. Here is a batter-fried oyster recipe which is truly delicious.

oil for deep frying
3 quarts shucked fresh oysters
1 cup flour
3 eggs, beaten with 3 tbsp. milk
2 cups bread crumbs or cornmeal

1. Pour oil into your deep fryer to a depth of 2½ to 3 inches, and heat to 375°. If you are using a stove-top fryer which is not equipped with a thermostat, be sure to use a fat thermometer clipped to the side to monitor the temperature.

2. While the oil is heating drain the oysters and pat dry on paper towels.

3. When the oil is ready, dust the oysters lightly with the flour (you don't want gobs of flour), then dip them into the beaten-egg mixture and roll them in the bread crumbs or cornmeal.

4. Pop them into the oil. Fry only 8 or 10 oysters at a time. When they turn golden, remove them to a warm platter lined with paper towels to drain, and keep putting fresh oysters in the oil.

5. When they are all done and drained, serve hot. I advise not salting them, but leaving that to each individual at the table. You may serve tartare sauce or a tomato sauce if desired, although I personally like them best plain.

Scallops in White Wine Sauce

    3 lbs. scallops
    1 quart dry white wine
  ½ cup chopped parsley
    1 bay leaf
  ½ cup chopped shallots
   12 tbsp. butter (1½ sticks)
 1½ cups sliced fresh mushrooms
  ½ cup flour
    1 cup heavy cream
    2 egg yolks
    2 tbsp. lemon juice

1. Put the scallops in a medium-size saucepan with the wine, parsley, bay leaf and shallots, and bring to a simmer. Simmer for 5 minutes, turn off heat, remove scallops with a slotted spoon, and set aside. Strain the cooking liquid through cheesecloth and reserve it.

2. Melt 4 tablespoons of the butter in a skillet, add the mushrooms, and sauté them over medium heat until soft. Remove mushrooms with a slotted spoon, leaving the butter in the pan. Hold the mushrooms aside to add later.

3. Add the remaining butter to the skillet and melt it. Stir in the flour to make a paste, and cook for about 3 minutes, stirring frequently, without allowing the roux to brown.

4. Add the strained wine broth, a little at a time, stirring constantly to form a smooth sauce. When all the broth is mixed

into the sauce, pour off about 1 cup of the sauce into a mixing bowl. Turn off heat.

5. Add the heavy cream to this 1 cup of sauce, then with an egg beater beat the egg yolks and lemon juice into the mixture.

6. Preheat oven to 350°.

7. Return the egg and cream mixture to the main body of sauce, stir it in, and blend well over medium heat. If at this point the sauce seems too thick, add a little more wine or some more cream. Do not allow the sauce to boil.

8. Arrange the partially cooked scallops in a large baking dish. Stir the cooked mushrooms into the hot sauce, then pour the sauce over the scallops.

9. Bake the scallops in the sauce for about 15 minutes, or until the surface of the sauce begins to brown a little in spots.

10. Remove from oven and serve hot. Rice is an excellent accompaniment to this dish.

Cracked Crab with Mustard Sauce

This dish makes a perfect summer luncheon, but it can also be used as a first course in an elaborate meal in any season.

> 10 to 12 lbs. cooked crab in the shell, Dungeness, Alaskan King, Blue or any other
> 4 cups mayonnaise
> 4 tbsp. dry mustard, or 1 cup prepared mustard (your preference of strength)
> 2 tbsp. lemon juice
> 2 tbsp. Worcestershire sauce
> 1 tsp. paprika
> 3 lemons, cut into wedges for 12

1. Using a cleaver or heavy chef's knife on a board, separate the crabs into convenient pieces and crack the shells so that there is easy access to the meat.

2. Prepare 12 dishes of crushed ice, and arrange pieces of crab on them.

3. Mix the remaining ingredients except the lemon wedges together in a mixing bowl and blend well to make the mustard sauce.

4. In the center of each dish of crushed ice, put a small cup full of the sauce. Add lemon wedges to each dish and serve.

Deep-Fried Soft-Shell Crabs

4 dozen fresh or frozen, cleaned soft-shell crabs
1 to 2 quarts cooking oil
1 cup flour
2 eggs, beaten
1 cup cornmeal
½ cup water
3 lemons cut into wedges for 12

1. Wash the crabs and dry on paper towels. If they are frozen, before starting, defrost them at room temperature until all ice melts off.

2. Heat the oil in a deep saucepan or deep fryer to 375°. If you do not have an electric fryer with a thermostat (which I strongly recommend), make sure you use a fat thermometer and carefully monitor the temperature of the oil.

3. Mix the flour, beaten eggs, cornmeal and about ½ cup of water together in a bowl. The batter should be liquid, but quite thick.

4. With tongs, dip each crab into the batter, coating it on all sides, then slip it into the hot oil. The crabs require about 2 to 3 minutes of cooking; they are ready when they turn golden brown. The best system for cooking them is to continuously keep 4 to 6 crabs cooking at any one time, putting the fresh ones in and removing the ready ones as they get done. Remove the crabs

to a warm platter lined with paper towels to drain the grease, and keep warm until serving time.

5. Serve with lemon wedges and tartare or mayonnaise sauce, or with tomato-based cocktail sauce.

Baked Alaskan King Crab

6 lbs. frozen Alaskan King crab legs
1 cup melted butter
2 tsp. paprika
3 lemons cut into wedges for 12

1. Defrost the crab legs thoroughly, then slit them with a sharp knife to expose the meat.

2. Preheat oven to 375°.

3. Using a pastry brush, brush melted butter generously in the slits of the crab legs.

4. Arrange the crab legs in a baking pan, and cover with a sheet of aluminum foil. Bake for 15 minutes.

5. Serve hot with additional melted butter and the lemon wedges.

Fried Frogs' Legs

6 dozen fresh or frozen cleaned frogs' legs
  oil for frying
2 cups flour
1 tbsp. garlic salt
1 tsp. freshly ground black pepper
1 egg, beaten with 1½ cups milk

1. Dry the frogs' legs thoroughly, particularly if they are just defrosted.

2. Pour cooking oil into a heavy skillet to a depth of about ⅛ inch, and heat until it is very hot but not smoking.

3. Mix the flour, garlic salt and pepper together and place in a shallow dish near the stove.

4. Dip the frogs' legs, a few at a time, into the milk and egg mixture, then roll them in the flour mixture.

5. Fry them in the hot oil to a golden brown, turning once. As they are done, remove the frogs' legs to a warm platter lined with paper towels to drain. Keep warm until serving time.

Steamed Live Lobsters

This is perhaps the very finest food from the sea available in fresh form in North America. As with many other things, the simpler the treatment, the better the result. Although lobster can be prepared in dozens of ways with all sorts of aromatic and tasty herbs and spices, the best way to me is still steaming them live and serving them with hot melted butter, large bibs, and sturdy lobster crackers. To prepare 12 lobsters at the same time you will need a large clam steamer (see description in recipe for Steamed Clams, p. 109) or 2 very large deep pots with covers.

> 12 live Maine lobsters, 1 to 1½ lbs. each
>   hot melted butter
> 3 lemons cut into wedges for 12

1. Bring 3 or 4 quarts of water to a boil in the lower vessel of the steamer, or about 3 inches of water in the bottom of 2 large stockpots.

2. When the water begins to give off steam, put the live lobsters into the upper vessel of the steamer, or divide them between the 2 pots. Cover tightly and steam for 30 minutes.

3. To serve, remove lobsters from steamer with tongs,

place them on their backs on a board, one by one, and split them with the cleaver to crack them. Serve hot with individual cups of melted butter for each person, and lemon wedges.

Lobster Thermidor

12 *live Maine lobsters, 1 to 1½ lbs. each*
½ *lb. butter (2 sticks)*
¾ *lb. fresh mushrooms, sliced*
 1 *tbsp. sherry*
½ *cup flour*
1½ *quarts light cream*
 1 *tsp. salt*
½ *tsp. freshly ground white pepper*
 3 *egg yolks*

1. Steam the lobsters according to the recipe for Steamed Live Lobsters (p. 117) or boil them in slightly salted water for 30 minutes. For this recipe you do not need to cook the lobsters all at once, so if your pot is not large enough, do it in 2 or 3 shifts. When the lobsters are cooked, let them cool.

2. Split lobsters, carefully remove the tail meat without breaking the shells, clean out the body cavity, and save the shells. Remove the meat from the claws, and cut it together with the tail meat into bite-size pieces.

3. In a large saucepan melt the butter and simmer the sliced mushrooms in it over medium heat for a few minutes until they soften. Add the sherry, sprinkle on the flour, and mix it into the butter. Cook for about 3 minutes longer.

4. Add the cream to the pan, a little at a time, stirring into the mixture to keep the sauce smooth. Add the salt and pepper. Reduce heat and beat in the egg yolks, then cook a little longer, adding the cut-up lobster meat.

5. Spoon the lobster in the sauce into the reserved lobster

shells. Arrange the shells on a heatproof platter, then place the platter under the broiler for a minute or so to brown the surface of the sauce slightly. Serve hot.

Broiled Lobster Tails

24 *frozen South African rock lobster tails*
 1 *cup melted butter*
 2 *tbsp. chopped fresh or frozen chives*
 1 *tbsp. chopped parsley*
 1 *tbsp. lemon juice*
 2 *tbsp. soy sauce*
 2 *cups bread crumbs*

1. Allow the lobster tails to thaw completely at room temperature. With a small sharp knife loosen the meat in the shells without removing it completely. If the shell covering the flat side of the tail has not been removed before freezing, cut that away with shears first.

2. Turn on your broiler and also preheat the oven to 400°.

3. Mix the melted butter with the chives, parsley, lemon juice and soy sauce in a saucepan and put on top of the stove over very low heat to keep warm. Do not allow this butter sauce to brown or even simmer.

4. Arrange the lobster tails, flat side up, in a broiling pan. Baste lightly with the butter mixture, then bake in the preheated oven for 10 minutes, basting once more halfway through the time.

5. With tongs turn the tails over, round side up, and place under the broiler for 2 minutes. Remove from oven, turn shells over again to the flat side, baste liberally, and broil for 6 minutes.

6. After 6 minutes, sprinkle the bread crumbs over the flat side of the lobster tails, dividing the quantity as evenly as possible. Pour the rest of the butter mixture over the bread crumbs.

Return the pan to the broiler and broil for another minute or two, until bread crumbs begin to brown.

7. Remove from heat and serve immediately. You can serve additional melted butter at the table.

Deep-Fried Shrimps in Batter

oil for deep frying
2 eggs
1 tsp. seasoned salt
1 cup milk
1 cup flour
3 lbs. fresh shrimps, shelled and deveined

1. Heat the oil in your deep fryer to 375°, using either a fat thermometer or the thermostat on an electric fryer. The oil should be about 3 inches deep.

2. Beat the eggs, salt, milk and flour together in a mixing bowl to make the batter.

3. Line a platter with paper towels and put it in a warm oven to keep the shrimps hot as they are cooked.

4. Wash the shrimps under cold running water and dry them well with paper towels.

5. Dip the shrimps into the batter and fry them in the oil, not more than 6 or 8 at a time, depending on the size of your fryer. When they are golden brown, remove them to drain on the paper towels in the hot platter, and continue frying until all are done.

6. Serve the shrimps hot. Serve them with Chinese-style plum sauce and hot mustard, or with tartare sauce or tomato cocktail sauce.

Curried Shrimps

4 quarts water
1 tbsp. salt
3 lbs. fresh shrimps, shelled and deveined
12 tbsp. butter (1½ sticks)
2 cups finely chopped shallots
⅓ cup curry powder
¾ cup flour
3 cups clam juice
3 cups scalded milk
1 cup heavy cream
3 tbsp. sherry
1 tbsp. Maggi liquid seasoning
2 tbsp. lemon juice
2 tsp. sugar

1. In a large stockpot bring the 4 quarts of water to a boil with the salt.

2. Put the shrimps into the water and simmer for about 5 minutes, or until they turn opaque with pink lines.

3. When done, remove shrimps from the water, drain and set aside.

4. In a large saucepan melt the butter and sauté the chopped shallots in it over medium heat for 3 or 4 minutes, until they soften but do not brown. Stir in the curry powder and blend well.

5. Stir in the flour, making a paste. Cook the paste for about 3 minutes, stirring constantly.

6. Add the clam juice, a little at a time, stirring constantly into a smooth sauce. After the clam juice, do the same with the scalded milk, then the heavy cream. At no time during this process should the sauce be allowed to boil.

7. Add the sherry, Maggi, lemon juice and sugar, and blend into the sauce. If the sauce is too thick at this point, add a little

more clam juice to thin it to the desired consistency. It should not be too runny but thick enough to coat a spoon dipped into it.

8. Add the cooked shrimps to the sauce and keep over low heat until they are heated through, about 5 minutes.

9. Serve the curried shrimps hot with steamed rice, and garnish with chutney.

Shrimp Newburg

¼ lb. butter (1 stick)
3 lbs. fresh shrimps, shelled and deveined
1 cup sherry
12 egg yolks
3 cups heavy cream
1 tsp. paprika
½ tsp. salt

1. Cover a burner on your stove with an asbestos pad; it is very important that this recipe be prepared over low heat to avoid scrambling the egg yolks or curdling the cream.

2. Melt the butter in a large saucepan over low heat. Wash the shrimps and pat dry, then add them to the melted butter and cook over low heat for 2 to 3 minutes, turning them frequently so that the ones on the bottom do not get overcooked while leaving the top ones too raw.

3. Add the sherry and continue cooking for another 15 minutes.

4. Beat the egg yolks separately in a bowl with 1 cup of the cream and add to the shrimps in the saucepan, then add the rest of the cream and the seasonings.

5. Continue to cook and stir until the sauce thickens. Be careful at all times to keep the heat low and avoid spoiling eggs or cream. When ready, serve hot with steamed rice.

5

Poultry

You will find that most of the recipes are for easily available domestic poultry—chicken, turkey and duck. Since there is always a problem deciding on quantity for a particular number of people, here are the guidelines I have followed. For small birds such as squabs and quails, one per person. For chickens, I calculate that one 4- to 5-pound bird will serve four, that is, 2 breast portions, and 2 leg and thigh portions. For turkey, calculate about 1½ pounds precooking weight per person for roast turkey (an 18-pound turkey will serve twelve). For duck, taking into account the larger proportion of fat and the thinner breasts, half of a 4- to 5-pound duckling per person, or 6 ducklings to feed twelve.

Chicken in the Pot

For this recipe you will require a large stockpot, large enough to accommodate 3 trussed chickens. The pot should be 12 to 18 inches deep and have a capacity of 15 to 20 quarts.

3 roasting or frying chickens, each 4 to 5 lbs.
3 tbsp. olive oil
2 tbsp. butter
3 large onions
1 bunch of leeks

(cont'd)

1 head of celery
2 dozen medium-size carrots, peeled
1 bay leaf
3 large sprigs of fresh parsley
1 tsp. dried thyme
1 tsp. salt

1. Truss the 3 chickens with white string, place them in the pot, add enough cold water to cover them, and bring the water to a boil.

2. While the water is heating, heat the olive oil in a black cast-iron skillet, then melt the butter in the hot oil. When the butter is melted, peel the onions and cut them into halves. Place the onions, flat side down, in the skillet, and let them cook until the flat side is very dark brown, almost black. Then turn the onions and brown the rounded sides. Use tongs for this operation.

3. Wash the leeks and cut them into large pieces, discarding the green parts. Do the same for the celery, cutting it into 2- or 3-inch lengths.

4. When the water comes to a boil, turn off heat and skim the surface with a flat spoon or ladle to remove impurities and scum.

5. Add the browned onions, leeks, celery, carrots, bay leaf, parsley, thyme and salt to the pot, bring to a simmer, and cook covered for 1 hour and 20 minutes.

6. When the chickens are almost ready, warm 1 large or 2 medium-size platters.

7. When the chickens are done, turn off heat and remove the chickens from the broth to a cutting board. Remove the trussing strings, and with a sharp knife separate them into serving pieces—breasts, legs, thighs and wings. Arrange the pieces on the warm platter alternating with the carrots, pieces of celery and leeks. Serve hot with rice.

Poached Chicken Breasts in Dill Sauce

    7 tbsp. butter
    1 cup chopped onions
   12 large chicken breasts (breasts of 6 chickens), boned
    3 cups chicken broth or stock
    1 large bunch of fresh dill
   ½ tsp. seasoned salt
   ¼ tsp. freshly ground white pepper
    2 tbsp. flour
    1 cup heavy cream

1. In a large skillet which has a cover, melt 3 tablespoons of the butter and sauté the onions in it until they are transparent.

2. Add the chicken breasts, skin side up, to the skillet, then add the broth.

3. Strip the dill stalks, chop the delicate green tendrils fine, and set aside. Chop the dill stalks into 1-inch pieces and add them to the skillet.

4. Add the salt and pepper, and simmer the chicken breasts, covered, over low heat for 15 minutes.

5. While the chicken is cooking, melt remaining 4 tablespoons of butter in a small saucepan. Stir the flour into it, make a paste, and cook for about 3 minutes without browning. Stir the chopped dill into the paste, turn off heat, and let stand.

6. When the chicken is almost ready (cooked through but still firm), add the heavy cream to the skillet, and cook for 5 more minutes, not allowing the cream to boil.

7. Set up a bowl with a fine sieve, or a sieve lined with cheesecloth. Holding the cover of the skillet to keep the pieces of chicken from falling out, pour all the liquid out of the skillet into the sieve. Set the warm skillet containing the chicken aside, covered to stay warm.

8. Turn on the heat under the butter-dill paste, and stir the strained cooking liquid into it, a little at a time, stirring con-

stantly. Keep adding the liquid and stirring until the sauce reaches a medium-thick consistency, sufficiently thick to coat a metal spoon, but not thick enough to hold a mass.

9. Transfer the chicken breasts to a warm platter, spoon the hot dill sauce over them, and serve hot. This is another dish that goes very well with steamed rice.

Southern Fried Chicken

3 fryers, each 3½ lbs., cut into parts
½ cup melted butter
oil for deep frying
1 cup flour
1 tsp. salt
½ tsp. pepper

1. Preheat oven to 350°.

2. Arrange chicken parts, skin side up, in a baking pan, brush them with melted butter, and bake in preheated oven for 10 minutes, brushing on additional butter after 5 minutes.

3. While the chicken is baking, heat the oil in your deep fryer to 375°.

4. After the chicken is baked, put the flour, salt and pepper in a large paper bag. Toss 1 or 2 pieces of the baked chicken in the paper bag until coated, then set them out handy to the deep fryer. Continue this process until all the chicken is coated.

5. Line a platter with paper towels and place in warm oven.

6. Fry the pieces of chicken in the hot oil for 10 to 12 minutes, until golden brown, only a few pieces at a time depending on the size of your fryer. When done, remove them to the warm platter to drain.

7. When all the chicken has been fried, remove paper towels from platter and serve the chicken hot. This chicken can also be refrigerated for up to 3 days and eaten cold, on a picnic, etc.

Roast Chicken with Herb Stuffing

Although there are many prepared foods which are over-priced and sadly lacking in quality and freshness of taste, prepared stuffing mixes tend to be an exception. If you are short of time or do not wish to go to the trouble of making stuffing from scratch, follow the directions on the package of a good-quality herb stuffing mix so as to yield about 6 cups of stuffing (2 cups per bird). I generally hesitate to recommend brands of products, but in this case the exception proves the rule. The best brand I have tasted in the United States is called Pepperidge Farm Herb Stuffing Mix.

FOR THE STUFFING:

½ lb. butter (2 sticks)
1 cup chopped onions
1 cup chopped celery
3 cups chicken stock or broth
8 cups soft bread crumbs
¼ cup chopped fresh parsley
2 tsp. dried thyme
1 tsp. dried rosemary

1. In a skillet melt 4 tablespoons of the butter and sauté the onions and celery in it over medium heat until the onions are softened. Turn off heat.

2. In a large saucepan melt the remainder of the butter in the broth. When it is melted, add the bread crumbs, parsley, herbs, and the onions and celery from the skillet. Toss until everything is well mixed. Set stuffing aside to cool for a few minutes before stuffing the chickens.

FOR THE CHICKENS:

3 roasters, 4 to 5 lbs. each
coarse (Kosher) salt
¼ lb. butter (1 stick), softened

(cont'd)

> 6 slices of bacon or thin slices of fatback
> 3 tsp. poultry seasoning
>   fresh black pepper in a pepper mill
>   livers, giblets and necks from the chickens
> 2 cups chicken broth

1. Wash the chickens with cold water and pat dry, making sure the cavities are dry. Salt the inside of the cavities lightly with Kosher salt.

2. Divide the stuffing into 3 equal portions, and stuff the chickens. Truss the birds and sew up the cavity openings.

3. Butter the skins of the chickens with the softened butter, and place 1 slice of bacon or fatback over each side of each breast. Sprinkle the chickens with poultry seasoning and a little pepper (one or two turns of the mill).

4. Preheat the oven to 400°.

5. Arrange the chickens on roasting racks in baking pans. You may be able to get 2 chickens in 1 large baking pan, and the other in a small one. Put the chickens into the preheated oven and reduce the temperature setting immediately to 350°.

6. In a saucepan put the necks, livers and giblets in the broth, turn on low heat, and keep hot.

7. Roast the chickens for about 2 hours, until the juice runs clear from a prick in the thickest part of the leg. During the cooking, baste frequently with the drippings, using a basting bulb. About 30 minutes before the end of the cooking, remove the bacon or fatback from the breasts and continue to baste.

8. When the chickens are done, remove them to a carving platter. Pour off about half the fat from the baking pans and reserve remaining liquid. Quickly remove the necks from the broth and discard them. Chop the giblets and livers very fine and add them to the large baking pan. Pour the giblet broth into the small baking pan, hold it over medium heat, and deglaze the pan by scraping down the drippings. Pour the contents of the small pan into the large pan and repeat the operation. Pour the resulting gravy into 1 or 2 gravy boats. Once the chickens

are cooked, it is important to carry out all the last steps quickly. Have a board ready to chop the giblets nearby, and a chopper or knife handy. Have potholders handy to hold the baking pans over the heat with one hand while you scrape up the drippings with a spoon in the other. Have the gravy boats convenient for pouring out the gravy from the pan, which is a slightly clumsy operation.

9. Carve the chickens at the table. Don't forget to have a large serving spoon available to serve the stuffing. I suggest not serving potatoes or any other starch when you have stuffed chicken, because that tends to make the meal too heavy. Serve the gravy, and have a light salad or a green vegetable for accompaniment.

Chicken Florentine

12 large chicken breasts (breasts of 6 chickens), boned
½ cup melted butter
4 cups chicken broth or stock
1 tsp. seasoned salt
¼ tsp. freshly ground black pepper
3 lbs. fresh spinach
4 quarts water
12 tbsp. butter (1½ sticks)
1 cup heavy cream
½ cup flour
3 cups milk
2 tsp. salt
1 cup grated Parmesan cheese
1 cup grated Swiss cheese

1. Remove the skin from the chicken breasts. Arrange them in a large skillet with a cover available, or in 2 smaller ones. Pour the melted butter over the breasts. Add 2 cups of the chicken

stock to the pan without pouring it over the breasts. Sprinkle with the seasoned salt and pepper, cover, and simmer gently for 30 minutes.

2. While the breasts are cooking, wash the spinach and remove any thick ribs. Bring the 4 quarts of water to a boil in a large pot or saucepan. Drop in the washed spinach and simmer for 20 minutes. When done, remove from heat and drain.

3. Shift the spinach to a chopping bowl or board, and chop it roughly. Do not chop it very fine.

4. Prepare 2 baking dishes large enough to accommodate all the chicken breasts in one layer on top of the spinach without crowding. Butter the baking dishes generously with 4 tablespoons of butter.

5. Mix the chopped spinach in a bowl with ½ cup of the heavy cream. Make a bed of the spinach about ¾ to 1 inch deep in the baking dishes.

6. Melt remaining butter in a large saucepan, then quickly stir flour into it; keep stirring the resulting paste over medium heat for another 2 minutes.

7. Off heat, add the milk, remaining cream and the salt and cook, stirring constantly, over medium heat for 1 minute. Add remaining 2 cups of the chicken broth and bring to a boil. Turn off heat immediately, stir in the grated cheeses, and let them melt into the sauce without any more cooking.

8. Arrange the poached chicken breasts on top of the spinach in the baking dishes. Spoon a thick layer of the cheese sauce over the chicken.

9. Using the position in the broiler farthest from the source of heat, heat under the broiler until the top of the sauce begins to brown in spots. Remove from the broiler and serve hot.

Chicken Mousse with Velouté Sauce

For this recipe use either 12 1-cup molds or 2 6-cup decorative molds, whichever you prefer. The individual servings are easier to handle, but the decorative molds may be more attractive.

    4   cups cooked chicken (no bones or skin)
    4   tbsp. butter
    4   tbsp. flour
    2   cups chicken broth or stock
    ½   tsp. salt
1 ¾   cups heavy cream
    2   tsp. Worcestershire sauce
    4   eggs
    3   tbsp. Madeira wine
    ½   tsp. freshly ground white pepper
        softened butter for the molds

1. Preheat the oven to 325°.

2. Run the cooked chicken through a meat grinder until very finely ground. Do it twice if necessary.

3. In a saucepan melt the butter, add the flour, and stir into a paste. Cook the paste while stirring for about 2 minutes.

4. Add the stock, stirring constantly. Reduce heat, stir in the salt, ½ cup heavy cream and the Worcestershire sauce. Turn off heat and leave on stove while doing the next step.

5. Separate the eggs. Beat the yolks slightly, then add them to the ground chicken. Beat the whites until they form soft peaks. In a separate bowl, beat remaining 1 ¼ cups of heavy cream until it forms soft peaks.

6. Add the Madeira and the pepper to the ground chicken mixture, then pour in half of the prepared velouté sauce.

7. Mix the chicken with the sauce and egg yolks thoroughly, then fold the chicken mixture first into the beaten egg whites, then that mixture into the whipped cream.

8. Butter the molds (either individual or decorative) and prepare 1 or 2 pans of hot water in which to set the filled molds before baking.

9. Pour the mousse mixture into the molds, set them in the pans of water, and bake in the preheated oven. If you use individual molds, allow about 1 hour. If you use larger molds, allow 1¼ hours. When the mousse is ready a cake needle plunged into the center will come out clean.

10. During the last few minutes of baking, heat up the remaining velouté sauce in the saucepan again, so that it is ready to serve hot with the mousse.

11. Unmold the mousse onto serving platters or individual plates. Coat the mousse with the hot sauce and serve.

Casserole of Chicken in Burgundy

¼ lb. butter (1 stick)
3 stewing chickens (5 to 6 lbs. each), separated into cooking pieces (legs, thighs, wings, breasts)
6 slices of bacon
2 cups finely chopped onions
3 carrots, peeled and sliced thin
½ cup very thinly sliced leek (white part only)
½ cup flour
½ cup chopped fresh parsley
1 bay leaf
1 tsp. ground thyme
3 tsp. salt
1 tsp. freshly ground black pepper
1 quart dry Burgundy wine
1 lb. fresh mushrooms
1 to 2 tbsps. arrowroot (optional)

1. Use a large enamelware casserole or pot which will hold

all the ingredients comfortably. Melt the butter in the casserole, then over medium heat, brown the pieces of chicken on all sides. Remove the chicken pieces as they are browned and set them aside.

2. Cut the bacon slices into 1-inch pieces and add them to the pot. Let them continue to cook as you add the onions, carrots and leek. Stir these vegetables in the butter and bacon, and let them brown slightly.

3. Add the flour to the pot; stir it into the mixture until it has been absorbed and there are no white bits of flour showing.

4. Return the browned chicken pieces to the pot; add the parsley, bay leaf, thyme, salt, pepper and wine. Cover the casserole and simmer for 1 to 1¼ hours. The chicken meat should be cooked through but not falling off the bone.

5. While the casserole is cooking, wash the mushrooms and slice thin. Add them to the casserole about 30 minutes after it is fully assembled.

6. Before serving, skim any fat floating on top of the liquid in the casserole. If the cooking liquid seems too thin, dip a little bit out of it with a measuring cup, add 1 or 2 tablespoons of arrowroot to the cup, and stir to dissolve it well. Return the mixture to the casserole and stir it in, continuing to cook for a minute or two. This will provide a slight thickening with no aftertaste.

7. The ideal accompaniment for this dish is steamed white rice.

Broiled Half Chickens à la Joy

This recipe was invented by my wife, and is named after her. In the first place she is a chicken lover surpassed by no one, so you can be sure it's good. In the second place this recipe has probably been tested more often than any other in this book, so you can be sure it works.

2 cups soy sauce (please use Japanese, not Chinese)
1 cup fine olive oil
2 tbsp. minced fresh garlic
2 tbsp. dried onion chips
6 squab chickens, 2 to 2½ lbs. each, split into halves (12 halves)

1. Mix together the soy sauce, olive oil, garlic and onion chips.

2. Wash and dry the chicken halves, put them in any large pan, pour the mixture over them, and marinate, basting occasionally with a spoon, for about 4 hours. You can even leave them in the marinade in the refrigerator overnight if you wish, as long as you remember to baste them occasionally.

3. Preheat the oven to 350°.

4. Transfer the chicken halves to 1 or 2 baking pans, or throw-away foil pans, and bake in the preheated oven for 50 minutes, basting every 10 minutes. Be careful not to use up all the marinade, because you will need some later.

5. Remove the chickens from the oven. Using either a stove-top grill or the broiler in the stove, broil on each side for about 3 minutes, until golden brown. Baste generously with the marinade during the broiling and serve hot. Any remaining marinade should be poured over the chickens on the serving platter.

Individual Chicken Potpies

To make these little potpies you need a dozen deep oven-proof pie dishes. They should be made of thick earthenware with straight sides, and should have a capacity of about 1½ cups each.

3 roasters, 4 to 5 lbs. each, cut up into parts
2 cups chopped celery
2 cups sliced carrots

2 cups diced raw potatoes
2 cups sliced fresh mushrooms
2 cups pearl onions
1 bay leaf
1 tbsp. salt
½ tsp. freshly ground black pepper
¼ lb. butter (1 stick)
½ cup flour

FOR THE CRUST:

4 cups all-purpose flour
3 tbsp. baking powder
2 tsp. salt
5 tbsp. shortening
1½ cups milk

1. In a deep covered casserole combine the chicken pieces, celery, carrots, potatoes, mushrooms, onions, bay leaf, salt and pepper. Add enough cold water to cover by about 1 inch. Bring to a boil, then reduce heat and simmer, covered, for about 1 hour. To test for doneness, remove a piece of chicken with tongs and see if it is tender all the way to the bone.

2. Remove all the pieces of chicken to a large cutting board. Separate the meat from the bones and discard all bones and skin. Strain the remaining contents of the pot to separate the cooked vegetables from the liquid. Reserve the liquid.

3. In a separate saucepan melt the butter, stir in the flour, and make a smooth paste, stirring constantly.

4. Add the reserved cooking liquid, little by little, stirring all the time, until you have a smooth fairly thick (but not pasty) gravy. If there is not enough liquid, add some canned chicken broth or consommé to bring the gravy to the desired consistency.

5. When the gravy is ready, pour it back into the original casserole. Add the boned and skinned cooked chicken meat and the cooked vegetables, making sure to remove the bay leaf, and

combine well with the gravy. Set this aside while making the crust.

6. Preheat oven to 450°.

7. Sift the flour, baking powder and salt into a mixing bowl. With your fingers, rub the shortening into the flour, combining it well. Pour in the milk, and mix just enough to moisten all the flour.

8. Gather the dough into a mass, and transfer it to a floured board. Knead the dough for about 1 minute, then roll it out into a sheet about ¼ inch thick.

9. Hold one of your earthenware pie dishes upside down on the dough and score 12 circles into the surface of the dough. With a sharp knife or cutter, cut around the outside edge of each circle, making the dough about ¼ inch larger all around the circumference than the scoring indicates.

10. Divide the chicken and vegetable mixture evenly among the 12 pie dishes, filling them up to the top. Lay 1 circle of dough over each, pressing down the edges to make them adhere to the edges of the dish. Cut 2 or 3 slashes into the surface of the dough.

11. Bake the pies in the preheated oven for about 20 minutes, or until the crust is golden brown.

12. The pies should be served immediately, but if there is some delay they will keep hot for a long time in a warm oven because the earthenware dishes retain heat.

Optional: You can substitute green peas, lima beans, diced turnips or other vegetables for the ones in the recipe if you like.

Chicken Breasts Maryland

12 *chicken breasts (breasts of 6 chickens), boned*
1 *tbsp. salt*
1 *tsp. freshly ground black pepper*
  flour for dusting

4 eggs, beaten
2 cups unflavored bread crumbs
   olive oil for frying
¼ lb. butter (1 stick)
12 thin ham steaks, ¼ inch thick
12 Baked Tomatoes (see recipe, p. 224)

1. Sprinkle the chicken breasts with salt and pepper, then dust them with flour.

2. Dip the breasts into the beaten eggs, then roll them in the bread crumbs, making sure a good layer of the bread crumbs adheres to both sides.

3. Heat 2 large cast-iron skillets, one for the ham steaks, one for the chicken.

4. Heat about ¼ cup of olive oil in one skillet, add the butter to it, and let the butter melt. Sauté the chicken breasts in the butter and oil until they are golden brown on both sides.

5. When you turn the breasts over to cook the second side, put the ham steaks into the other skillet and fry them for about 2 minutes on each side. Try to time the cooking so that both ham and chicken are ready at about the same time.

6. Use either a large platter or individual plates. Place 1 chicken breast on each ham steak and garnish with a baked tomato. Serve hot with mustard or horseradish.

Tarragon Chicken

---

1 large bunch of fresh tarragon
3 fryers, each 3½ lbs., cut into parts
1 tbsp. salt
1 tsp. freshly ground black pepper
4 tbsp. olive oil
¼ lb. butter (1 stick)
2 cups pearl onions   (cont'd)

2 cups tiny mushrooms or small mushroom caps
½ cup dry white wine

1. Carefully separate the fresh tarragon leaves from the stalks. Using a small sharp paring knife, slip 1 or 2 tarragon leaves under the skin of each piece of chicken. Chop the remaining tarragon leaves fine, and reserve.

2. Sprinkle the salt and pepper over the chicken pieces. Heat the oil in a heavy casserole, then melt the butter in the oil.

3. Brown the chicken in the oil and butter until golden brown on both sides.

4. Remove the pieces of chicken with tongs and set aside.

5. Add the chopped tarragon, onions, mushrooms and white wine to the casserole, cover, and simmer the vegetables for 5 minutes. Return the chicken to the casserole, cover, and simmer for 30 minutes, until the chicken is tender.

6. Serve hot with steamed white rice.

Note: This dish can be prepared in advance, subtracting about 15 minutes of the final cooking time. Reheat in the casserole just before serving.

Chicken Marengo

This is the famous Napoleonic dish, for which there are dozens of different versions. I don't hesitate to add one more to the list because it is truly delicious.

3 fryers, each 3½ lbs., cut into parts
½ tsp. salt
¼ tsp. freshly ground black pepper
1 cup flour
¼ cup olive oil
12 tbsp. butter (1½ sticks)
¼ cup Cognac or brandy
1 cup finely chopped shallots

1 lb. mushrooms, caps separated from stems, the stems chopped very fine

4 cups finely chopped peeled, seeded tomatoes

2 cups thin strips of cored, seeded green peppers

2 small cans (about 1⅓ cups) thick tomato paste

2 cups dry white wine

2 cups pitted black olives, without liquid

1. Sprinkle the chicken parts with the salt and pepper, and dust them with flour.

2. Heat the olive oil in a large casserole and melt 8 tablespoons of the butter in the oil. Add the chicken pieces and brown them to a golden brown on all sides. This will require some agile work with long tongs. You can also do this in shifts if you wish, but all the pieces must be in the casserole at the same time for the next step.

3. Sprinkle the Cognac over the browned chicken in the casserole. Flame it immediately and let it alone until the flames burn down completely. This takes only a few seconds, but be sure to light the Cognac with a long fireplace match held at arm's length, or a twisted piece of newspaper held the same way.

4. Remove the pieces of chicken from the casserole and set them aside.

5. Add the chopped shallots and the finely chopped mushroom stems to the casserole, and sauté them for a minute or two until they soften.

6. Add the chopped tomatoes, green peppers, tomato paste and 1 cup of the white wine. Let the vegetables simmer, covered, over medium heat for 5 minutes.

7. Return the chicken pieces to the casserole, and baste them with the sauce a few times. Cover and cook at a gentle simmer for 45 minutes.

8. Once the casserole is assembled, melt remaining 4 tablespoons of butter in a smaller saucepan, add the remaining wine and the mushroom caps to it, cover, and simmer gently for 20 minutes while the casserole is cooking.

9. Add the mushrooms, wine and all, to the main casserole, as well as the black olives.

10. The chicken Marengo is ready when the chicken meat is tender and the other ingredients have combined well into a sauce. Serve hot, making sure each person gets some mushroom caps and olives on his plate.

Optional and a little unwieldy: A traditional garnish for this dish is a fried or poached egg on a buttered toast round with each portion, but I find it too difficult to try to do this for 12 people and still serve everything hot.

Chicken Hash

---

  6 *cups cubed cooked chicken meat*
  3 *cups light cream or half and half (½ milk, ½ cream)*
¼ *lb. butter (1 stick)*
  6 *tbsp. flour*
  4 *cups milk*
  6 *egg yolks*
  2 *tsp. salt*
  1 *tsp. chopped fresh chives*
⅓ *cup grated Parmesan cheese*

1. In a saucepan gently simmer the cooked chicken meat in the light cream until the amount of liquid is substantially reduced and the cream has thickened.

2. While the chicken is cooking, melt the butter in a saucepan, stir in the flour, and stir into a smooth paste.

3. Scald the milk in a separate pan and add it to the flour mixture, stirring constantly.

4. Stir the egg yolks into the sauce, beating well with a whisk, and add the salt.

5. Add the white sauce to the chicken, stir in the chopped chives, and transfer the whole thing to 1 or 2 ovenproof dishes.

6. Turn on the broiler. Sprinkle Parmesan cheese on the surface of the sauce.

7. Heat the chicken hash under the broiler just long enough to brown the top, and serve hot.

Chicken Fricassee

3 fryers, 3½ lbs. each, cut up into parts
4 large carrots, peeled and cut into chunks
3 celery ribs, cut into 2-inch pieces
1 bay leaf
1 tsp. black peppercorns
2 tsp. salt
¼ lb. butter (1 stick)
¾ cup flour
3 egg yolks, beaten
1½ cups light cream or half and half (½ milk, ½ cream)
3 tbsp. lemon juice
2 tbsp. chopped parsley

1. In a large stockpot or casserole simmer the chicken pieces with the carrots, celery, bay leaf, peppercorns and salt, in enough water to cover the chicken and vegetables by 1 inch, covered, for 1 hour, or until the chicken is tender and cooked through but not falling off the bones.

2. Remove the pieces of chicken to a warm platter and keep warm while preparing the sauce. Strain the liquid in which the chicken was cooked, and have it ready.

3. In a medium-size saucepan melt the butter and stir in the flour, making a smooth paste.

4. Stir in the strained cooking liquid, a little at a time, until you have the desired consistency for the sauce. It should be smooth and fairly thick, but it should pour easily and not form a mass.

5. Stir in the beaten egg yolks, cream and lemon juice with a wire whisk, keeping heat low to avoid boiling the sauce and scrambling the yolks.

6. Pour about half the sauce over the chicken on the platter (or platters), and sprinkle the chopped parsley over the top for decoration.

7. Transfer the remaining sauce to a sauceboat and serve at table with the chicken.

Chicken Livers in Port Wine

¼ lb. butter (1 stick)
3 cups finely chopped onions
4 lbs. fresh chicken livers
2 tsp. salt
½ tsp. freshly ground black pepper
3 cups port wine
1 tbsp. arrowroot
12 slices of white bread, toasted

1. Melt the butter in a large skillet, add the chopped onions, and sauté them until they have softened, about 3 minutes.

2. Wash the livers in cold water, pat dry, and add to the skillet over high heat. Toss the livers as they cook, browning them on all sides quickly. As they are browning sprinkle on the salt and the pepper.

3. As soon as all the livers have been browned, reduce heat and pour in the wine.

4. Bring it to a simmer, and simmer until the volume of liquid has been reduced by half or more. Dip out ½ cup of liquid, blend it with the arrowroot until all the powder dissolves, then pour the mixture back into the pan.

5. Cook for a few more minutes, stirring the sauce while it thickens slightly from the arrowroot.

6. Arrange the slices of toast on individual plates, spoon a good portion of the livers in their sauce over the toast, and serve hot.

Chicken and Turkey Cutlets

1 loaf of packaged white bread, crusts trimmed off
¼ lb. butter (1 stick), melted
1 cup chicken broth
4 lbs. boned and skinned chicken breasts (weight after skinning and boning)
4 lbs. boned and skinned turkey breasts (weight after skinning and boning)
3 eggs
1 cup very finely chopped onions
1 tbsp. Maggi liquid seasoning
1 tsp. salt
¼ tsp. freshly ground white pepper
flour for dusting the cutlets
shortening for frying the cutlets
2 cups heavy cream

1. Put the white part of the bread in a mixing bowl, add the melted butter and chicken broth, and mash into a paste with a wooden spoon.

2. Run the chicken and turkey meat through a meat grinder (or have the butcher do it), and add the meat to the bowl. Add the eggs, chopped onions, Maggi, salt and pepper. Knead the mixture together with your hands, blending all the ingredients thoroughly.

3. Lay out a piece of wax paper near the stove. Form the cutlets by hand, about the size of a large ice-cream scoop, dust them with flour, and arrange them on the wax paper ready to cook. This recipe should yield about 24 cutlets, depending on the size you make them, but you can make them smaller or larger if you wish.

4. Melt shortening in a heavy black cast-iron skillet, and brown the cutlets on both sides to a medium brown color. This should take 2 or 3 minutes for each side and will have to be done

in shifts. As the cutlets are browned, remove them to a shallow ovenproof dish (or two) and arrange them in the dish with their sides touching.

5. Preheat the oven to 325°.

6. Divide the cream evenly among the dishes of cutlets, and bake them in the preheated oven for 45 minutes. The cream should be gently simmering but not boiling.

7. Serve the cutlets hot, spooning a little of the cream over as a sauce.

Optional: You can bake the cutlets and let them get cold, to serve as a cold dish for luncheon or supper. They can be sliced and used for sandwiches or as cold cuts.

Large Roast Turkey

Although it takes some time, roasting a large turkey is one of the easiest ways to feed a crowd. Your butcher probably won't have a 20- to 25-pound turkey on hand whenever you ask for it, unless it's the week before Thanksgiving, so be sure to drop in on him a week or so before you need it and place an order. Cooking time for a big turkey is about 20 minutes per pound, so be sure you allow the better part of the day for the job. Once the turkey is in the oven, it merely requires basting every 30 minutes or so. Have the butcher provide some pieces of salt pork, cut into ¼-inch-thick slices, to place over the breast of the turkey while it's roasting.

> *1 hen turkey, 20 to 25 lbs.*
> *¼ lb. butter (1 stick), softened*
> *2 tbsp. poultry seasoning*
> *salt pork slices for turkey breast*
> *4 cups chicken broth*

1. Preheat oven to 325°.

2. Spread the softened butter all over the skin of the turkey, then sprinkle with the poultry seasoning. Arrange salt pork to cover the entire breast of the bird.

3. Place the turkey on a rack in a large roasting pan and put in the preheated oven. Make a careful note of the time you started and at what time the turkey should be ready, calculating 20 minutes to the pound.

4. After the turkey is in, put the giblets and neck in a saucepan with the chicken broth. After about 3 hours, turn on low heat under this broth and let it get hot.

5. While the turkey is roasting, baste thoroughly with a basting bulb every 20 or 30 minutes after the first hour and a half. For the last hour, remove the salt pork from the breast. If the drippings are too scant, or if they begin to burn, add a little of the hot chicken broth to the pan, let it soak up some taste, then baste with it.

6. When you puncture the thick part of the leg, and the juice runs clear with no traces of red, the turkey is ready. Remove the turkey to the carving board, and quickly make the gravy.

7. Strain the chicken broth into the roasting pan. Chop up the giblets and livers from the saucepan and add them to the roasting pan. Hold the roasting pan, using a potholder, over one burner of the stove. Scrape all the drippings into the simmering broth, and cook it down so that the liquid is reduced by about one third. If there is too much fat in the gravy, carefully pour off some of it before transferring to the gravy boat.

8. Carve the turkey at the table and serve the gravy separately.

STUFFING THE TURKEY:

1. Follow the recipe for Herb Stuffing (p. 127), in the recipe for roast chicken.

2. To make oyster stuffing, add 1 cup of chopped fresh oysters to the herb stuffing.

3. To make sausage stuffing, slice 1½ cups of breakfast

sausages into thin slices, brown them in a frying pan for 2 minutes, and mix them into the other ingredients for herb stuffing.

4. When you are stuffing the turkey, insert the stuffing in the cavity, truss up the opening and proceed with the roasting, *adding 5 minutes per pound to the roasting time.*

Turkey Tetrazzini

1½ lbs. thin egg noodles (*you can use the recipe for Home-made Egg Noodles, p. 69*)
 4 quarts water
 5 tsp. salt
 6 tbsp. olive oil
 2 garlic cloves, minced
 3 tbsp. chopped parsley
1½ lbs. mushrooms, sliced thin
 ½ tsp. freshly ground black pepper
 ½ lb. unsalted butter (2 sticks)
 6 tbsp. flour
 3 cups chicken broth
1½ cups light cream or half and half (½ milk, ½ cream)
 1 cup dry white wine
 6 cups cubed cooked turkey meat
 1 cup grated Parmesan cheese

1. Bring 4 quarts of water with 3 teaspoons of the salt to a boil. Add the noodles, and cook them for 8 minutes. Drain through a colander and set aside.

2. Heat the oil in a large skillet and add the garlic, parsley, mushrooms, 2 teaspoons salt and the pepper. Stir over medium to low heat for about 5 minutes, until the mushrooms soften.

3. In a separate saucepan melt the butter; stir in the flour, blending well.

4. Add the broth to the mixture, stirring constantly until the

sauce thickens. Stir in the cream, then the wine, and continue to cook until heated through but not boiling.

5. Preheat oven to 325°.

6. Pour a little of the cream sauce into a 4-quart deep oven-proof casserole. Add the drained cooked noodles to the casserole, followed by the contents of the mushroom skillet, then the cubed turkey and finally the rest of the cream sauce. Sprinkle the surface of the sauce with the Parmesan cheese.

7. Bake the casserole for about 20 minutes.

8. Serve hot.

Optional: Just before serving put the casserole under the broiler for a minute to brown the top slightly.

Braised Duck in Wine Sauce

The main problem with serving duck to 12 people is that, unless you want to appear stingy, you must allow ½ duck per person. The reason is that although the duck looks as big as a chicken, it has much less meat and more fat and thicker bones. The breast meat is often only thick enough to yield 2 decent slices, and the thighs and drumsticks are not very large. To serve this dish you will need a large pan with a cover, capable of holding 6 ducks, that is at least 5 inches deep, preferably 6 inches. The ideal would be a square or rectangular cast-aluminum pan, 6 inches deep, 24 inches wide and 30 inches long, fitted with a cover. You can buy such a pan at a restaurant supply house. If it is not possible, you may have to use 2 or 3 casseroles to accommodate the ducks, in which case you should apportion the sauce accordingly.

> ¼ *lb. butter (1 stick)*
> 6 *ducklings, each 4 to 4½ lbs., cleaned and oven ready*
> 8 *slices of bacon, cut into 2-inch lengths, blanched in boiling water*
> (cont'd)

3 cups small white onions
3 cups chicken broth
3 cups red wine
1 bay leaf
1 large sprig of parsley
1 tbsp. salt
1 tsp. freshly ground black pepper

1. Melt the butter in a large skillet. Using tongs, brown the ducks, 1 duck at a time, on all sides in the butter, then set them aside.

2. Add the blanched bacon to the skillet, and cook over medium heat for 2 minutes.

3. Add the small onions to the skillet, and cook over medium heat until they just begin to turn brown.

4. Pour off most of the fat from the skillet. Add the chicken broth, wine, bay leaf, parsley, salt and pepper, and simmer the sauce very gently for about 10 minutes, until it is slightly reduced in volume. If the skillet you used to brown the ducks is not big enough, move this whole operation into one of the casseroles after pouring off the fat.

5. While the sauce is cooking, arrange the ducks in the large casserole described at the beginning of the recipe, or in 2 or 3 smaller casseroles.

6. Pour the wine sauce over the ducks, cover the casserole tightly, and cook over medium heat for about 1 hour and 15 minutes. Ducks should be tender and cooked through.

7. The best way to make the serving easy is to cut the ducks into halves, right down the backbone, with large poultry shears. You can choose between arranging the duck halves neatly on serving platters, or serving them on individual plates. In any case, after halving the ducks return the halves to the warm casserole while you do the rest.

8. When they are all cut, arrange them on platters or plates, spoon a little sauce over them, and serve. Serve the remaining sauce in a gravy boat at the table. Be sure to skim excess fat from the surface of the sauce before using it.

Roast Duckling with Apple Stuffing

FOR THE STUFFING:

¼ lb. butter (1 stick)
4 cups chunks of peeled cored apples
4 cups chicken broth
8 cups soft bread crumbs
1 tbsp. ground cinnamon
¼ cup chopped fresh parsley
2 tsp. dried thyme
1 tbsp. salt

1. In a large saucepan melt the butter, then add the apple chunks. Cook, covered, for 6 to 7 minutes, but not long enough to let the pieces disintegrate.

2. Add the chicken broth, bread crumbs, cinnamon, parsley, thyme and salt, and toss together thoroughly so that all the ingredients are well blended and the bread crumbs well moistened.

3. Allow the stuffing to cool before stuffing duck cavities.

FOR THE DUCKS:

6 ducklings, each 4 to 4½ lbs., oven ready
salt shaker
pepper mill

1. Season the cavities of the ducks with salt and pepper, then stuff loosely with the apple stuffing. Sew the cavities tightly with white string and trussing needles. Prick the thighs and fatty portions of the ducks in several places to help the fat cook off during roasting.

2. Preheat oven to 350°.

3. Arrange the trussed and stuffed ducks on racks in roasting pans. Roast in the preheated oven for 1½ hours, until a puncture in the fleshy part of the thigh yields clear juice with no trace of red.

4. During the roasting time it is not necessary to baste the

ducks, but rather to periodically remove the accumulated fat with a basting bulb. One duck will normally yield about 1½ cups of fat.

5. When the ducks are ready, turn off oven and remove them, one at a time. Cut the ducks into halves down the backbone with poultry shears, then cut through the stuffing with a knife to separate the halves.

6. Arrange the duck halves on a warm platter, each with its own half-cavity filled with stuffing. Serve hot.

Optional: You can make some gravy by pouring off the fat from the roasting pans and adding a little wine and beef consommé, scraping down the pan while holding it over a burner of the stove, then pouring off the liquid into a gravy boat. It is not essential to do this because the apple stuffing helps keep the meat of the ducks quite moist.

Casserole of Duck with Cherries

> 6 *ducklings, each 4 to 4½ lbs., ready to cook*
> *salt shaker*
> *pepper mill*
> ¼ *lb. butter (1 stick)*
> 1 *cup Cognac or brandy*
> 4 *cups chicken broth or consommé*
> 1 *cup dry white wine*
> 2 *tbsp. sugar*
> 6 *cups pitted sweet red cherries*

1. Season the inside of the ducks with salt and pepper. Preheat oven to 350°.

2. Arrange the ducks on racks in baking pans and roast them in the preheated oven for 1 hour, occasionally removing accumulated fat from the pans with a basting bulb.

3. Remove the ducks to a carving board, and cut them apart into pieces (leg, thigh, breast).

4. In a large casserole or stockpot melt the butter, add the duck pieces, and sauté them lightly for 1 or 2 minutes. Pour the Cognac or brandy over the pieces and flame it. Let the flames die down by themselves; they will only burn for a few seconds.

5. Add the chicken broth, wine and sugar to the pot and simmer for 5 minutes. Add the cherries and cook for 5 more minutes.

6. Transfer the duck pieces to a warm platter and spoon some sauce over them, serving the remaining sauce with the cherries separately at the table.

Roast Goose

---

2 geese, each 8 to 10 lbs., cleaned and oven ready
salt shaker
pepper mill
2 cups chopped onions
1 tsp. dried thyme
2 cups water
1 cup chicken broth
1 cup Madeira wine
2 tsp. arrowroot

1. Season the cavities of the geese with salt and pepper. Insert 1 cup of onions into the cavity of each goose. Sprinkle ½ teaspoon of thyme into each.

2. Preheat oven to 325°.

3. Prick thighs and other fatty places on the geese in several places to help the fat run off. Truss the geese.

4. Set up 2 racks in 2 roasting pans, and set a goose, breast side up, on each one. Add 1 cup of water to each pan.

5. Roast in the preheated oven for about 3½ hours, fre-

quently removing the accumulated fat from the surface of the water with a basting bulb, and adding water to replace evaporation.

6. Check for doneness by pricking thick part of thigh. If the juice runs clear, the goose is ready, but if the juice is a little bloody, the bird requires more time.

7. When done, remove geese to warm serving platters while you make the gravy.

8. Remove as much fat as possible from the roasting pans, then scrape the remaining drippings into one pan from the other. There should be very little water left. Add the chicken broth and the Madeira with the arrowroot dissolved in it to the pan and hold over a burner on the stove. Let the liquid simmer and thicken as you scrape down the pan drippings. Transfer the gravy to a gravy boat and take to the table.

9. Carve the geese in the same manner as a turkey, remembering that there is less breast meat on a goose. The meat is very rich so do not serve excessively large portions.

Roast Squabs

12 young 1-lb. squabs
   salt shaker
   pepper mill
12 tbsp. butter (1½ sticks), softened
1½ tsp. dried thyme
12 thin squares of salt pork, each large enough to cover the entire breast of 1 squab

1. Season the cavities of the squabs with salt and pepper.

2. Rub the outside of the skins liberally with the softened butter and sprinkle with the dried thyme. Lay 1 square of salt pork over each breast.

3. Preheat oven to 325°.

4. Arrange the squabs, breasts up, in 1 or 2 roasting pans. They may be arranged quite close together. Roast in the pre-heated oven for 1 hour and 10 minutes, basting frequently with a basting bulb. It is important not to neglect the basting because squabs are not very fat and will dry out quickly in the oven if not kept moist.

5. To check for doneness, simply check to see that a leg moves easily. Or you may prick a thigh to see that the juice does not run bloody. During the last 15 minutes of cooking time, remove the squares of salt pork with tongs, and baste the breasts liberally with the pan drippings.

6. When the squabs are done, remove them quickly to a warm serving platter. Add a little water to the roasting pan and scrape down the drippings, holding the pan over a burner and simmering the gravy. Serve hot, 1 squab per person, and pass the gravy in a gravy boat.

Broiled Quail

These marvelous little birds have a distinctive flavor and need very little in the way of seasonings. The directions given are for a normal broiler in a stove with the heat source above the pan. The quail can also be broiled over charcoal with excellent results. Try to remove any lead shotgun pellets which may remain in the flesh; they can destroy a tooth for you if not found.

    12 quail, cleaned and ready to cook
        salt shaker
        pepper mill
    ½ lb. butter (2 sticks), softened

1. Preheat oven broiler.
2. Split the quail from the back, not cutting through the skin completely so that the halves stay connected. Sprinkle them

with a little salt and freshly ground black pepper.

3. Spread the quail on both sides with softened butter.

4. Broil for about 5 minutes on each side, starting with the skin side down. If you must do this in 2 shifts, have a warm oven ready to keep the first batch warm while you broil the second batch.

5. If the quail are fresh and plump, they will not require any gravy or sauce.

Meat

Roast Sirloin of Beef

I much prefer a roast sirloin to a standing rib roast because, invariably, the rib roast contains enormous amounts of fat, while the sirloin has much less waste.

6- to 8-lb. sirloin roast, tied and trimmed, leaving ¼ inch outside layer of fat
2 tsp. freshly ground black pepper
1 cup beef consommé

1. Preheat oven to 300°.
2. Weigh the meat exactly, and figure out the roasting time at 20 minutes to the pound for medium rare, 18 minutes for rare, and 25 minutes per pound for medium to well done.
3. Rub the meat all over with the pepper.
4. Roast to the desired degree of doneness according to your calculation.
5. When ready, remove the roast from the oven and transfer the meat to the carving board, cutting and removing the strings.
6. Add the consommé to the roasting pan; hold the pan over a burner and simmer the consommé, reducing it by a third in volume and scraping down the drippings. If there is too much

fat in the gravy, carefully pour some of it off before using.

7. Carve into *thin slices,* and serve hot with the gravy. Do not attempt to serve thick slices of this roast; it will not be soft and tender like a rib roast. The thin slices are more attractive and the meat is tastier.

Pot Roast of Beef, Onion Sauce

6 cups roughly chopped onions
4 cups beef broth or consommé
1 tsp. black peppercorns
1 bay leaf
2 first-cut pieces of brisket of beef, about 4 lbs. each
2 garlic cloves, peeled and crushed

1. Using a large casserole or stockpot, simmer the onions in the broth with the peppercorns and the bay leaf over medium heat for about 30 minutes.

2. While the onions are cooking, rub each of the briskets with 1 crushed garlic clove. This will have to be done by hand, and I suggest a rubber glove if you don't want the garlic odor to cling to your hand.

3. When the onions have cooked for about 30 minutes, place the 2 pieces of meat in the pan, right on top of the onions. Baste them a little with the juice, and cover.

4. Reduce the heat to low, and cook slowly for about 4 hours, basting occasionally, and turning the meat about once every hour.

5. Remove the pieces of brisket carefully from the pot, and transfer them to a carving board. Cut thin slices against the grain. Smother the slices with the onion sauce from the pot, and serve hot. If you prefer, you can slice all the meat and arrange the slices on a warm platter, then cover the slices with sauce. Serve any remaining sauce in a gravy boat.

Short Ribs of Beef

6 slices of bacon, cut into 1-inch pieces
8 lbs. short ribs of beef, cut into 2-inch sections
3 cups chopped onions
2 tsp. seasoned salt

1 tsp. freshly ground black pepper
2 cups beef broth or consommé
½ cup red-wine vinegar
1 garlic clove, peeled and crushed

1. Have an ovenproof casserole or large Dutch oven ready. Preheat oven to 350°.

2. In a large skillet fry the bacon until the bottom is well coated with bacon fat.

3. Add the short ribs and brown them on both sides in the bacon fat, then remove the meat with tongs and place it in the casserole.

4. Add the onions to the skillet and brown them in the remaining fat. Remove them with a slotted spoon and add them to the casserole, discarding the remaining fat.

5. Season the meat with the salt and pepper. Add the broth, vinegar and garlic to the casserole, cover, and bake in the preheated oven for 2½ hours. Baste every 30 minutes or so; if all the liquid dries up, add a little more broth.

6. When the ribs are ready they can be kept warm in the oven with the heat turned off. Serve them hot with rice or egg noodles or boiled potatoes.

Marinated Roast Fillet of Beef

2 cups finely chopped onions
4 garlic cloves, minced fine

(cont'd)

½ cup olive oil
1 cup red-wine vinegar
¾ cup Cognac or brandy
2 tbsp. soy sauce
1 cup beef consommé
1 tsp. freshly ground black pepper
1 cup chopped fresh parsley
1 bay leaf
1 whole fillet of beef, about 5 lbs.

1. In a saucepan simmer the onions and garlic in the olive oil just long enough to soften them.

2. Add the vinegar, Cognac, soy sauce and consommé, and bring to a simmer. Turn off heat and add pepper, parsley and bay leaf.

3. Set the fillet of beef in any utensil large enough to hold it that also has a cover. The ideal would be an enamel or stainless steel fish poacher, because its elongated shape would fit the fillet best, and the enamel or stainless steel will not react with the acid of the marinade. Pour the marinade from the saucepan over the meat, baste several times, cover, and refrigerate. Leave in the marinade overnight, basting occasionally.

4. Preheat oven to 450°.

5. Pour off the marinade, but reserve it. Roast the beef in a roasting pan for 10 minutes to the pound. It is important to have the exact weight of the meat before roasting. Baste with the marinade occasionally during the roasting.

6. When done, remove from over, transfer fillet to carving board, and pour the remaining marinade into the roasting pan. Hold the pan over a burner of the stove and scrape down the drippings. Reduce the volume of the gravy to about 2 cups. This is a very strong-tasting gravy and only a spoon or two will be needed for each serving of meat.

7. Slice the fillet into ½-inch steaks and serve hot with the gravy.

Cold Fillet of Beef with Aspic

This is an elegant and luxurious dish, ideal for a buffet or for a warm-weather meal. Since this is a decorative as well as a tasty production, you should keep in mind that the key element of decoration is the clarity of the aspic. If it is crystal clear with a dark golden-brown color and shining surface, then you have succeeded.

> 1 whole fillet of beef, 5 lbs., tied with thin strips of salt pork
> 4 cans, 10½ oz. each, concentrated beef consommé
> 2 eggs
> 6 envelopes unflavored gelatin
> 12 slices of black truffle (or substitute black olive slices)

1. Preheat oven to 450°. Weigh the fillet accurately.

2. Roast the whole fillet in a roasting pan for 12 minutes to the pound.

3. Remove from oven and allow to cool at room temperature. Remove strings and salt pork. Slice the fillet into ¼-inch slices, as evenly as possible.

4. Mix the consommé with sufficient water to make 2 quarts of liquid. Place the consommé in a clean, greaseless saucepan. Bring to a simmer, not a boil.

5. Separate the eggs and store the yolks for use elsewhere. Stir the whites into the simmering consommé with a whisk, and add the crumbled shells of the eggs to the saucepan. Simmer for 10 minutes. While it is simmering, dip out about a cupful of the liquid, stir the gelatin with it until all the grains are dissolved, then return it to the simmering consommé.

6. Remove from heat and let the consommé stand for about 1 hour. Then strain it through several thicknesses of cheesecloth into a clean pan. This will remove all the impurities and leave a clear aspic.

7. Use a long loaf pan, or any other decorative mold shaped so that the slices of beef can stand up in it on end and leave some clearance. Pour about ¼ inch of aspic into the mold, and arrange the truffle slices in the bottom. Refrigerate the mold and let this layer set.

8. Refrigerate the rest of the aspic to allow it to set *partially*. You want the aspic to thicken but not to jell solid. Check it frequently. When it has thickened but is still loose enough to pour slowly, you are ready for the next step.

9. Arrange the slices of beef in the mold, standing upright, then fill with the partly set aspic, making sure it works in between the slices, separating them from each other with a thin aspic layer, and also making sure there are no air bubbles.

10. Refrigerate the mold and allow it to set solidly. Save the remaining aspic.

11. A few hours before serving, unmold the beef in aspic onto a silver platter or other suitable serving platter. Bring the extra aspic to a liquid by warming it up if necessary, and pour it onto the platter, making a layer about ⅛ inch deep surrounding the beef. Refrigerate the platter and allow it to set, creating the appearance of the mold standing on a shiny surface of aspic.

12. For additional decoration, you can jell the remaining aspic in a jelly roll pan, let it set, cut it into cubes, and sprinkle the cubes artistically over the platter. Keep the whole thing refrigerated until shortly before serving time. Service is easy because the slices of meat are already separated and need no carving.

Minute Steaks for Twelve

The "minute" in the name is truly the secret of preparing this always popular dish. The steaks must be pounded thin enough so that merely touching a hot pan causes them to cook immediately.

12 minute steaks, about ¼ inch thick before pounding
1 tbsp. olive oil
6 tbsp. softened butter
1 tbsp. lemon juice
1 tbsp. chopped fresh parsley
pepper mill

1. Pound the steaks between two pieces of wax paper with a meat mallet or the side of a heavy cleaver to reduce their thickness by almost half.

2. Lightly oil a large griddle, 2 heavy skillets or other good frying surface with the olive oil. Heat the griddle so that a drop of water sprinkled on it immediately steams away without rolling.

3. Spread both sides of the steaks with a thin coating of the soft butter.

4. Lay the steaks on the cooking surface. By the time you have placed the last one, the first one is ready to turn. Turn them all in the same order. Immediately sprinkle them with the lemon juice, then the parsley, then quickly grind a little pepper from the mill over them (4 or 5 turns in all).

5. Remove the steaks from the griddle and serve immediately.

Swiss Steak

This favorite dish is made with a big piece of round steak, about 1 inch thick. One such piece is sufficient to serve 6 people, so for 12 you will need 2 large skillets equipped with covers.

2 large slices of round steak, 1 inch (or more) thick, 5½ to 6 lbs. altogether
2 garlic cloves, peeled and crushed
¾ cup flour
4 tsp. salt

(cont'd)

1 tsp. pepper
6 tbsp. olive oil
2 cups chopped onions
1 cup diced peeled carrots
1 cup finely sliced celery
2 cups canned stewed tomatoes, drained of their liquid
2 cups beef broth or consommé

Note: In following these instructions, all the ingredients must be divided evenly between the 2 skillets as you go along.

1. Rub each steak with crushed garlic on both sides.

2. Mix the flour, salt and pepper together, then pound the powder into the steaks on both sides with a meat mallet or the side of a heavy cleaver.

3. Put the steaks into hot olive oil in the skillets, brown on first side, then turn over.

4. Add the onions, carrots, celery, tomatoes and beef broth to the skillets. Cover and simmer over low heat for at least 1 hour, until the steaks are tender and can be cut with a fork. Depending on the amount of heat, this may take 1 hour and 20 or 30 minutes.

5. To serve, transfer the steaks to a warm platter, smother in the cooked vegetables, and slice at the table. The use of a carving board is not necessary because the meat should be tender enough to cut easily into even slices on the platter.

Beef Stew

---

8 lbs. stewing beef, cut into 1-inch cubes
4 tbsp. olive oil
4 medium-size to large onions, peeled and cut into halves
¼ lb. butter (1 stick)
8 carrots, peeled and sliced
1 head of celery, trimmed of leaves and sliced

4 cups beef broth or consommé
1 bay leaf
1 cup tomato paste
3 cups canned stewed tomatoes
¼ cup freshly ground black pepper
3 tsp. salt
½ cup dry red wine
2 tbsp. Worcestershire sauce
2 quarts water
6 medium-size potatoes

1. Place a large casserole or stockpot on one front burner of the stove.

2. In a heavy cast-iron skillet brown the cubes of beef on all sides in the oil, just long enough to brown, then transfer them to the casserole. This will require several shifts.

3. When the beef cubes are all browned, place the onion halves flat side down on the hot skillet and leave them until the flat side is very brown, almost burned. Transfer the onion halves to the casserole.

4. Pour off the fat in the skillet and reduce the heat slightly. Add the butter and let it melt. Simmer the sliced carrots and celery in the butter for about 8 minutes, turning or tossing frequently and browning just a little. Transfer the vegetables to the casserole with a slotted spoon, discarding butter left in the skillet.

5. Add the broth, bay leaf, tomato paste, stewed tomatoes with their liquid, pepper, 1 teaspoon salt, the wine and Worcestershire sauce to the casserole. Bring to a boil, then reduce heat, cover, and simmer gently for about 2 hours or more, until meat is tender.

6. While the stew is cooking, bring the water to a boil in a separate saucepan. Peel the potatoes, add remaining 2 teaspoons salt to the water, cut potatoes into rough quarters, and boil them for 10 minutes. Remove them from the water and add them to the stew for the last hour of cooking time.

7. The stew can be kept hot for several hours until serving.

It may also be stored overnight and reheated another day; this stew tends to taste even better after a day or two. You will find the portions here, even for 12 people, rather large, but you will be delighted that you have some left over.

Meat Loaf

    4 lbs. freshly ground beef
    2 lbs. freshly ground shoulder of pork
    6 tbsp. butter, softened
    ½ cup fine unflavored bread crumbs
    ½ cup chopped fresh parsley
    ½ tsp. freshly ground black pepper
    2 tsp. salt
    6 hard-cooked eggs, shelled
    4 carrots, scraped and boiled
    2 cups bottled chili sauce

1. Combine the meats, 5 tablespoons of the butter, the bread crumbs, parsley, pepper and salt in a mixing bowl, making sure all the ingredients are well blended throughout.

2. Preheat oven to 350°.

3. Butter a flat baking pan (18 × 14 inch) with the remaining butter.

4. Mold the meat mixture into a loaf, arranging the hard-cooked eggs near the center, end to end for the length of the loaf, and the carrots in 2 lines in a similar manner, end to end. The idea is that each slice of the loaf will have incorporated a round slice of egg and 2 round slices of carrot.

5. Place the molded loaf on the buttered baking pan and bake in the preheated oven for 1¼ hours. Halfway through the cooking time, pour the chili sauce over the top and let it cook in to moisten the loaf.

6. Slip the loaf off the pan onto a serving platter, baste with

any remaining sauce and drippings, and serve. Slice at the table, and serve additional chili sauce to go with it.

Meat Loaf Variations: You can vary the proportions of meat in the loaf, and you can use lamb as well. You can use different vegetables, and you can use different sauces, such as a thickened meat sauce with mushrooms in it, for example. When you have made the meat-loaf recipe once, you will see how easy it is to add your own special touches.

All-purpose Meatballs

These meatballs can be used in a spaghetti sauce, or served plain, or used in combination with just about anything.

6 slices of plain white bread, crusts trimmed
1 cup beef consommé
3 lbs. freshly ground beef, preferably round steak
¼ cup minced onion
3 tbsp. chopped fresh parsley
1 egg
½ cup grated Parmesan cheese
1 tsp. salt
½ tsp. freshly ground black pepper
1 cup olive oil

1. Soak the trimmed white bread slices in the beef consommé

2. Pour off excess consommé, then add the beef, onion, parsley, egg, cheese, salt and pepper, and blend together thoroughly with your hands; no other implement will do.

3. Form the meatballs by hand, making them about 1 inch in diameter. One way I use to make them uniform is to use a small ice-cream scoop, scooping up a full measure each time, scraping it off against the side of the bowl, then ejecting the meat.

4. Heat the olive oil in a large skillet, and brown the meatballs on all sides. Serve hot with spaghetti and tomato sauce, or with egg noodles, or rice.

Spicy Hamburgers

6 lbs. freshly ground round steak or other good cut of beef
1 cup very finely chopped onions
1 egg
½ tsp. freshly ground black pepper
⅛ tsp. cayenne pepper
4 to 6 drops of Tabasco

1. Combine all the ingredients in a large mixing bowl. Blend well with a wooden spoon, making sure the onions aren't concentrated in bunches anywhere.

2. Form the meat into patties. You can use a hamburger press or an ice-cream scoop, but the main thing is to make them all of equal size.

3. Broil or fry the patties for 3 or 4 minutes on each side, depending on desired doneness.

4. Serve on toasted hamburger buns or rolls.

Meatballs in Dill Sauce

3 lbs. freshly ground lean beef
2 cups finely minced onions
1 cup finely minced green peppers
1 cup chopped fresh dill
½ tsp. freshly ground black pepper
¼ cup olive oil
¼ lb. butter (1 stick)

½ cup flour
2 to 3 cups beef broth or consommé
1 cup milk
1 tsp. salt
2 tbsp. Worcestershire sauce

1. In a mixing bowl combine the beef, onions, green peppers, ½ cup of the dill and the pepper. Blend the mixture well by hand.

2. Form the beef mixture into 1½-inch-diameter balls.

3. Heat the oil in a cast-iron skillet, and quickly brown the meatballs in the oil on all sides.

4. In a large saucepan melt the butter, add the flour to it, and mix over medium heat into a paste. Mix the other ½ cup of chopped dill into the paste.

5. Add the beef consommé and milk, stirring constantly, until you have a smooth sauce. Continue stirring and cooking as you add the salt and Worcestershire sauce.

6. When the sauce is ready, add the meatballs to it and heat through over low heat, not allowing the sauce to boil.

7. Serve hot, as a buffet dish or over rice.

Corned Beef Hash

4 lbs. cooked corned beef
4 tbsp. butter
1 cup finely minced onions
½ cup finely minced celery
4 large potatoes, peeled, boiled and diced very small (4 to 5 cups)
2 tbsp. Worcestershire sauce
2 tbsp. tomato paste
1½ cups beef broth or consommé
12 eggs
tomato ketchup or chili sauce

1. Put the corned beef through the coarse blade of your meat grinder.

2. Melt the butter in a large saucepan and sauté the minced onions and celery in it until the onions are soft and transparent.

3. Add the meat, potatoes, Worcestershire sauce and tomato paste to the pan, and toss well to blend all ingredients.

4. Add the beef broth, a little at a time, stirring over medium heat, until all the liquid is absorbed into the hash.

5. Poach the eggs and keep them warm on a platter while the hash is being finished.

Optional: You can heat a heavy cast-iron skillet, add a little butter to it, and carefully place the whole mass of the hash into it. Let it brown, then turn the whole thing over to brown the other side. This creates a crust which some people find tasty.

6. Serve the hash hot, with 1 poached egg on top per person, and serve with one of the prepared tomato sauces.

Roast Leg of Veal

1 whole leg of veal, 12 to 15 lbs.
2 garlic cloves, crushed
1 tsp. freshly ground black pepper
2 onions, sliced
1 cup beef broth
1 cup Madeira wine

1. Rub the meat with the crushed garlic and the pepper.

2. Preheat oven to 325°.

3. In a large roasting pan scatter the sliced onions, making a layer.

4. Put the meat, fat side up, on the onions and roast for 12 minutes to the pound, about 2½ hours for 12 pounds of roast. During roasting time, baste with the pan drippings occasionally; add a little water if the onions start to get blackened.

5. When roast is done, transfer meat to the carving board.

6. Add the beef broth and the wine to the roasting pan and simmer, holding pan over a burner and stirring and scraping down the drippings. Reduce the volume of liquid by about a third, then strain and use the liquid as gravy.

Stuffed Shoulder of Veal

>   3 tsp. salt
>   1 tsp. freshly ground black pepper
>   1 tbsp. lemon juice
>   1 boned shoulder of veal, 6 lbs. after boning
>   12 tbsp. butter (1½ sticks)
>   ½ cup chopped onion
>   ½ cup chopped celery
> 1½ cups chicken broth
>   4 cups soft bread crumbs
>   ¼ cup chopped fresh parsley
>   1 tsp. dried thyme
>   ½ tsp. dried rosemary
>   1 cup beef broth, or more

1. Mix the salt, pepper and lemon juice together and rub the veal with it inside and out.

2. In a skillet melt 4 tablespoons of the butter and sauté the onion and celery over medium heat until the onion is softened. Turn off heat.

3. In a saucepan melt another 4 tablespoons butter in the chicken broth. When it is melted, add the bread crumbs, parsley, herbs and the cooked onion and celery; toss until well mixed. Let the stuffing cool for a few minutes before stuffing the veal.

4. Lay out the veal shoulder with the skin side down. Spread the stuffing over it in a thick layer, then roll up the meat and tie

it with several pieces of white string so that it holds together firmly.

5. Preheat oven to 350°.

6. Using a large roasting pan equipped with a cover, or a Dutch oven, bake the meat uncovered for about 30 minutes. Add the cup of beef broth to the pan, then the remaining 4 tablespoons of butter. Baste the meat, cover, and bake for 2 hours. During this time, baste the meat once every 20 minutes or so. If the liquid evaporates too fast, add a little more beef broth.

7. To serve, remove the roast from the oven, transfer to carving board, and strain remaining liquid from the pan to use as gravy.

Baked Veal Chops with Sour Cream and Mushroom Sauce

---

  1 cup flour
3½ tsp. salt
  ¾ tsp. freshly ground white pepper
 12 loin chops of veal, each ¾ to 1 inch thick
  ¼ lb. plus 6 tbsp. butter
  1 cup dry white wine
  ½ lb. mushrooms, sliced thin
  3 cups sour cream

1. Mix the flour, 3 teaspoons salt and ½ teaspoon pepper together in a bowl or dish.

2. Coat the chops with the flour mixture on both sides.

3. Heat ¼ pound of the butter in a skillet, and brown the chops on both sides to a medium-brown color, not burned.

4. Preheat the oven to 350°.

5. Put the browned chops into a covered baking dish, add the wine, cover, and bake in the preheated oven for 1 hour.

6. While the chops are baking, sauté the sliced mushrooms in remaining 6 tablespoons butter, seasoning them with remaining salt and pepper, until they are softened but not browned very much.

7. Pour off excess butter from the pan, and add sour cream. Heat over very low heat without allowing the cream to boil and curdle.

8. When the chops are done, remove them from the oven and arrange on a warm platter or individual plates. Spoon the sour cream sauce over them and serve.

Veal Cutlets Milanese

 2 eggs
½ cup milk
¼ tsp. freshly ground white pepper
 1 cup grated Parmesan cheese
 1 cup dry unflavored bread crumbs
12 5 to 6 oz. veal cutlets (cut from the leg, each ⅜ to ½ inch thick)
 2 tbsp. olive oil
 4 tbsp. butter

1. Beat the eggs in the milk.

2. Separately, mix together the pepper, grated Parmesan and bread crumbs.

3. Dip the cutlets into the egg mixture, then roll in the crumbs and cheese, pressing down on the crumbs so that they adhere.

4. Heat the oil in a large skillet, melt the butter in the oil, then fry the cutlets in the oil and butter mixture until they are golden brown on both sides. Serve hot.

Veal Cutlets with Cheese Sauce

¼ lb. plus 4 tbsp. butter
½ cup flour
3 cups milk

1½ cups heavy cream
1 tsp. salt
¼ tsp. freshly ground white pepper
2 egg yolks
1 cup grated Parmesan cheese
12 5 to 6 oz. veal cutlets (cut from the leg, each ⅜ to ½ inch thick)
½ cup grated Swiss cheese

1. Melt ¼ pound of butter in a medium saucepan over low heat. Add the flour, stir into a paste, and cook the paste for 3 minutes, stirring constantly and not allowing it to brown.

2. Stir in the milk, a little at a time, stirring constantly into a smooth sauce. Bring the sauce almost to a boil, then remove from heat. Stir in 1 cup of the heavy cream and the salt and pepper and set aside.

3. Beat the egg yolks with remaining ½ cup heavy cream, then add this mixture to the sauce. Stir in the grated Parmesan cheese and return to heat. Heat just enough to melt the cheese without boiling, then remove from heat and set aside.

4. Pound the cutlets with a meat mallet until they are about ¼ inch thick. Using a large skillet, and doing only one or two at a time, sauté the cutlets in remaining 4 tablespoons of butter for about 3 minutes on each side, until they are lightly browned.

5. Make a layer of the sauce in a large baking dish, then alternate layers of the cooked cutlets with layers of sauce until they are all in and the top layer is sauce.

6. Sprinkle the surface with the grated Swiss cheese, then put the baking dish under the broiler as far as possible from the source of heat using medium-low heat for about 5 minutes or until the surface of the sauce browns in spots. Serve hot.

Wiener Schnitzel Holstein

12 5 to 6 oz. veal cutlets (cut from the leg, each ⅜ to ½ inch thick)
 2 tsp. salt
¾ cup flour
24 anchovy fillets (about two 2-oz. cans)
¼ lb. butter (1 stick)
    butter for frying eggs, about 4 tbsp.
12 eggs
 3 lemons, cut into quarters

1. With a meat mallet or other heavy utensil, pound the cutlets so that they are reduced in thickness by half.

2. Mix the salt and the flour together. Coat the cutlets with the flour-salt mixture on both sides. Open the cans of anchovy fillets and drain them; separate and count out the fillers.

3. Heat a griddle for cooking the cutlets, melt butter on it, and sauté the cutlets on both sides until they are golden brown. Remove the cutlets to a warm platter and keep warm while frying the eggs.

4. Scrape the griddle clean, and quickly fry the eggs "sunny side up."

5. While the eggs are frying, quickly place 1 cutlet on each of 12 plates. Put 1 fried egg on each cutlet, cross 2 anchovy fillets over the yolk, and add a lemon wedge to each plate. Serve immediately.

Veal Scaloppine Marsala

12 veal scallops, each ½ inch thick
 2 tsp. salt
 1 tsp. freshly ground black pepper

(cont'd)

¾ *cup flour*
½ *cup olive oil*
6 *tbsp. butter*
3 *cups thinly sliced mushrooms*
1 *cup Marsala wine*

Note: The scallops will have to be cut to order for you by your butcher because they are thicker than usual.

1. Pound the scallops with a meat mallet until they are ¼ inch thick.

2. Mix the salt, pepper and flour together, and coat the pounded scallops with the mixture on both sides.

3. Using a large skillet equipped with a cover, heat the olive oil and melt the butter in the hot oil. Sauté the veal scallops on both sides, just browning them.

4. Add the mushrooms and the wine to the skillet, cover, reduce heat, and simmer together with the veal for 10 minutes.

5. Transfer the meat to a hot platter, pour the sauce and mushrooms over, and serve.

Veal Stroganoff

 1 *lb. fresh mushrooms*
 7 *tbsp. olive oil*
10 *tbsp. butter*
½ *cup minced shallots*
½ *tsp. salt*
⅛ *tsp. freshly ground black pepper*
 5 *lbs. loin of veal, cut into 2-inch strips*
 2 *cups beef broth or consommé*
½ *cup dry white wine*
 2 *cups heavy cream*
 1 *tbsp. arrowroot*

1. Slice the mushrooms. Heat 3 tablespoons of the oil and 6 tablespoons of the butter in a large skillet. Sauté the mushrooms for a few minutes until slightly browned, then add the shallots, salt and pepper, and cook for 2 minutes more. Remove from heat. Transfer the contents of the skillet to another container because you will need the skillet again.

2. Heat remaining 4 tablespoons oil and 4 tablespoons butter in the skillet, and brown the pieces of veal on both sides slightly. Remove the meat from the skillet after it has browned.

3. Add the broth and the wine to the skillet. Boil down the liquid until it has reduced by about two thirds. Reduce heat and add heavy cream, stirring well.

4. Dip up ½ cup of the cream sauce, blend it with the arrowroot, and return the mixture to the pan, stirring until the sauce thickens.

5. Return first the mushrooms, then the meat, to the skillet, and continue to heat just long enough to heat the meat without overcooking.

6. Serve hot with rice.

Veal Kidneys with White Wine Sauce

 4 *quarts water*
12 *veal kidneys*
 2 *cups dry white wine*
 4 *cups thinly sliced onions*
½ *cup chopped fresh parsley*
¼ *lb. butter (1 stick), melted*
 1 *tbsp. Maggi liquid seasoning*
 2 *tsp. salt*
½ *tsp. freshly ground black pepper*

1. Bring 4 quarts of water to a boil in a large saucepan. Cut the kidneys into halves and remove the cores. Drop the halves

into the boiling water and cook for about 3 minutes. Remove from water and drain in a colander.

2. Put the drained kidneys in a bowl, pour the wine over them, and let them soak in the wine for 2 to 3 hours, basting and turning occasionally. Do this at room temperature.

3. In a large skillet or saucepan simmer the onions and parsley in the melted butter until the onions soften but do not brown.

4. Add the kidneys to the skillet, add Maggi, salt and pepper, and half of the wine in which the kidneys soaked. Cover the skillet and simmer for about 20 minutes, until the kidneys are tender.

5. Serve hot, slicing each half kidney into several slices at the table and spooning some wine sauce over them.

Rabbit Stew

3 rabbits (3 lbs. each), ready to cook, disjointed into legs, thighs and back pieces
salt shaker
pepper mill
flour for dusting
¼ lb. butter (1 stick)
12 slices of bacon, cut into 2-inch lengths, blanched in boiling water
2 cups pearl onions
4 large carrots, peeled and sliced thin
1 cup beef broth or consommé
1 cup dry red wine
1 lb. fresh mushrooms, sliced thin

1. Sprinkle the rabbit pieces with salt and pepper, then dust with flour.

2. Using a large casserole, brown the meat in the butter on

all sides, then remove the meat from the casserole and set aside.

3. Add the pieces of blanched bacon to the casserole, then the onions and carrots. Toss the vegetables in the butter over medium heat until the onions are slightly browned.

4. Return the rabbit pieces to the casserole, add the beef broth and wine, and simmer gently, tightly covered, for 1 hour.

5. Add the mushrooms to the pot, and simmer for 10 or 15 minutes longer, still tightly covered. Skim off fat wherever possible and serve the stew hot.

Note: It is important to keep the stew tightly covered while cooking. If you fail to do so, there will not be enough liquid to keep it moist. Be prepared to double the quantities of consommé and wine if necessary.

Roast Haunch of Venison

---

3 cups red wine
1 cup beef consommé
1 garlic clove, minced
1 cup finely minced onions
4 tbsp. soy sauce
4 tbsp. lemon juice
1 bay leaf
1 haunch of venison, without lower part of leg, 8 to 9 lbs.
  several ¼-inch-thick slices of salt pork, sufficient in size
  to cover the venison on one side

1. Mix the wine, consommé, garlic, onions, soy sauce, lemon juice and bay leaf in a container large enough to hold the meat. Immerse the meat in it and marinate for at least a whole day, turning the meat over several times during this period and basting occasionally.

2. Preheat oven to 450°.

3. Arrange the meat on a rack in a large roasting pan, and

cover with the salt pork. Strain the marinade, discarding the bits of onion, but save the liquid for basting.

4. Roast the meat at high temperature for 30 minutes. Reduce oven temperature to 350°, and roast for 2 hours and 20 minutes. This will yield a medium-rare roast. For well done, increase cooking time by about 20 minutes.

5. To serve, remove roast to carving board, discarding salt pork. Add the marinade to the roasting pan; holding the pan over a burner of the stove, scrape down the drippings and simmer the gravy. Reduce volume by about half, skim off the fat, and serve in a gravy boat.

Calf's Liver and Smothered Onion Casserole

---

12 large slices of fresh calf's liver, each about ¼ inch thick
¾ cup flour
¼ cup olive oil
¼ lb. butter (1 stick)
6 cups thinly sliced onions
2 tbsp. Worcestershire sauce
1 tsp. paprika
1 tsp. salt
1 cup beef broth or consommé

1. Dust the slices of liver with the flour, making a thin even coating.

2. Heat a cast-iron skillet, add the oil to it, and brown the liver on both sides in the hot oil. Cook only long enough to brown, less than 1 minute each side. Set the browned liver aside on a platter.

3. Add the butter to the same skillet, let it melt, then add the sliced onions. Season them with the Worcestershire sauce, paprika and salt, and cover. Stirring occasionally, let them get soft and begin to brown a little.

4. Preheat oven to 350°.

5. In a deep casserole, arrange alternate layers of the liver slices and the softened onions. Add the beef broth, cover, and bake for about 45 minutes.

6. Remove from oven and serve when ready.

Calf's Liver on Skewers

Please read the information on skewers at the beginning of the recipe for Shish Kebab (p. 193). For this dish, you will have to ask your butcher to cut the liver into 1-inch cubes for you. It cannot be done with liver sliced in the normal way.

> 6 tbsp. butter
> 4 lbs. fresh calf's liver, cut into 1-inch cubes
> 2 quarts water
> 12 strips of bacon, cut into 1-inch lengths
> 12 medium-size onions, cut into quarters
> ½ cup olive oil
> 1 tsp. salt

1. Melt the butter in a large skillet. When it is sizzling hot, quickly toss in the cubes of liver and brown them on all sides very quickly—you don't want to cook them through—and immediately remove from heat and set aside.

2. Bring the 2 quarts of water to a boil in a saucepan, drop the sliced bacon pieces into it, and boil for 1 minute. Remove the bacon from the water and drain on paper towels.

3. Arrange the food on the skewers in the following order: 1 cube of liver, 1 piece of bacon, 1 onion quarter; repeat until the skewers are full.

4. Heat the broiler of the stove. Broil the loaded skewers for about 2 minutes on each side (remember, there are *four*

sides), brushing them occasionally with the olive oil and sprinkling with salt as they cook.

5. When they are done, serve hot, pushing the food off each skewer with a two-tined fork onto individual plates at the table.

Roast Whole Suckling Pig

1 whole young suckling pig, 14 to 16 lbs., cleaned and
  oven ready
½ lb. butter (2 sticks), softened
1 cup flour
3 cups beef bouillon or consommé
1 small apple (for the mouth)
2 raisins (for the eyes)

1. Preheat oven to 325°. Weigh the pig accurately.

2. Rub the pig with the softened butter, all over the skin. Sprinkle it with flour and pat it down so that there is an even, light coating of flour but no lumps.

3. Arrange the pig in a large roasting pan. If the pan is big enough, the front legs may extend forward, but if not they can be in a kneeling position. Put something that won't burn, like a block of wood or a ball of aluminum foil in the pig's mouth to keep it open. Cover the ears with aluminum foil, and wrap the tail with it too, to prevent burning.

4. Roast the pig for 25 minutes to the pound, calculating the time carefully. During the roasting, add some of the beef bouillon to the pan drippings, a little at a time, then baste the pig thoroughly. Repeat the process of adding broth and basting every 20 minutes.

5. Transfer the pig to a platter, remove all foil, put the apple in the mouth and the raisins in the eye holes. You can garnish the roast pig with a large variety of foods: apples, pine-

apples, onions, roast potatoes, sweet potatoes or whatever you prefer.

6. To serve, carve from the rear first, separating the hams from the body and dishing out the ham meat, then cutting the sections of chops from the loin.

Roast Loin of Pork

2 large center-cut pork loin roasts, about 12 chops each
2 garlic cloves
2 tsp. freshly ground black pepper
2 cups beef broth or consommé

1. Preheat oven to 325°. Weigh one of the loins; they should be of equal size.

2. Rub the meat with cut garlic cloves, then sprinkle with pepper.

3. Put the loins on racks in 2 roasting pans, and roast in the preheated oven for 30 minutes per pound. You may use a meat thermometer, inserted in the center of each loin without touching bone. Roast to an internal temperature of 170°. During the roasting, add some broth to the pan drippings and baste occasionally.

4. When done, remove meat to a carving board, add the remaining beef broth to the roasting pans, and scrape down the drippings while holding the roasting pan over a burner of the stove. Strain the liquid and serve it as gravy.

Roast Fresh Ham

It is important to know the difference between fresh ham and smoked ham. The ham which has a pink color and appears in many varieties, hot, cold, sliced, deviled, etc., has been cured and smoked. Fresh ham is the fresh leg, which has not been cooked or processed in any way. You could call it leg of pork. When it is cooked, the meat has the white color and texture of roast pork, and does not look at all like pink ham.

1 whole fresh ham, bone in, 7 to 8 lbs.
1 tbsp. salt
1 tsp. freshly ground black pepper
½ tsp. dried thyme
2 cups chopped onions
1 cup beef broth or consommé

1. Weigh the ham accurately. Preheat oven to 325°.

2. Mix the salt, pepper and thyme together, and rub the surface of the ham with the mixture.

3. Roast in the preheated oven on a rack for 30 minutes per pound, calculated accurately. To be absolutely sure of sufficient cooking, insert a meat thermometer in the thickest part of the ham without touching a bone, and roast until the instrument reads 170°.

4. During the last 45 minutes of roasting, add the chopped onions and beef broth to the roasting pan; after a few minutes, baste the ham with the pan juices.

5. When ready, remove the ham to a carving board and allow it to cool slightly.

6. Meanwhile, scrape down the drippings in the pan, adding a little more beef broth if necessary. Strain, rubbing onions through the strainer, and use the liquid as a gravy. Carve and serve.

Crown Roast of Pork

A crown roast is a loin roast of pork, with the backbone removed, and the rib bones exposed, tied in a circle so that the bones are sticking up. The bone side of the chops is outside, and the meaty side is inside the circle. For 12 people you will require 2 crowns, allowing 2 ribs per person, with seconds for some.

2 *crown roasts of pork, tied and oven ready*
2 *tbsp. salt*
2 *tsp. freshly ground black pepper*
3 *cups water*
¼ *lb. butter (1 stick)*
4 *cups chopped, peeled and cored apples*
1 *cup chopped celery*
4 *cups bread crumbs*
½ *tsp. dried thyme*
½ *cup chopped parsley*
2 *eggs, beaten*

1. Preheat oven to 325°.

2. Cover the bones of the crown roasts with aluminum foil to prevent their burning. Rub the meat with the salt and pepper. Set 1 roast in each of 2 roasting pans and roast in the preheated oven for 3 hours.

3. After the meat has begun to cook, prepare the stuffing. Bring 3 cups of water to a boil in a large saucepan. Melt the butter in the water. Add the chopped apples, then the celery. Simmer for 2 minutes. Add the bread crumbs, thyme, parsley and beaten eggs, and toss the whole together until well blended.

4. Cut 2 round pieces of aluminum foil roughly the size of the inside circular area of the crown roasts.

5. After the meat has cooked for 1½ hours, remove the roasts from the oven, leaving the oven on. Divide the stuffing into halves, and fill the center of each roast, covering the stuffing with one of the foil circles. Return to oven and finish roasting for the remaining 1½ hours.

6. Carefully remove the roasts from the roasting pans, holding a spatula under the stuffing or sliding a cookie sheet under the roast to get it out. Carve at the table, removing the string and cutting between the bones for each portion.

Grilled Pork Chops

24 *center-cut pork chops, each ¾ inch thick, almost all fat trimmed off*

2 *tsp. freshly ground black pepper*

4 *tbsp. olive oil*

1. The best way to do this is to use a stove-top cast-iron grill with raised ridges. Two of these grills, each of which fits over two burners of the stove, would be enough to cook 24 chops. If you do not have them or don't want to buy them, then use the broiler of the stove or even several cast-iron skillets.

2. Heat the grills or skillets until a drop of water sprinkled on the surface steams off immediately, without sliding around. Or preheat the broiler of the stove for about 10 minutes.

3. Rub the chops on both sides with the pepper.

4. Brush the hot cooking surfaces quickly with olive oil, and with long tongs put the chops on right away, close together. Grill them on each side for about 6 minutes. If you are using a skillet, remove accumulated melted fat with a basting bulb. The grills have a well to gather fat.

5. Serve piping hot with mashed potatoes and applesauce.

Baked Pork Chops in Sherry

6 *tbsp. butter*

1½ *cups chopped onions*

1 *tbsp. Worcestershire sauce*

12 *center-cut loin pork chops, each 1½ inches thick*

1 tsp. salt
½ tsp. freshly ground black pepper
2 cups sherry

1. In a large skillet melt the butter and sauté the onions in it until they soften. Add the Worcestershire sauce.

2. Rub the chops with the salt and pepper, and brown them on both sides in the skillet with the onions. If this must be done in shifts, remove about half of the onions, and put them back for the second shift.

3. Preheat oven to 350°.

4. Transfer the browned chops and cooked onions to an ovenproof baking dish equipped with a cover. Add the sherry, cover, and bake for 1 hour and 20 minutes, removing the cover for the last 20 minutes. Baste the chops with the pan liquid after removing the cover. The chops should be cooked through and white throughout. Check one with a small knife cut before removing from the oven.

5. Serve, using the pan liquid as gravy. Strain the liquid before using if the onions look too burned, otherwise it's not necessary.

Baked Spareribs

4 racks of spareribs (3 to 4 lbs., each rack), cracked through center
6 to 8 quarts water
4 large onions, peeled and sliced
4 apples, peeled, cored and thinly sliced
2 cups apple juice
2 tsp. salt
1 tsp. freshly ground black pepper

1. Trim any large pieces of fat or loose gristle from the ribs with a small sharp knife.

2. Using your largest pot, bring the water to a boil. Parboil the racks of ribs, one at a time, in this boiling water for about 3 minutes each.

3. Preheat oven to 350°.

4. Use 2 roasting pans. Make a layer of the onion slices on the bottom of both pans. Cover the onions with a layer of apple slices. Put 2 racks of ribs in each pan on top of the apple layer.

5. Bake for 1½ hours, occasionally adding apple juice to keep onions and apples moist, and basting with the combined juice and drippings. During the cooking, turn the racks of ribs every 30 minutes, exposing different surfaces. Season.

6. Serve the ribs hot when ready. They should be browned, and no trace of redness should appear in the meat between the bones.

Pork Stew with Tomatoes

---

4 lbs. boneless pork loin, shoulder or butt, cut into 1-inch cubes

3 large onions, cut into rough slices

6 large carrots, peeled and cut into 1-inch lengths

6 cups beef broth or consommé

1 cup dry red wine

1 bay leaf

2 tsp. salt

½ tsp. freshly ground black pepper

3 cups chopped, peeled and seeded fresh tomatoes

½ cup tomato paste

1. In a cast-iron skillet brown the cubed pork on all sides, then transfer the meat to a large casserole or stockpot.

2. Sauté the sliced onions in the skillet, browning slightly, and add to the casserole.

3. Add the carrots, beef broth, wine, bay leaf, salt and pep-

per to the pot, cover, and simmer, uncovered, for about 3 hours, until the meat is tender.

4. For the last 45 minutes of the cooking time, add the chopped tomatoes and the tomato paste, mixed in well.

5. The stew can be prepared in advance and reheated, but should be served hot.

Pork and Beans

This might strike you as a dish not worth bothering with because it is so easily available in canned form. Don't be deceived! Like most other recipes, when you make it yourself from the raw materials and do not include the various preservatives that commercial canners use, the taste is *different*. On a winter night when you are expecting a group of hungry people, this dish is both satisfying and fairly inexpensive to make. Also, it can be prepared well ahead of time and reheated.

> 6 *cups dried white or Navy beans*
> 4 *lbs. pork shoulder meat, cut into ¾- to 1-inch cubes*
> 1 *cup finely chopped onions*
> 1 *cup molasses*
> 1½ *cups chili sauce or tomato ketchup*
> 1 *tbsp. salt*
> 1 *tbsp. red-wine vinegar*
> 2 *tbsp. Worcestershire sauce*
> 4 *slices of bacon*

Note: The ideal cooking utensil is a large, deep earthenware crock for baking, equipped with a cover.

1. Put the dried beans in a large stockpot or casserole, and cover them by 1 inch with cold water. Bring the water to a boil, reduce heat, and simmer the beans about 45 minutes.

2. Drain the beans, saving the water they cooked in, and place them in the baking crock.

3. In a large cast-iron skillet brown the cubed pork on all sides to a dark-brown color. This is not the entire cooking process for the meat, but it still should not be bloody or rare after browning. Put the meat in the baking crock with the beans, leaving some of the fat in the skillet.

4. Add the chopped onions to the skillet, and sauté them for about 1 minute. With a slotted spoon or spatula transfer the onions to the crock. Discard whatever excess fat is left.

5. Add the molasses, chili sauce, salt, vinegar and Worcestershire sauce to the crock, and mix everything together so that the meat and flavorings are well distributed throughout the beans.

6. Preheat oven to 250°.

7. Lay the slices of bacon over the surface of the beans, cover the crock, and bake the beans in the preheated oven for 8 hours. Check every hour or so during the baking time; if the edges appear dry, add a little of the reserved cooking water from the beans to moisten.

8. Remove the bacon before serving. Serve the beans hot. The earthenware crock, covered, will keep the beans inside hot for 1 hour or more at room temperature, so there is no need to use a hot tray of any kind at the table.

Pork Pâté

---

  thin strips of salted fatback, enough to line a 12-inch loaf pan, plus to cover the open side
2 lbs. boned pork loin
¼ lb. slices of lean cooked ham
1 lb. pork liver
½ cup finely chopped onion
2 tsp. salt
½ tsp. freshly ground black pepper
1 garlic clove, crushed
¼ tsp. ground ginger

½ cup dry white wine
2 eggs, beaten
1 large truffle, chopped fine (optional)

1. Line the loaf pan with thin strips of salt fatback.

2. Grind the pork loin and ham, liver and onion through the finest blade of your meat grinder or food chopper. Transfer to a mixing bowl.

3. Add the salt, pepper, garlic, ginger, wine, eggs and truffle to the ground meat and onions, and blend well.

4. Put the mixture into the lined pan, and cover surface with the remaining slices of salt pork.

5. Cover the loaf pan as tightly as possible with heavy aluminum foil, tucked all around. Make 3 holes in the top for steam to escape.

6. Preheat oven to 375°.

7. Bake the pâté for 2½ hours, until it shrinks from the sides of the pan. Remove from oven, cool at room temperature, then refrigerate.

8. To serve, unmold the pâté onto a serving platter and slice thin with a sharp knife. This is an ideal buffet dish; it can be decorated with cubes of aspic, parsley, hard-cooked egg quarters, or anything else that looks attractive.

Ham with Madeira Sauce

1 whole processed ham (approximately 10 lbs.), ready
   for baking
2 cups brown sugar
½ cup apple juice
2 tbsp. whole cloves
1½ cups Madeira wine
½ cup raisins

1. Weigh the ham accurately, and preheat the oven to 325°.

2. Bake the ham on a rack in a roasting pan in the preheated oven for 25 minutes to the pound, calculated accurately.

3. After 2 hours of baking, increase temperature of oven to 450°.

4. At the same time, remove the ham from the oven, and using a sharp chef's knife, cut off the rind, exposing the fat. The rind should come off easily because the fat holding it down has been softened by the baking process.

5. Mix the brown sugar and apple juice together into a paste, and glaze the ham with it.

6. With a sharp knife, score the fat covering the ham with parallel lines, forming a pattern of diamonds. Insert the cloves at the intersections of the lines.

7. Return the glazed, studded ham to the oven for the remaining baking time.

8. Transfer the ham to a carving board. Add the wine to the pan and scrape down the drippings and coagulated juices. Pour off excess fat, strain, and add the raisins to the sauce. Carve the ham and serve with the sauce.

Ham Mousse

For this mousse you should use two 1½-quart molds, either the ring type or any decorative form as long as it is not too tall. The mousse is rather heavy and should not be expected to stand very high.

 3 cups clear rosé wine
 6 cups beef consommé
 6 envelopes unflavored gelatin
24 black olives, pitted and cut into round slices
 4 hard-cooked eggs, cut into round thin slices
 6 cups finely ground lean ham
 ¾ cup tomato paste
 ½ lb. butter (2 sticks), softened at room temperature

2 cups heavy cream, whipped (measured before whip-
ping)

1. Combine the wine and consommé. Pour off 2 cups of the mixture into a separate container and soften the gelatin in it. Meanwhile, heat the remainder in a saucepan. When the gelatin is softened, add it to the hot liquid, and heat over low heat until gelatin is completely melted. Refrigerate until cold but not jelled solid.

2. Coat the molds with some of the gelatin, and refrigerate them until it sets. Arrange the olive and egg slices in a decorative pattern in the molds, keeping in mind that they should be placed with the best side down. "Glue" them in place with a little more gelatin and refrigerate again to set.

3. Make another layer of gelatin over the decorations and let it set.

4. While this last layer is setting, combine the ground ham with the tomato paste and softened butter. Fold this mixture into the whipped cream.

5. Fill the molds loosely with the ham mousse mixture then fill with the remaining, still liquid, gelatin mixture. Refrigerate to set mousse.

6. If you have some of the liquid gelatin left, pour it into a flat container like a jelly-roll pan, refrigerate to set, then cut into cubes.

7. Unmold the mousse onto serving platters and decorate the platters with the cubes. Slice the mousse at the table.

Roast Leg of Lamb

---

2 garlic cloves

1 whole leg of lamb, 10 lbs. (make sure the butcher under-
stands that you want a whole leg, and not the usual
truncated cut)

2 tsp. freshly ground black pepper

(cont'd)

¾ *cup red wine*
2 *tbsp. butter*

Note: If you have hearty eaters, you may want to substitute two 6-lb. legs for the single larger one.

1. Preheat the oven to 350°. Weigh the leg accurately.

2. Peel the garlic cloves and cut them into slivers. With a small sharp knife make numerous little slits near the bone and under the fat layer, and insert the garlic slivers in the slits. Rub the surface of the meat with pepper.

3. Roast, fat side up, on a rack, at 20 minutes to the pound for medium rare, 25 minutes to the pound for medium, and as much as 30 minutes to the pound for well done, although that is not advisable. The lamb requires no basting.

4. When done, remove the leg to a carving board or platter.

5. Carefully pour off excess fat from the roasting pan, but do not lose any of the dark-colored particles in the drippings. Holding the pan over a burner of the stove, add the wine and let it simmer while you scrape down the coagulated drippings from the roast. Add the butter, simmer just until it melts into the gravy, then transfer to a gravy boat or two.

6. Carve at the table, because if you carve in the kitchen and lay out slices of meat on a platter, they get cold quickly and are not so appetizing. Slice the meat thin when you carve and serve the gravy.

Rack of Lamb

Rack of lamb comes from the rib section of the animal. Order from your butcher four 9-rib roasts, or two racks of 9 double-rib chops, split in half. Each rack contains two rib roasts. These cuts will yield 36 chops altogether, or 3 per person for 12 people. This is an adequate portion, but not excessive; the 3 chops are rather small, and each has only 1 eye of meat, unlike the loin chops further along which have an additional smaller eye of meat on the other side of the bone.

> 4 racks of lamb, trimmed
> 2 tsp. salt
> ½ tsp. freshly ground black pepper
> ¼ cup white wine
> 4 tsp. dry mustard
> 1 cup unflavored bread crumbs
> ½ cup chopped fresh parsley

1. Preheat oven to 400°. Weigh all four rib roasts accurately and write down the weights, from the lightest to the heaviest. Stick 1 wooden toothpick into roast number 1, 2 toothpicks into number 2, etc. Then you will know which to remove first from the oven.

2. Rub the meat with the salt and pepper. Arrange in 2 roasting pans, fat side up and bone side down. Roast in preheated oven for 15 minutes per pound.

3. While the meat is roasting, mix the wine and mustard into a paste, and also mix the bread crumbs with the chopped parsley in a bowl.

4. When there are only 10 minutes of roasting time left, remove the meat from the oven, spread with the mustard paste, and sprinkle on a coating of the bread-crumb mixture, as evenly as possible. Return the meat to the oven for the final 10 minutes.

5. To carve, cut between all the bones, serving 3 small chops to each person. Rack of lamb is traditionally served with a selection of fresh spring vegetables.

Shish Kebab

This dish requires a set of skewers. You can get a quite inexpensive set which consists of little more than steel spikes with an eye at one end. You can also get very expensive ones, made like dueling *épées* with copper handguards and tempered shafts. The latter are beautiful and impressive but definitely not necessary. One advantage of this dish is that you can remove from the heat the portions for the people who like lamb on the rare side, and leave in longer the ones for those who prefer it well done.

 1 cup olive oil
 2 garlic cloves, crushed
½ tsp. salt
 1 tsp. freshly ground black pepper
 4 lbs. boneless leg of lamb, cut into 1-inch cubes
¼ lb. butter (1 stick)
 1 cup dry white wine
 4 dozen medium-size fresh mushrooms, about 1½ lbs., but count to be sure
 2 quarts water
12 strips of bacon, cut into 1-inch lengths
 4 dozen small onions, 1 inch in diameter, or 12 larger onions, cut into quarters
 4 dozen cherry tomatoes

1. In a large mixing bowl combine the olive oil, crushed garlic, salt and pepper; blend well. Add all the lamb cubes to the bowl, and turn occasionally so that the oil coating is distributed evenly over the meat.

2. While the meat is soaking (30 to 40 minutes) melt the butter in the white wine in a large saucepan. Reduce heat to low and add the mushrooms (caps only—save the stems for another meal). Cover, and simmer for 20 minutes, turning occasionally so that all the mushroom caps cook evenly.

3. Bring the 2 quarts of water to a boil in another saucepan, and drop the pieces of bacon into it. Boil for 2 minutes, remove the bacon and drain. Set aside.

4. When the mushrooms are done, remove them from the liquid and let them cool on paper towels. Reserve the cooking liquid.

5. Now you are ready to assemble. On each skewer, follow

this order: 1 lamb cube, 1 piece of bacon, 1 mushroom cap, 1 onion or onion quarter, 1 tomato; then repeat until all the skewers are filled. If you have some pieces left over, assemble a couple of extra skewers for second helpings. Mix the mushroom cooking liquid with whatever is left in the bowl of the olive oil mixture, and use that for basting during the cooking.

6. Heat a stove-top grill, or the broiler of the stove. Broil or grill the skewered food for about 3 minutes on each side, remembering that there are *four sides*, not two. For those who like it well done, add about 1 minute for each side.

7. Bring the finished kebabs to the table on a platter, and remove food from the skewer onto each plate by pushing it off with a two-tined fork.

Curried Lamb

    1 cup very finely minced onions
 ¼ lb. butter (1 stick)
    6 tbsp. curry powder
    1 cup flour
    2 cups beef broth or stock
    2 cups milk
    1 cup heavy cream
    3 tbsp. chopped fresh parsley
    3 tbsp. Worcestershire sauce
 ¼ cup lemon juice
    2 tbsp. sugar
    2 tsp. salt
 ½ tsp. freshly ground white pepper
    4 tbsp. olive oil
    4 lbs. boneless shoulder or leg of lamb, cut into 1-inch cubes

1. In a large saucepan sauté the onions in the butter slowly

without allowing them to brown for about 5 minutes, until they are softened. Stir the curry powder into the onions, making a fairly dry paste, and cook for another 3 or 4 minutes, stirring and turning the whole time.

2. Add the flour to the paste, stir well while cooking, gathering all of it into one mixture.

3. Add the liquids, first the beef broth, then the milk, a little at a time, stirring well and blending with the curry paste to make a smooth sauce. When all the liquid is incorporated, add the heavy cream, parsley, Worcestershire sauce, lemon juice, sugar, salt and pepper, and stir well. Put the sauce over very low heat to keep hot but not to cook while you prepare the meat.

4. Heat a heavy skillet and add the oil. Brown the cubed lamb on all sides in the oil to a medium brown color. Cut 1 cube open to check; it should be deep pink but not bloody rare in the center.

5. Add the cubed meat to the curry sauce and continue to heat, stirring occasionally, until the meat is heated through, 15 to 20 minutes.

6. Serve hot with steamed rice and condiments.

Lamb Stew with Baby Onions

5 lbs. boneless lamb shoulder, cut into 1-inch cubes
2 lbs. small white onions (silverskins), dry outer skin removed
3 lbs. potatoes, peeled and sliced into ¼-inch slices
3 tsp. salt
1 tsp. freshly ground black pepper
2 tbsp. chopped fresh parsley
2 cups thinly sliced celery

1. Using a deep casserole equipped with a cover, arrange the food in layers as follows : 1 layer lamb cubes, 1 layer onions, 1 layer sliced potatoes. Sprinkle on some salt, pepper, parsley and

sliced celery, then begin again with a layer of lamb.

2. Preheat oven to 375°.

3. Add enough water to the pot to cover the top layer by about ½ inch. Cover, and bake in the preheated oven for 2½ hours, until lamb is cooked all the way through and is tender. Check by removing 1 lamb cube and cutting open.

4. Remove the casserole from the oven and serve the stew hot.

Cassoulet

1½ lbs. dried white or Navy beans
2 onions
1 bay leaf
4 tbsp. chopped fresh parsley
6 tbsp. lard
2 lbs. boneless lamb shoulder, cut into 1-inch cubes
2 lbs. pork loin, cut into 1-inch cubes
1 lb. spicy garlic sausage, sliced into ½-inch-thick slices
8 cups beef consommé
½ cup tomato paste
1 tsp. freshly ground black pepper

1. Put the dried beans into a large pot, along with the onions, bay leaf and parsley, cover by 1 inch of cold water, and simmer for about 1 to 1½ hours, until the beans are tender. Turn off heat and drain.

2. Melt the lard in a large casserole. Brown the lamb and pork cubes in the lard, then add the sliced sausage, cover, and cook over low heat for 15 minutes.

3. Add half the consommé to the casserole, cover, and simmer for another hour. Add the drained beans to the casserole containing the meat, and stir in the tomato paste and pepper. Cover and, still over low heat, cook for 1 more hour.

4. Serve very hot.

Paella

The paella is one of the great national dishes of Spain. There are literally dozens of different recipes, containing almost any kind of combination of fish, shellfish, meat and poultry. One common denominator is rice, and the second is saffron.

    3 lbs. chicken parts (breasts, thighs, legs)
    2 lbs. pork loin, cut into 1-inch cubes
    2 lbs. fillets of white fish (swordfish, cod or haddock), diced
    ½ cup olive oil
    1 tsp. freshly ground pepper
    1 tbsp. salt
    1½ cups chopped onions
    8 cups chicken broth or consommé
    2 tsp. saffron
    1 cup chopped sweet red peppers (pimientos)
    4 cups canned stewed tomatoes
    2½ cups uncooked rice
    1 lb. shrimps, shelled, deveined and simmered
    2 cups canned peas
    2 dozen clams, scrubbed and steamed long enough to open

1. Brown the meat and fish in a skillet on all sides in the oil. Sprinkle with pepper and salt while browning. Remove meat and fish from skillet with a slotted spoon and set aside to drain.

2. Add the onions to the same skillet, reduce heat, and cook until soft.

3. Transfer onions to a large casserole equipped with a cover. Add the chicken broth to the onions and bring to a boil. Add to the casserole the saffron, red peppers, tomatoes, uncooked rice and shrimps. Add browned meat and fish.

4. Preheat oven to 350°.

5. Cover casserole and bake in the preheated oven for 30 minutes.

6. When ready, remove from heat and taste rice to make sure it is sufficiently tender. Mix in the peas and the steamed clams in their shells, toss several times, and serve hot.

Variations: You can replace the pork with beef, the fish with other firm-fleshed fish. You can use more shrimps and no fish. You can add pieces of lobster, in or out of the shell, instead of or with the shrimps. You can use mussels as well as clams. You can use fish stock instead of the chicken broth for a more fishy taste. Also the vegetables can be changed, using beans or lima beans instead of peas, green peppers instead of red.

Bigos (Polish Hunters' Stew)

 4 lbs. sauerkraut
 8 dried black mushrooms
 4 green apples, cored and sliced but not peeled
 2 cans, 20 oz. each, stewed tomatoes
10 black peppercorns
 2 garlic cloves, crushed
 1 bay leaf
 2 tbsp. ground thyme
 2 cups brown sugar
 2 large onions, cut into halves
 6 cups diced Polish or Hungarian garlic sausages, and left-over cooked meat such as pork, ham or beef, diced; the proportion of meat to sausages should be about 3 to 1.
 2 cups cubed salt pork or bacon

1. Put the sauerkraut with its liquid into a large stockpot or casserole.

2. Soak the dried mushrooms in cold water for 2 hours.

3. Add the soaked mushrooms to the sauerkraut, and add all

the other ingredients to the pot except the sausages and meat.
Simmer, covered, over low heat for 2 hours, stirring occasionally.

4. Add the meats to the pot, mix them in, cover, and cook
slowly for at least 1 more hour. If the stew looks too dry, add a
little apple juice or red wine. The stew is particularly good if left
to sit overnight, to be reheated next day.

5. Serve hot with steamed or boiled potatoes.

CHAPTER 7

Vegetables
and
Salads

In this chapter on vegetables you will find that most often I recommend steaming. The advantages of steaming vegetables are very basic. When you cook vegetables on a raised platform over live steam coming from boiling water (sometimes seasoned) the vegetables do not become waterlogged and the taste does not cook away into the water. To realize the truth of this assertion, you need only consider *why* you put vegetables *into* the water when you are making soup or stock. In that case you are trying to transfer the flavors from the vegetables into the liquid, which will eventually be served in one form or another. But here, we are trying to do just the opposite. We want to *preserve* the flavor of the vegetables in themselves, and *not* let it cook away into the liquid. Therefore, steaming is best. Also, I personally have a horror of the typical American restaurant's way of serving vegetables in a puddle of gray water, in a little saucer as a side dish. Vegetables should *never* be served that way. In a sauce, yes. But not in water!

For a vegetable steamer, the best thing to get is the French platform type, with hinged leaves around the sides. The legs are adjustable, and the leaves contract or expand to accommodate to any size of pot. It might be advisable for the purpose of large-quantity cooking to own at least two of these, so that you can have 2 pots going at once for vegetables that are bulky. A steamer, at this writing, costs about $4.

When you see a salad recipe in this chapter without a dress-ing, it is because the salad dressings are at the end of the chapter, and the choice is yours. If the dressing is an integral part of the recipe it will appear with it. Otherwise, some choices may be recommended.

Steamed Artichokes with Melted Butter

12 *medium-size to large artichokes*
 3 *lemons, halved*
 2 *garlic cloves, crushed*
10 *peppercorns*
 3 *tbsp. olive oil*
½ *cup vinegar*
 1 *lb. butter (4 sticks)*

1. Using a large sharp kitchen knife, cut off the stems of the artichokes evenly to make flat bottoms. Then cut ½ inch off the tops of the leaves. With kitchen shears, trim off the sharp points of all the leaves on the sides.

2. Squeeze the lemon halves over the artichokes, applying the lemon to all the cut surfaces of the artichokes.

3. Using 1 or 2 deep pots or saucepans equipped with cov-ers, put in enough cold water to reach the bottom of your steamer platforms. Add the garlic, peppercorns, oil and vinegar to the water. If using 2 pots, divide these ingredients equally.

4. Place the artichokes base down on the steaming plat-forms over the water, cover, and turn on high heat. When water boils, set timer for 25 minutes. If the artichokes are very small,

you need less time. During the last 5 minutes of this time, melt the butter and divide it into 12 small cups.

5. To test readiness of artichokes, pull out 1 leaf and taste it. If the meat clinging to the leaf is tender but not hard, they are ready. Do not overcook. Serve the artichokes hot on large plates with room for discarding leaves, with melted butter.

Cold Artichokes Vinaigrette

1. Prepare 12 artichokes according to the instructions in the preceding recipe, omitting the butter.

2. When artichokes are removed from the steamers, chill them in the refrigerator.

3. Prepare 1 recipe of Vinaigrette Dressing (p. 240) and serve it in small cups alongside the artichokes.

Steamed Asparagus with Bread Crumb Sauce

For this operation you should have an asparagus steamer. This is a round or square pan which is extra tall, containing a divider. The divider separates the space in the pot into quarters, and is about half as tall as the pot. It makes it possible to stand up the asparagus spears in the pot for cooking. If you do not have such a pot and do not want to buy one, there is a simple solution. Any deep pot with a cover will do. Tie the asparagus spears in bunches with string in such a way that the whole bunch will stand up.

 6 *dozen fresh asparagus spears*
½ *lb. butter (2 sticks)*
 2 *cups unflavored bread crumbs*
½ *tsp. salt*

1. Wash the asparagus in cold water and trim the thick ends by about 1 inch.

2. Pour about 2 inches of cold water into the asparagus steamer or pot you plan to use. Place the asparagus, thick ends down, standing in the steamer. Or tie them into 3 bunches of 24 pieces each with white string, and stand up the tied bunches in the pot.

3. Turn on heat and bring water to a boil. When it boils, cover the pot and steam the asparagus for 20 minutes. Test by feeling tips to see if they are tender and not hard.

4. While asparagus is steaming, melt the butter in a saucepan. When melted, add bread crumbs, season with salt, stir, and keep hot.

5. Serve asparagus, 6 stalks per person, with 1 or 2 spoonfuls of the sauce spooned over the tips.

Broccoli and Bacon Bits

4 lbs. broccoli
1 cup heavy cream
2 tsp. salt
6 slices of bacon

1. Wash the broccoli in cold water, and cut off the tough, thick lower part of the stems.

2. Steam the broccoli over boiling water on a steamer platform, covered, for 20 minutes. Or you can use an asparagus steamer and cook the broccoli standing up, thick stems down, in 2 inches of boiling water, covered.

3. When the broccoli is tender, transfer it to a wooden bowl and chop it medium fine with a food chopper. Do not use an electric blender.

4. Place the chopped broccoli in a saucepan and add the

heavy cream. Heat over very low heat, mixing occasionally. Season with the salt.

5. Fry the bacon until crisp but not burned. Drain it on paper towels. Crumble the bacon into the broccoli and stir. Serve hot.

Brussels Sprouts with Cream Sauce

---

    3 *lbs. Brussels sprouts*
    2 *tsp. salt*
    2 *tbsp. lemon juice*
    1 *tbsp. sugar*
  ¼ *tsp. freshly ground black pepper*
  ¼ *lb. butter (1 stick)*
  ½ *cup flour*
    1 *cup chicken broth*
    1 *cup heavy cream*

1. Wash the Brussels sprouts in cold water. Soak them in cold water to cover, with the salt added, for 30 minutes.

2. Boil about 1 quart of water in your teakettle.

3. Put the sprouts in a large saucepan, add the lemon juice, sugar and pepper.

4. Pour enough boiling water into the saucepan to make it about 1 inch deep.

5. Cover, and cook the Brussels sprouts over medium heat for 15 minutes, until tender.

6. While they are cooking, melt the butter in another saucepan, stir the flour into it, and mix into a smooth paste. Add first the chicken broth, then the cream, a little at a time, stirring constantly to form a sauce.

7. When the Brussels sprouts are done, pour the sauce into the pan in which they were cooked. The small remaining amount of water will blend with the sauce as you stir. Serve hot.

Red Cabbage Cooked in Wine

6 tbsp. butter
2 cups sliced onions
2 medium-size heads of red cabbage, shredded
1 tsp. salt
½ tsp. freshly ground black pepper
1½ cups dry red wine

1. In a large saucepan melt the butter and cook the onions in it until they are quite soft but not browned.

2. Add the shredded cabbage, season with salt and pepper, and add the wine.

3. Cover the saucepan, and cook over a very low heat for 30 minutes, stirring occasionally, until cabbage is tender. If not enough wine has evaporated near the end of the cooking time, remove cover and increase heat to boil off some wine quickly before serving.

Buttered Carrots

If you can get young, tender, baby carrots, please do. However this recipe will work fine with the larger, more mature ones.

2½ lbs. carrots
1 tsp. salt
2 tsp. sugar
¼ lb. butter (1 stick)
½ cup chopped fresh parsley

1. Peel the carrots and cut them into 1½- to 2-inch pieces. If they are very thick, split them lengthwise first.

2. Boil about 1 quart of water in your teakettle.

3. Put the carrots in a saucepan and add the salt, sugar and butter.

4. Pour over enough boiling water from the kettle to make the liquid about 2 inches deep.

5. Cook, covered, over low heat for 20 minutes. Test carrots to see if they are tender. Remove cover and cook for another 5 minutes to reduce liquid.

6. Turn into serving dish and sprinkle with chopped parsley before serving.

Steamed Cauliflower Baked in Cheese Sauce

---

2 *large heads of cauliflower*
6 *tbsp. butter*
6 *tbsp. flour*
3 *cups milk*
1 *cup grated Swiss cheese*
1 *cup grated American cheese*
2 *tbsp. Worcestershire sauce*
4 *tbsp. sherry*
½ *tsp. salt*
¼ *tsp. freshly ground black pepper*

1. Wash the cauliflower, and remove the coarse leaves from the outside.

2. Steam the cauliflower heads, either in 2 pots, or one head at a time, over boiling water on a steamer platform, covered, for 30 minutes until medium tender. Remove when ready and cut apart into 2-inch pieces.

3. In a saucepan melt the butter and stir the flour into it, making a smooth paste. Cook the paste over low heat for 2 minutes.

4. Stir in the milk, a little at a time, until it makes a smooth sauce. Add the grated cheeses and stir over medium heat until

the cheese is melted and blended into the sauce. Add Worcestershire sauce, sherry, salt and pepper to the sauce.

5. Preheat oven to 375°.

6. Pour a little sauce into an ovenproof baking dish, enough to cover the bottom. Arrange the pieces of cauliflower in the baking dish. Pour the remaining sauce over. Bake in preheated oven for 15 minutes. Remove from oven and serve hot.

Braised Celery

    4 *lbs. celery*
  ¼ *lb. butter (1 stick)*
    1 *cup chicken broth or consommé*
1½ *tsp. salt*
  ½ *tsp. freshly ground white pepper*
  ¼ *cup lemon juice*
    2 *tbsp. sugar*
  ½ *cup chopped fresh parsley*

1. Wash the celery, trim leaves, and cut ribs into 3-inch pieces.

2. In a large casserole melt the butter, then add the celery pieces and all the remaining ingredients.

3. Cover and simmer over medium heat for 30 minutes, until celery pieces are tender but not too soft.

4. Transfer to a serving dish and serve hot, with a few spoonfuls of the cooking liquid poured over.

Creamed Sweet Corn

    8 *quarts water*
12 *to 18 ears of fresh corn*

2 tbsp. sugar
1 cup heavy cream
2 tsp. seasoned salt
½ tsp. freshly ground black pepper

1. Bring the 8 quarts of water to a rolling boil in a large kettle or pot.

2. Strip the skin and silk from the corn.

3. Add the sugar to the boiling water, then drop the peeled ears of corn into it. Boil for exactly 5 minutes from the time the water resumes boiling.

4. After 5 minutes, remove the ears of corn from the water and set aside to cool.

5. When cool, take a sharp paring knife and cut the kernels of corn off the ears into a saucepan.

6. Add the cream, salt and pepper to the saucepan, and heat over low heat without boiling the cream. Serve hot.

Baked Corn Pudding

6 cups canned corn kernels (not cream-style)
6 tbsp. butter
6 tbsp. flour
1½ cups heavy cream
5 eggs, separated
2 tsp. salt

1. Drain the canned corn kernels, reserving the liquid.

2. In a saucepan melt the butter and stir in the flour, mixing until you have a smooth paste.

3. Add the reserved liquid from the corn, a little at a time, then the cream, stirring constantly until you have a smooth sauce.

4. Add the corn kernels. Heat to just below boiling point. Turn off heat.

5. Beat the egg yolks well in a mixing bowl, then stir them

into the corn, a little at a time. Turn on heat after all yolks are in, and allow mixture to thicken slightly. Stir in the salt.

6. Beat the egg whites to soft peaks in a mixing bowl. Fold the corn mixture into the beaten egg whites.

7. Preheat oven to 375°.

8. Butter the inside of a deep baking dish, then turn the mixture into the baking dish. Bake in the preheated oven for 30 minutes. Serve hot.

Eggplant Parmigiana

4 medium-size eggplants
2 tbsp. salt
   olive oil for frying
6 tbsp. butter
2 cups tomato paste
1 lb. mozzarella cheese
¾ cup grated Parmesan cheese

1. Peel the eggplants and cut them into slices ¼ inch thick.

2. Salt the slices and drain them in a colander for 1 hour, until most of the moisture has dripped out.

3. Heat oil to a depth of about 1 inch in a heavy skillet, and fry the dried slices of eggplant, a few at a time, to a golden brown. Drain them on paper towels.

4. Grate the mozzarella cheese through a medium grater.

5. Butter 1 or 2 ovenproof baking dishes with a little of the butter. Arrange the ingredients in layers in the baking dish(es) as follows: 1 layer fried eggplant slices, thin layer of tomato paste, 1 layer grated mozzarella, a little grated Parmesan. Begin again with a layer of eggplant and continue until all is used. The top layer should be eggplant, with a little Parmesan on top.

6. Preheat oven to 375°.

7. Dot the top of the eggplant with the remaining butter,

and bake in the preheated oven for 40 minutes.

8. Serve hot from the oven, or allow the eggplant to cool to room temperature without losing any flavor.

Green Peppers Stuffed with Meat

    12 medium-size to large green peppers
     4 quarts water
  1½ tsp. salt
     1 cup chopped onions
  2½ lbs. ground beef
     4 tbsp. olive oil
     4 cups cooked white rice
     1 cup beef broth or consommé
    ¼ tsp. freshly ground black pepper
    ¼ lb. butter (1 stick)
  1½ cups unflavored bread crumbs
     1 cup tomato juice

1. Wash the outer skins of the peppers in lukewarm water, removing any wax. Cut off tops of the peppers and remove cores and seeds from the inside with a spoon.

2. Bring the 4 quarts of water to a boil with 1 teaspoon salt in a large saucepan. Drop the peppers into water and boil for about 3 minutes. Remove from water with a slotted spoon and drain upside down.

3. In a skillet cook the onions and ground beef in the oil until the beef is browned. Stir frequently.

4. Add the rice, beef broth, remaining ½ teaspoon salt and the pepper to the skillet, and stir.

5. Allow the mixture in the skillet to cool, then stuff the drained peppers with it, being careful not to tear the skins.

6. Melt the butter in a saucepan and mix the bread crumbs into it. Put a layer of the bread-crumb and butter mixture on

top of each stuffed pepper, covering the meat.

7. Preheat oven to 325°.

8. Arrange the stuffed peppers in an ovenproof baking dish. Pour the tomato juice into the dish. Bake in the preheated oven for about 1 hour.

9. Serve the peppers hot, basted with the pan liquid.

Braised Leeks

6 bunches of leeks
4 tbsp. butter
½ cup finely diced carrot
½ cup chopped onion
½ cup chopped celery
4 tbsp. chopped parsley
¼ tsp. salt
⅛ tsp. freshly ground black pepper
2 cups chicken broth or consommé

1. Cut off the green tops of the leeks and discard. Cut the roots off the white ends, as close as possible. Wash the leeks under cold running water, removing all dirt.

2. Melt the butter in a small saucepan. Pour the melted butter into a baking dish equipped with a cover. Make a layer of the diced carrot, chopped onion and celery on the bottom of the baking dish. Arrange the washed leeks on top of this layer.

3. Preheat oven to 325°.

4. Sprinkle the parsley, salt and pepper on the leeks, and pour the chicken broth into the baking dish on the side.

5. Cover, and bake for 45 minutes, until leeks are tender. Serve hot; spoon pan liquid over leeks as you serve them.

Braised Lettuce

    4 tbsp. butter, softened
    3 heads of lettuce, cut into quarters
    ¼ cup lemon juice
    1 cup beef consommé or stock
    ¼ tsp. salt
    ⅛ tsp. freshly ground black pepper
    4 tbsp. parsley

1. Butter a casserole equipped with a cover generously with the softened butter. Use all the butter.

2. Arrange the quarters of lettuce in the dish. Pour the lemon juice over them, then the beef consommé. Sprinkle with salt, pepper and parsley.

3. Cover, and simmer over medium heat for about 20 minutes, until the lettuce is tender. Baste once or twice with the pan liquids. Serve hot.

Buttered Lima Beans

    6 lbs. fresh lima beans (weight in the pods)—yields about
       2 quarts of shelled beans
    4 tbsp. butter
    1 tsp. salt
    ¼ tsp. freshly ground black pepper
    3 tbsp. chopped fresh parsley

1. Shell the beans just before you plan to use them.

2. Put enough water in a large saucepan equipped with a cover to come up to the bottom of your steamer platform. Bring the water to a boil. Insert the steamer platform in the pot.

3. Put in the shelled beans, and cover. Steam for 20 to 25

minutes until tender; test a bean to check. If the water boils down too low, add some *boiling* water from the kettle during the steaming process.

4. When the beans are done, transfer them to another saucepan, add the butter, salt, pepper and parsley, toss, and keep hot until time to serve.

Mushrooms in White Wine

This method of preparing mushrooms is simple, and the result fits with many different main dishes. The mushrooms can be served with almost any meat—grilled, roasted or broiled. They can accompany fish or chicken dishes too.

> 1 *lb. fresh mushrooms*
> ¼ *lb. butter (1 stick)*
> 1½ *cups dry white wine*
> 1 *tsp. salt*
> ½ *tsp. freshly ground black pepper*
> 2 *tbsp. Worcestershire sauce*
> 3 *tbsp. chopped fresh parsley*

1. Wash the mushrooms carefully with a damp cloth, removing all dirt. Do not soak them under running water. It is not necessary to separate the caps from the stems. If there is a great variety in the size of the mushrooms, cut some of the biggest ones into halves so that the halves are about equal in size to the average or smaller whole ones. The quantity given here is intended only to use as a garnish, and not as a full vegetable course. For a full course, please triple the quantity.

2. Melt the butter in a large saucepan. Add the wine, salt, and Worcestershire sauce, then the mushrooms. Cover, and simmer them for 25 minutes, turning them occasionally so that they are all moistened in the wine and butter.

3. Sprinkle the parsley over them during the last 5 minutes of cooking time. Serve hot with some, but not all, of the liquid.

Mushroom and Onion Garnish (for use with meats)

This is meant as a side dish to go with fried or grilled steak, liver, chops or other meats. You will notice the quantity is not large because it is not intended as a full portion of vegetable.

6 tbsp. butter
2 tbsp. olive oil
3 cups sliced onions
3 cups (½ lb.) sliced fresh mushrooms
1 tsp. salt
¼ tsp. freshly ground black pepper
2 tbsp. Worcestershire sauce
2 tbsp. sherry

1. Melt the butter in the oil in a large cast-iron skillet.
2. Add the onions to the pan and simmer them for about 3 minutes, until they begin to soften.
3. Add the mushrooms, and cook over medium heat, stirring. Add salt, pepper, Worcestershire sauce and wine.
4. When seasonings are added, cover the skillet, leaving a little vent, and reduce heat. Cook over low heat for 20 minutes, stirring about three times during this period. Serve hot.

Mushroom Purée

The purpose of this delicious purée is not primarily to be used as a portion of vegetable, although, of course, it can be so served. The ideal use of it is for a garnish or stuffing. You can stuff poultry with it, spread toast rounds with it to be used as hors d'oeuvre or under a small steak or chops. You can stuff a small fish with it—a trout or a sole—and you can use it in combination with other vegetables.

5 lbs. fresh mushrooms
6 tbsp. butter
2 tbsp. lemon juice
½ tsp. freshly ground black pepper
½ tsp. sugar
2 tbsp. sherry or Madeira
2 tbsp. flour
¾ cup milk
¼ cup heavy cream

1. Wash the mushrooms, then purée them in a blender or food mill.

2. Melt 4 tablespoons of the butter in a saucepan. Add the lemon juice, pepper, sugar and wine, then the mushrooms, and simmer over low heat for about 10 minutes, stirring. Turn off heat.

3. In a separate saucepan melt remaining 2 tablespoons butter. Stir in the flour to make a smooth paste, and cook for 2 minutes.

4. Stir in first the milk, then the cream, a little at a time, stirring constantly to produce a smooth sauce.

5. Pour the contents of the second saucepan into the first. Turn on low heat and heat through without boiling. The purée is ready to serve or use in the various ways described.

Fried Onion Rings

oil or shortening for deep frying
3 cups flour

2 tsp. salt
3 tbsp. melted butter
4 eggs, beaten
2 cups milk
6 large onions
   salt

1. Put a large platter in the oven set at a keep-warm temperature (175°); line the platter with paper towels.

2. Pour about 3 inches of cooking oil or shortening into your deep fryer, and preheat to 375°. Use a thermometer if your fryer does not have a thermostat.

3. Combine the flour, salt, melted butter, eggs and milk in a mixing bowl with an egg beater or a whisk.

4. Peel the onions and slice them perpendicularly to the line of the stem, making rings about ¼ inch thick. Soak the rings in ice water for 20 minutes, then remove them from the water and drain them on paper towels.

5. When the oil has reached the desired temperature, dip the onion rings, a few at a time, in the batter mix, and fry them until they turn light golden brown. Remove them as they get done to the warm platter, and continue until all are done.

6. Sprinkle a little salt over the fried onion rings before serving.

Young Peas and Onions

6 lbs. young peas in pods
2 lbs. pearl onions
2 tsp. salt
½ tsp. freshly ground black pepper
4 tbsp. butter
2 tsp. Maggi liquid seasoning

1. Shell the peas and wash in cold water. Remove the dry skins from the onions.

2. Set up a large saucepan with enough water in it to reach the bottom of your steaming platform, and bring the water to a boil. When it is boiling, put the peas into the steamer and cook, covered, for 5 minutes.

3. Then add the onions to the steamer and steam, covered, for 10 minutes more. If necessary, add some boiling water to the pot during the steaming process. Do not add cold water.

4. When the peas and onions are done, remove them from the steamer to a saucepan. Add the salt, pepper, butter and Maggi, and stir until the butter is melted. Serve hot.

Baked Stuffed Potatoes

---

12 *baking potatoes*
½ *cup olive oil*
¼ *lb. butter (1 stick), softened*
2 *tsp. salt*
½ *tsp. freshly ground black pepper*
1 *cup very finely minced onions*
2 *cups sour cream*

1. Preheat oven to 450°.

2. Scrub the skins of the potatoes; using a paper towel, rub them with olive oil.

3. Bake the potatoes in the preheated oven for about 1 hour, until soft.

4. Remove the potatoes from the oven, but leave oven on. Cut a thin lengthwise slice off the top of each potato. Scoop out the potatoes, leaving a shell of skin as thin as possible without tearing.

5. Mix the scooped-out potato with the butter, salt, pepper,

onions and sour cream. Blend well, using a potato masher or electric mixer.

6. Using a large pastry bag, pipe the potato mixture back into the shells, filling them very full, mounding the mixture about ½ inch above the opening.

7. Put the potatoes back in the oven for about 15 minutes to reheat, and serve hot.

Potato Pancakes with Applesauce

12 medium-size old potatoes (do not use new potatoes)
2 medium-size onions
6 eggs
6 tbsp. flour
1 tbsp. salt
  shortening for frying
6 cups applesauce

1. Peel the potatoes and run them through the coarse blade of your grater. Squeeze the grated potatoes in a towel to remove as much moisture as possible.

2. Peel the onions, and grate them through the next to the finest blade of the grater (finer than the potatoes). Put the grated potatoes and onions into a bowl.

3. Beat the eggs in a separate bowl, then add them to the potato mixture. Stir in the flour and salt, and combine the batter thoroughly.

4. Turn on oven to 175°. Put in a large platter to keep warm.

5. Heat a heavy skillet, and melt the shortening in it. Fry the pancakes, making them about 2½ inches in diameter, browning the first side, turning once, and browning the bottoms. Transfer to paper towels to drain as they are done, then to the warm platter in the oven.

6. Serve the pancakes hot, with applesauce.
Optional: Serve with sour cream, and/or crisp bacon.

Balls

12 *large potatoes*
¼ *lb. butter (1 stick)*
2 *tsp. salt*
½ *tsp. freshly ground black pepper*

1. Peel the potatoes, and cut them into balls with a melon-ball or potato-ball cutter. Use the smaller cutter if you have a choice.

2. Melt the butter in a skillet, then reduce heat to medium. Prepare a warm platter in the oven or on a hot tray to receive the potatoes.

3. Fry the potatoes in the butter on all sides until golden brown. Do only 1 layer in the pan at a time, then remove to the platter, and do the next batch. If the butter burns, scrape it out, wipe the skillet with paper towels, and start with fresh butter. Sprinkle the salt and pepper over the potatoes while they are frying.

Home-Fried Potatoes

5 *quarts water*
2 *tsp. salt*
12 *medium-size to large potatoes (4 to 5 lbs. total)*
¼ *lb. butter (1 stick)*
2 *cups chopped onions*
12 *strips of bacon, cut into ½-inch-square pieces*
½ *tsp. freshly ground black pepper*

1. Bring the 5 quarts of water to a boil in a large pot, and add the salt to it.

2. Boil the potatoes, unpeeled, in the water for 25 or 30 minutes, until cooked through but not very soft.

3. Remove them from the water and let them cool for a few minutes. Peel the potatoes, and slice them into ¼-inch-thick round slices.

4. Using a large skillet, or even a casserole, melt the butter and add the onions. Cook the onions over medium heat for about 2 minutes, stirring them, then add the potato slices, the bacon pieces and the pepper.

5. Toss the potatoes and other ingredients, browning them on both sides in the butter and allowing the pieces of bacon to cook. Serve hot.

French Fried Potatoes

12 large baking potatoes
   oil for deep frying
 2 tsp. salt

1. Peel the potatoes; cut them lengthwise into slices about ¼ inch thick. Cut each slice into sticks ¼ inch thick. Wash the potatoes in cold running water, then spread out on towels and allow them to dry thoroughly.

2. Heat the oil in the deep fryer to 375°. Use a fat thermometer if the fryer is not equipped with a thermostat.

3. Prepare a large platter, and keep it warm in the oven on a low setting.

4. Fry the potatoes, a handful at a time, until they are golden brown. Transfer them to paper towels to drain, then onto the warm platter. Continue until all are done.

5. Sprinkle salt over the platter of potatoes before serving.

Mashed Potatoes with Sour Cream

    12 large potatoes
     2 tsp. salt
     2 cups sour cream
    ½ cup chopped fresh chives
    ½ tsp. freshly ground black pepper
     4 tbsp. butter, softened

1. Peel the potatoes, and put them in boiling water to cover, adding the salt. Boil them for 25 to 30 minutes until fairly soft. You can test them with a knife point, which should go in easily in the center of a potato.

2. Drain the boiled potatoes and put them in a casserole over low heat. Using a potato masher, mash them well and mash in the sour cream. When the potatoes are smooth with no lumps, add the chives, pepper and softened butter. Stir in well.

3. Serve hot. The potatoes may need a little more salt, depending on your taste.

Boiled Parsley Potatoes

    12 large potatoes
     2 tsp. salt
     6 tbsp. butter
     1 cup chopped fresh parsley

1. Peel the potatoes and cut them into halves or thirds.

2. Boil them in enough water to cover, with the salt added, for about 20 minutes, until soft.

3. Drain the water from the pot, leaving in the potatoes. Add the butter and parlsey, and toss the cooked potatoes in it

until the parsley is well distributed and the butter is melted and coats the potatoes. Serve hot.

Creamed Spinach with Mushrooms

3 to 4 lbs. fresh spinach leaves
2 cups water
½ lb. butter (2 sticks)
1 garlic clove, minced fine
½ cup finely minced onion
2 cups finely minced fresh mushrooms
5 tbsp. flour
1½ cups heavy cream
1 tsp. salt
¼ tsp. freshly ground black pepper

1. Cut off the tough stems on the spinach leaves. Wash the leaves under cold running water at least twice, making sure you get all the sand and dirt out of them.

2. Bring 2 cups of water to a rapid boil in a large saucepan. Add the washed spinach, cover, and simmer over medium heat for 20 minutes.

3. When ready, drain the spinach, and chop it very fine with a chopper or electric blender. If you use the blender, let the spinach cool off before starting. It has a tendency to explode out of the blender if very hot.

4. Melt the butter in a saucepan, add the minced garlic, onion and mushrooms to it, and cook for about 2 minutes, stirring. Stir in the flour and mix into a fairly smooth paste.

5. Add the cream, a little at a time, stirring constantly, then add the chopped spinach, salt and pepper. Heat through without boiling, stir well, and serve hot.

Optional: For plain creamed spinach, follow the same directions, but leave out the garlic, onions and mushrooms.

Steamed Green Beans

3 lbs. fresh green beans
4 tbsp. softened butter
1 tsp. salt
¼ tsp. freshly ground black pepper
2 tsp. Maggi liquid seasoning

1. Cut the ends off the beans, and wash them in cold water. Push them through a bean cutter to French them. If you do not have a cutter, cut the beans into 3 or 4 thin *lengthwise* slices with a sharp knife.

2. Arrange your steamer platform over just enough water to reach the bottom of the platform. Bring the water to a boil, add the beans to the top of the platform, cover, and steam for 15 minutes.

3. When done, remove the beans to a hot serving dish, add the butter, salt, pepper and Maggi, and toss them to distribute the butter and seasonings well. Serve hot.

Baked Tomatoes

12 medium-size to large tomatoes, firm but not overripe
¼ lb. butter (1 stick)
2 tbsp. chopped fresh parsley
2 tsp. salt
½ tsp. freshly ground black pepper

1. Preheat oven to 350°.

2. Cut a small cap off the top of each tomato, reserving the caps. With a small, sharp paring knife make a few cuts into the center of the meat of each tomato, being very careful not to pierce the skin.

3. Divide the butter into 12 equal pieces, and push 1 piece into each tomato. Sprinkle the tomatoes with the parsley, salt and pepper, then put the caps back in place.

4. Arrange the tomatoes in an ovenproof baking dish, and bake them in the preheated oven for about 20 minutes.

5. Remove from oven and serve hot.

Stuffed Zucchini

6 large zucchini
1 tsp. salt
2 tbsp. butter
¾ cup chopped onions
4 tbsp. tomato paste
1 cup soft bread crumbs
1 egg, beaten
¼ tsp. freshly ground black pepper

1. Cut the zucchini lengthwise into halves, dividing them as evenly as possible.

2. Put them in a large saucepan or pot, add the salt and water to the depth of about 1 inch, cover, and simmer for 5 minutes.

3. Remove the cooked zucchini halves from the water, and place them flat side down on paper towels to drain and cool.

4. When they are cool enough to handle, scoop out the meat from the centers, leaving enough thickness so that the skin will not tear (⅜ inch).

5. Melt the butter in a saucepan and simmer the chopped onions in it until they soften but do not brown. Add the tomato paste, the scooped-out meat of the zucchini, the bread crumbs, beaten egg and pepper. Stir well and cook over medium heat for 2 or 3 minutes.

6. Preheat oven to 400°.

7. Using a small spoon, put the stuffing mixture into the zucchini shells, and arrange them in an ovenproof baking dish. Heat in the oven for about 10 minutes, or until the top of the stuffing just begins to brown. Serve hot.

Fried Zucchini

oil for deep frying
12 *medium-size zucchini*
1 *tbsp. salt*
1 *cup flour*

1. Heat the oil in a deep fryer to 375°. Use a fat thermometer if the fryer is not equipped with a thermostat.

2. While the oil is heating, wash the zucchini under cold running water. Slice them into ½-inch-thick slices, and sprinkle the slices with salt. Let stand for a few minutes.

3. Dry the sliced zucchini on paper towels, then dust them with the flour.

4. Line a platter with paper towels, and put it in a warm oven to receive the zucchini as they are cooked.

5. When the oil is heated to the proper temperature, fry the zucchini, a few at a time, to a golden brown, then transfer them to the warm platter to drain.

6. When all are done, remove paper towels and serve hot.

Steamed Zucchini with Parmesan

6 *large zucchini*
4 *tbsp. butter*
1 *cup grated Parmesan cheese*

1 tbsp. seasoned salt
½ tsp. freshly ground black pepper

1. Put enough water in a large pot equipped with a cover to reach the bottom of your steamer platform.

2. Put in the platform, and arrange the zucchini on top of it. Bring the water to a boil, cover, and steam for 15 minutes, until tender. If you use a very big pot, or if the lid does not fit very tightly, you may need a few more minutes.

3. If you are not going to serve the zucchini immediately, leave them in the steamer, heat off, but covered, until just before serving time.

4. To serve, transfer the zucchini to a warm platter with tongs. Quickly cut them lengthwise into halves. On the exposed surface, dot the butter, which should melt immediately. Sprinkle the buttered halves with Parmesan cheese, then with salt and pepper. Serve immediately.

A Few Words on Salads

To put salads together successfully for 12 people or more, there are certain things you *must* have and cannot do without. The first is a very large salad bowl. The bowl can be made of wood or glass or plastic or ceramic, but it should be easily big enough to accommodate 3 or 4 heads of lettuce leaves, torn apart. Do not think that you are wasting money on this, because a large salad bowl is always usable for smaller quantities, but a small one, overfilled, is a disaster when you try to toss the salad. As a general rule, I believe in mixing the dressing in the bottom of the salad bowl first, then adding the salad and tossing it. Every leaf should be well coated with the dressing, because there is nothing worse than being served a salad with a few wet leaves on top, and dry ones underneath. A second item I highly recommend is a large colander for draining and washing salad ingredients. Also, a set of large wooden or plastic tools (spoon and fork) for tossing and serving.

Celery Root Salad

4 lbs. celery root
5 quarts water
½ cup lemon juice
2 cups mayonnaise
1 tsp. dry mustard
1 tsp. salt
¼ tsp. freshly ground white pepper
1 tsp. curry powder

1. Peel the celery root carefully. Grate it through the coarsest blade of your grater, or cut with a knife into thin julienne strips.

2. Put all the strips into a colander or large strainer.

3. Bring the 5 quarts of water to a boil in a large saucepan or pot big enough to accommodate the colander or strainer. Add the lemon juice to the boiling water, then immerse the container of celery root in it for about 3 minutes.

4. Remove container from water and spread the pieces out on paper towels to drain and cool.

5. In a salad bowl, mix the mayonnaise, mustard, salt, pepper and curry powder well. Add the cooled celery root and toss to coat with the dressing evenly. Serve.

Hot Potato Salad

12 medium-size potatoes
12 slices of bacon, cut into small pieces
3 cups chopped onions
1 cup white vinegar
1 cup beef consommé
2 tsp. salt

½ tsp. freshly ground black pepper
3 egg yolks, beaten well

1. Peel the potatoes, put them in a pot of cold water to cover, and boil until tender, 25 to 30 minutes.

2. Drain the potatoes and slice them into ¼-inch-thick round slices. Put them in a salad bowl or serving bowl.

3. In a medium-size saucepan cook the bacon until it is browned, then add the chopped onions and continue cooking until onions are softened. Remove and drain the bacon.

4. Add the vinegar and consommé to the pan, bring to a boil, reduce heat, and simmer for 2 minutes. Remove from heat, and beat in the egg yolks with a wire whisk.

5. Crumble the bacon into the potatoes. Pour the dressing over the potatoes and toss. Serve the salad warm.

Caesar Salad

1 loaf of crusty French or Italian bread (a baguette, weighing 1½ lbs.)
¼ lb. butter (1 stick)
4 heads of romaine lettuce
2 cups olive oil
4 garlic cloves, minced very fine
3 tsp. salt
½ tsp. freshly ground black pepper
3 eggs
¾ cup wine vinegar
12 anchovy fillets, mashed into a paste
¾ cup grated Parmesan cheese

1. Using a sharp, serrated bread knife cut the bread into ½-inch cubes. My system is to cut the whole loaf through horizontally into about 3 or 4 lengthwise slices. Then, holding it to-

gether with one hand, make several lengthwise vertical cuts. Finally, cut as though making standard bread slices, producing the cubes.

2. Using a heavy skillet, melt about one third of the butter over medium heat. Fry the bread cubes in the butter to a golden brown. Add more butter, fry a new batch of cubes, and continue until all are done. Reserve the cubes in a bowl for addition to the salad later.

3. Wash the lettuce in cold running water, separating the leaves and tearing them into halves or thirds. Pat the leaves dry between towels.

4. Put the oil and garlic into a large salad bowl. Let the garlic soak for about 10 minutes. Add the dry lettuce, sprinkle with salt and pepper, then toss thoroughly to coat the lettuce with oil.

5. Break the eggs into the salad and toss well again.

6. Add the vinegar and anchovies, and toss again, making sure no little lumps of anchovies get caught in one place.

7. Add the bowl of fried bread cubes and sprinkle on the Parmesan cheese. Toss a final time and serve.

Green Goddess Salad

3 heads of Boston lettuce
4 ripe but firm avocados
2 tbsp. anchovy paste
1 cup sour cream
1 cup mayonnaise
4 tbsp. chopped fresh chives
¼ cup white vinegar
1 tbsp. lemon juice
½ cup chopped fresh parsley
½ tsp. freshly ground black pepper
1 garlic clove, peeled and minced
1 tbsp. sugar
1 cup julienne of red pimientos

1. Wash the lettuce, separate the leaves, tear them into halves or thirds, and pat them dry between towels. Peel the avocados, remove the pits by cutting the avocados into halves, then slice thin.

2. Put the anchovy paste, sour cream, mayonnaise, chives, vinegar, lemon juice, parsley, pepper, garlic and sugar in an electric blender, and blend at medium speed for 15 to 20 seconds to make a smooth dressing.

3. Pour the dressing in the salad bowl and add the dry lettuce leaves, avocado slices and pimientos. Toss well and serve.

Chef's Salad I

The chef's salad, an American invention, is the exception to my rule about putting the dressing at the bottom of the bowl and tossing before serving. In this recipe, and the one following, the salads are arranged for maximum eye appeal, and the dressing is served separately for adding and tossing at the table, after the diners have seen the arrangement of the salad. For serving, you may choose not to make one bowl, but to arrange individual bowls for each person at the table. In that case, you also have the opportunity to serve a choice of dressings.

3 heads of iceberg lettuce
2 bunches of watercress
1 lb. sliced ham, cut into julienne strips
1 lb. sliced Swiss cheese, cut into julienne strips
1 lb. sliced white meat of turkey or chicken, cut into julienne strips
6 medium-size tomatoes, quartered
3 cucumbers, peeled and sliced
6 hard-cooked eggs, peeled and quartered or sliced
12 pitted black olives

1. Wash the lettuce, separate the leaves, tear them into halves or thirds, and pat dry between towels. Trim the stalks from

the watercress, wash and dry the leaves. Put the lettuce and watercress into a large salad bowl or individual bowls, and toss them together, making a bed.

2. On top of the lettuce and watercress bed, arrange decoratively all the remaining ingredients, using contrasting colors for visual appeal.

3. Serve with your choice of the dressings at the end of this chapter.

Chef's Salad II

Please read the comments in the previous recipe about chef's salads.

> 3 heads of iceberg lettuce
> 1 tsp. sugar
> 2 tbsp. lemon juice
> ½ cup chopped fresh dill
> 36 shrimps, cooked and peeled (about 2 lbs.)
> 6 hard-cooked eggs, quartered
> 4 avocados, peeled, pitted and sliced thin
> 24 sardines, drained of their oil
> 12 anchovy fillets, drained of their oil
> 3 cups shelled cooked crab meat
> 3 cups cooked salmon
> 12 green olives, stuffed with pimiento
> 2 bunches of fresh scallions, washed and trimmed

1. Wash the lettuce, separate the leaves, tear them into halves or thirds, and pat dry between towels. Put them in a salad bowl.

2. Dissolve the sugar in the lemon juice. Add the dill to the lettuce, pour the lemon juice over, and toss well.

3. On top of the lettuce, arrange the remaining ingredients

in an attractive pattern. You can make some substitutions or omissions, but do not add any meats or cheeses.

4. Serve the salad with your choice of the dressings at the end of the chapter.

Fresh Green Bean Salad

3 lbs. fresh green beans
4 hard-cooked eggs, peeled and sieved

1. Follow steps 1 and 2 in the recipe for Steamed Green Beans (p. 224).

2. Allow the cooked beans to cool to room temperature, then chill.

3. Select one of the dressings at the end of the chapter and place it in the salad bowl. I recommend using the lemon dressing, vinaigrette or oil and vinegar.

4. Add the sieved eggs and the chilled beans to the bowl, toss well, and serve.

Potato Salad with Eggs and Onions

12 medium-size potatoes
3 quarts water
2 cups roughly chopped sweet onions
2 cups mayonnaise
2 tsp. salt
½ tsp. freshly ground black pepper
6 hard-cooked eggs, chopped

1. Peel the potatoes and boil in water to cover for about 25 minutes, until tender. Remove from water, drain, and allow the potatoes to cool.

2. Cut the potatoes into ½-inch cubes.

3. Bring the 3 quarts of water to a boil. Put the chopped onions into a colander or strainer. Dip the container of onions into the boiling water for about 2 minutes. Remove, drain, and cool the onions.

4. Combine the mayonnaise, salt and pepper in a salad bowl. Add the cubed potatoes, chopped onions and chopped hard-cooked eggs. Toss well to coat with dressing, and serve cold.

Russian Vegetable Salad (Salade Russe)

This is a wonderful way to serve vegetables in warm weather in the guise of a salad. Because of the great variety of vegetables included, it is a good idea to save an extra cup of whatever vegetables you are serving the previous week, to accumulate them in anticipation of making this salad. Naturally, quantities can be adjusted and a greater or smaller variety of ingredients may be used.

1 head of iceberg lettuce
1 cup each of the following:
  cooked green peas
  diced cooked carrots
  cooked corn kernels (canned or fresh)
  diced cooked potatoes
  cooked baby lima beans
  chopped cooked green beans
  peeled and chopped cucumbers
  seeded and chopped fresh tomatoes
  peeled and chopped radishes
  chopped raw onions (optional: *blanch them in boiling water to reduce strength*)

1. Wash and dry the lettuce leaves, without tearing them. Arrange them in a bowl, lining the sides and bottom.

2. Combine all the vegetables in a large mixing bowl with 3 cups of one of the mayonnaise dressings at the end of the chapter. Mix well.

3. Transfer salad to lettuce-lined bowl. Serve cold. You can also serve this salad on individual plates, spooned onto a lettuce leaf.

Endive and Beet Salad

6 *medium-size to large beets*
2 *cups vinegar*
2 *tsp. salt*
8 *heads of Belgian endive*

1. Wash the beets under cold running water. In a large pot equipped with a cover put enough water to reach the bottom of your steamer platform. Put the beets on the platform, bring the water to a boil, cover, and steam them for about 1 hour, until tender. You will have to add some *boiling* water from time to time during the hour.

2. When done, remove the beets from the steamer, and let them cool. Peel off the outside skin, then grate the beets through the coarsest blade of your grater, yielding thin strips.

3. Put the grated beets in a bowl, add the vinegar and salt, and soak them for several hours, turning occasionally.

4. Wash the endives, and separate the leaves without tearing them. With a knife cut the leaves into halves.

5. Choose one of the dressings at the end of the chapter— lemon, vinaigrette or oil and vinegar—and put it in the salad bowl. Drain the beets that were soaking and add them to the bowl along with the cut endives. Toss well and serve.

Cucumber Salad with Sour Cream

12 medium-size cucumbers
 3 medium-size onions
 3 quarts water
 3 cups sour cream
 3 tbsp. lemon juice
 1 tbsp. Worcestershire sauce
 3 tbsp. chopped fresh parsley
 1 tsp. seasoned salt
¼ tsp. freshly ground white pepper

1. Peel the cucumbers, and slice them thin through the slicing blade of your grater. Put them in a colander to drain.

2. Peel the onions, and slice them thin. Bring the 3 quarts of water to a boil. Put the onion slices in a strainer or colander, lower them into the boiling water, and blanch them for 2 or 3 minutes. Remove from water and drain.

3. In the salad bowl combine the sour cream, lemon juice, Worcestershire sauce, parsley, salt and pepper thoroughly.

4. Add the drained cucumbers and onions, mix well, and let stand for about 1 hour before serving.

Green Salad

2 heads of Bibb or Boston lettuce
1 head of romaine lettuce
1 head of iceberg lettuce
2 cups thinly sliced scallions, including the green part
½ cup chopped fresh parsley
2 green peppers, cored, seeded and chopped fine

1. Wash the various lettuces, separate the leaves, tear them

into halves or thirds, and pat them dry between towels.

2. Choose any of the dressings at the end of the chapter, and put it into the salad bowl.

3. Add the lettuce, scallions, parsley and peppers. Toss well and serve.

Baby Tomato Salad

---

4 pint boxes baby tomatoes
.2 heads of iceberg lettuce
2 cups thinly sliced scallions

1. Wash the tomatoes and cut each one into halves with a sharp knife, being careful not to squeeze them.

2. Wash the lettuce, separate the leaves, tear them into halves or thirds, and pat dry between towels.

3. Choose one of the dressings at the end of the chapter and put it in the salad bowl.

4. Add the tomatoes, lettuce and scallions. Toss well and serve.

Cucumber Salad with Dill

---

12 medium-size cucumbers
1 cup chopped fresh dill
2 cups white vinegar
1 tbsp. salt

1. Peel the cucumbers and cut them into thin slices with a knife or the slicing blade of the grater.

2. Put the slices in a large bowl, sprinkle the chopped dill

over them, and toss well to mix. Pour the vinegar over and sprinkle with salt.

3. Allow the cucumbers to soak in the vinegar, in the refrigerator, for several hours. Turn them occasionally so that all get soaked evenly.

4. Serve as is, pouring off some of the liquid first.

Optional: Add a little olive oil to the cucumbers and toss again before serving.

Cold Asparagus Salad

6 dozen fresh asparagus spears
1 head of iceberg lettuce (12 nice leaves are needed)
4 hard-cooked eggs, rubbed through a sieve
1 cup red pimientos, cut into julienne strips

1. Follow steps 1 through 3 in the recipe for Steamed Asparagus (p. 203).

2. Allow the cooked asparagus to cool in the refrigerator.

3. Arrange 1 leaf of lettuce, washed and patted dry, on each of 12 individual salad plates.

4. Arrange 6 asparagus spears on each plate, sprinkle with the sieved eggs, and arrange strips of pimiento over them in a decorative way.

5. Prepare the vinaigrette or oil and vinegar dressing at the end of the chapter, and spoon about 2 tablespoons of it over each portion.

Waldorf Salad

12 apples
3 quarts water

    4 cups chopped celery
    ½ cup lemon juice
    2 cups mayonnaise
    1 tsp. salt
    2 cups shelled, unsalted walnuts

1. Peel and core the apples and cut into approximately ½-inch pieces.

2. Boil the 3 quarts of water. Put the chopped celery in a large strainer or colander, and dip the container of celery into boiling water for 2 minutes. Remove, drain, and cool.

3. Combine the apples and celery with the lemon juice, and mix. Let stand for 2 hours, tossing occasionally.

4. In the salad bowl, mix the mayonnaise, salt, celery, apples and walnuts. Toss well, and serve.

Mixed Fruit Salad

    8 oranges
    4 grapefruits
    3 cantaloupes
    6 apples
    2 pints strawberries
    4 bananas
    2 cups seedless green grapes
    ¾ cup granulated sugar

1. Peel the oranges and grapefruits and separate into sections.

2. Cut the cantaloupes into halves, remove pulp and seeds, and cut into balls with a melon-ball cutter.

3. Peel, core, quarter, and slice the apples.

4. Wash and hull the strawberries, and cut them into halves.

5. Peel and slice the bananas.

6. Wash the grapes.

7. Combine all the fruits in a bowl and toss to mix well.

8. Sprinkle sugar over the fruits and refrigerate for 3 or 4 hours before serving.

Salad Dressings

Lemon Dressing

 1 cup olive oil
⅓ cup lemon juice
 2 tbsp. sugar
 2 tbsp. chopped fresh or frozen chives
½ tsp. salt
¼ tsp. freshly ground black pepper

Mix all the ingredients together well and let stand for 30 minutes before using. Make sure sugar is completely dissolved.

Vinaigrette Dressing

1½ cups olive oil
 ½ cup vinegar
 ½ tsp. salt
 ¼ tsp. freshly ground black pepper
  1 tbsp. capers
  1 tbsp. finely chopped onion, or dried onion chips
  1 tbsp. finely chopped fresh parsley
  1 tsp. chopped fresh chervil, or ½ tsp. dried chervil

1 tsp. chopped tarragon (½ tsp. if dried)
1 tsp. chopped fresh or frozen chives

Mix all the ingredients together well and let stand for 30 minutes before using.

Rémoulade Dressing

---

2 cups mayonnaise
1 tbsp. prepared mustard, Dijon style
1 tbsp. finely chopped gherkin pickles
1 tbsp. chopped fresh parsley
1 tsp. chopped tarragon
1 tsp. chopped fresh chervil, or ½ tsp. dried chervil
1 tsp. anchovy paste
¼ tsp. salt
¼ tsp. freshly ground white pepper

Mix all ingredients together well.

Thousand Island Dressing (Russian Dressing)

---

2 cups mayonnaise
½ cup chili sauce or tomato ketchup
¼ cup chopped pickles, sweet or dill
1 tsp. salt
½ tsp. freshly ground black pepper
1 tbsp. Worcestershire sauce
1 tbsp. chopped fresh parsley
2 drops of Tabasco

Mix all ingredients together well.

Garlic Italian Dressing

    1 garlic clove, peeled
    2 tsp. salt
1½ cups olive oil
    ½ cup red-wine vinegar
    ½ tsp. freshly ground black pepper

In the bottom of the salad bowl crush the garlic clove with the salt with the back of a wooden spoon. Remove the remaining strands of garlic and discard. Add the rest of the ingredients, mix well, and use in salad.

Oil and Vinegar Dressing

1½ cups olive oil
    ½ cup vinegar
    2 tsp. salt
    ½ tsp. freshly ground black pepper
    1 tbsp. chopped fresh or frozen chives

Mix all ingredients together well.

Green Mayonnaise Dressing

    2 cups mayonnaise
    2 tbsp. chopped fresh parsley
    1 tbsp. chopped fresh dill
    2 tsp. salt
    ½ tsp. freshly ground white pepper

1 tbsp. lemon juice
6 drops of green vegetable dye

Mix all ingredients together well.

Red Mayonnaise Dressing

2 cups mayonnaise
½ cup tomato ketchup
1 tbsp. chopped pimiento
1 tbsp. Worcestershire sauce
½ tsp. paprika
½ tsp. salt
6 drops of red vegetable dye

Mix all ingredients together well.

Sour Cream Dressing

1 tbsp. granulated sugar
2 tbsp. lemon juice
1 tbsp. Worcestershire sauce
2 cups sour cream
1 tbsp. chopped fresh parsley
1 tsp. seasoned salt
½ tsp. freshly ground white pepper

Dissolve the sugar in the lemon juice. Mix all ingredients together well, using a wire whisk.

Roquefort Dressing

1 cup crumbled Roquefort cheese (substitute Danish blue cheese if necessary)

½ cup white vinegar

1 cup olive oil

1 tbsp. chopped fresh parsley

½ tsp. freshly ground black pepper

Mash the cheese with a fork into the vinegar and oil until well combined. Add the remaining ingredients and mix well.

8

Cakes
and
Pastries

Génoise Layer Cake

This recipe provides first the directions for four 9-inch layers of the cake, which will yield two 9-inch, 2-layer cakes. Various suggestions for fillings follow, but of course you can choose different ones. The ideal type of cake pan to use is the kind that has a built-in cutter which can be pushed around the entire circumference of the pan, thus freeing the finished cake layer for removal.

> *softened butter for greasing pans*
> *flour for dusting pans*
> 12 *eggs*
>   2 *cups sugar*
>   2 *tsp. vanilla extract*
> ¾ *cup melted unsalted butter*
>   2 *cups all-purpose flour*

1. Preheat oven to 350°.

2. Butter the inside surfaces of the 4 cake pans and then dust them with a light coating of flour. The best way to do this is to put about a cup of flour in the first buttered pan, swish it around until a thin coating adheres to the bottom and sides, then spill the remainder into the next pan, and repeat the process.

3. Use a large double boiler for the next step. If you only have a small one, divide the ingredients in two and do it in 2 shifts. Mix the eggs and the sugar (do not *beat*) in the top of a double boiler, placed over simmering, not boiling, water. Insert an egg beater (either electric or manual) and beat steadily until the mixture increases in bulk by 3 times. You can estimate whether your double boiler is big enough from this. The beating process should take about 20 minutes. When almost done, add the vanilla and melted butter.

4. Sift the flour, and fold it gently into the mixture *off the heat*, using a rubber scraper or a spatula.

5. Pour the mixture into the 4 prepared pans and bake in preheated oven for 30 minutes. The cakes should be an even golden color, and dry and springy in the centers.

6. Reverse the pans onto cooling racks and operate the cutters to extract cake layers. After the layers are cooled they are ready to assemble with the various icings.

Chocolate Icing

6 oz. chocolate (cooking chocolate comes in 1-oz. squares)
1½ cups heavy cream
2 cups sugar
½ cup water
2 tbsp. corn syrup
2 eggs

1. In a heavy saucepan over medium to low heat, stir to-

gether the chocolate, cream, sugar, water and corn syrup. Stop stirring, and allow the mixture to thicken substantially after the chocolate has melted, 6 to 7 minutes.

2. Beat the eggs in a small mixing bowl with a whisk. Add a little chocolate mixture from the saucepan to the eggs, and beat it in. Now beat the egg mixture into the rest of the chocolate.

3. Cook for a little longer, allowing the icing to thicken, stirring constantly.

4. Allow the icing to cool completely at room temperature. Spread between layers and on top and sides of the *génoise* to form two 2-layer cakes.

White Vanilla Icing

4 cups sugar
2 cups water
4 egg whites
¼ *tsp. salt*
¼ *tsp. cream of tartar*
2 tsp. vanilla extract

1. Using a heavy enamelware saucepan, bring the sugar and water to a boil together. Cover, and cook for several minutes until the sugar crystals on the sides of the pan have been washed down into the mixture by the steam. Uncover, and insert a candy thermometer; this is very important.

2. Continue cooking until thermometer registers a temperature of *exactly* 240°.

3. Immediately after inserting the thermometer, beat the egg whites together with the salt until a thick froth forms on the surface. Do not overbeat; you do not want the whites to form peaks.

4. Pour the sugar syrup into the egg whites very slowly, continuing to beat all the while. This operation really demands a

hand-held electric mixer. After the syrup is all incorporated, beat in the cream of tartar and vanilla.

5. At this point, the icing should be fluffy and easy to spread, and may be used immediately. Or you may flavor or color it by beating in some powdered cocoa, a liqueur, powdered instant coffee, some raspberry or other fruit syrup, or simply some unflavored vegetable coloring for effect.

Other Fillings:

You can also finish the *génoise* layers by spreading any kind of jam or jelly between the layers, and whipped cream on top. Or you can serve the 4 layers as 4 separate thin cakes, dusted with confectioners' sugar.

Whipped Cream Topping

If you use this type of topping for the *génoise* layers, you should prepare it only shortly before serving.

> *3 cups heavy cream, well chilled*
> *4 tbsp. superfine granulated sugar*
> *2 tsp. vanilla extract*

1. Using a chilled metal bowl, beat the cream with an electric mixer set on high.

2. When the cream begins to form soft peaks, add the sugar and vanilla and continue beating until stiff. Be careful not to overbeat past this point.

3. Using a thin spatula, spread the whipped cream generously between and on the top and sides of the *génoise* layers, forming two 2-layer cakes.

Optional: In this recipe, instead of the vanilla, beat in 4 tablespoons of powdered cocoa, 1 tablespoon of instant coffee powder, or 6 tablespoons of your favorite liqueur or Cognac.

Coconut Layer Cake

This recipe will make four 9-inch layers for two 2-layer cakes.

> 1 tbsp. baking powder
> 3½ cups cake flour, sifted
> ¾ tsp. salt
> ⅝ lb. butter (2½ sticks)
> 2¾ cups sugar
> 5 eggs, separated
> 2 tsp. vanilla extract
> 1¼ cups milk
> 1 cup shredded coconut
> 2 tsp. grated lemon rind

1. Preheat oven to 350°.

2. Sift the baking powder with the cake flour and salt into a mixing bowl.

3. In a separate bowl cream together the butter and the sugar. Using an electric mixer, beat into the butter-sugar mixture the egg yolks, one at a time, followed by the vanilla extract.

4. Combine the egg yolk mixture and the dry ingredients, and beat them together with the milk. Beat until smooth, then stir in shredded coconut and lemon rind with a spoon.

5. Beat the egg whites in a separate bowl until they make stiff peaks, and fold the whites into the other mixture with a rubber spatula, being careful not to crush the whites.

6. Butter the cake pans, and pour a quarter of the mixture into each. Bake in the preheated oven for 40 minutes, until a cake needle inserted in the middle of a layer comes out clean and the surface is slightly browned.

7. Let the layers cool in the pans to room temperature. Then turn them out onto cooling racks while you make the icing.

Coconut Icing

    4 egg whites
    3 cups sugar
    ½ cup water
    2 tbsp. lemon juice
    ½ tsp. cream of tartar
    1 tbsp. corn syrup
    2 tsp. vanilla extract
    1 cup shredded coconut

1. Put the egg whites, sugar, water, lemon juice, cream of tartar and corn syrup in an enamelware saucepan. Using a hand-held electric mixer or a wire whisk, beat the ingredients together.

2. Turn on very low heat under the saucepan, and continue beating until the mixture thickens and stiffens. When almost thick enough to spread, add the vanilla extract and finally, when the icing is quite thick, add the coconut, stirring it in with a spoon.

3. Spread two of the cooled cake layers with the icing, add the other 2 layers, and spread the tops and sides of the cakes with icing. Transfer to cake platters for serving.

Angel Food Cake

This is a feather-light white cake baked in a deep tube pan. It can be served as is, or can be combined with other desserts such as a fruit compote.

    1¼ cups cake flour, sifted
    1½ cups superfine granulated sugar
    12 egg whites
    ¼ tsp. salt
    1¼ tsp. cream of tartar
    1¼ tsp. vanilla extract

1. Preheat oven to 375°.

2. Sift the flour with the sugar, and repeat the process twice more.

3. Using an electric mixer, beat the egg whites, salt, cream of tartar and vanilla extract together until soft peaks are formed.

4. Continue beating, and add about two thirds of the flour and sugar mixture, a little at a time, until blended.

5. Using a rubber scraper or spatula, fold the remainder of the flour and sugar mixture into the rest. Make sure there are no pockets of flour.

6. Transfer the mixture to a deep 10-inch angel food cake pan. Make sure the inside of the pan is dry and clean and completely greaseless. Grease will prevent the cake from rising.

7. Bake in the preheated oven for 30 minutes. Test the cake for doneness with a cake needle, which should come out clean.

8. Remove the cake from the oven and place the pan upside down on a plate. Let it cool completely, about 1 hour. Carefully insert a long thin spatula between the cake and the side of the pan. Do the same thing with the center tube. Cake should now slip out easily onto the plate.

Jelly Roll

This roll should be baked in a jelly roll pan 18 by 12 inches and 1 inch deep.

6 eggs, separated
1 cup granulated sugar
2 tsp. vanilla extract
1 cup cake flour
1 tsp. baking powder
softened butter for greasing jelly roll pan
1 cup confectioners' sugar
1 cup jelly or jam, your choice

1. Using an electric mixer beat the egg yolks, add the granulated sugar, and continue beating until the mixture is pale yellow and stiffens somewhat. Beat in the vanilla extract.

2. Sift the flour together with the baking powder and beat this mixture into the egg yolks. Turn mixer up to maximum speed and beat well.

3. Beat the egg whites separately until stiff, then fold them into the batter.

4. Preheat oven to 375°.

5. Butter the jelly roll pan, and turn batter into it, spreading to an even level with a spatula. Bake in preheated oven for 15 minutes.

6. Remove from oven and allow the cake to cool to room temperature.

7. Sprinkle the confectioners' sugar over an area on a pastry cloth or board equal in size to the jelly roll pan. Loosen the edges of the roll with a sharp knife, and quickly reverse the pan onto the sugar to unmold.

8. Spread the top side with an even layer of the jelly or jam, then roll it up the long way, making an 18-inch-long roll. Transfer to serving platter and slice to serve.

Alternative Fillings for Jelly Roll:

1. Substitute whipped cream (about 2 cups) for the jelly. Refrigerate after rolling until serving time.

2. Substitute French Pastry Cream (p. 266) for the jelly.

Chocolate Roll

softened butter for greasing pan
8 *eggs, separated*
1 *cup superfine granulated sugar*
8 *oz. cooking semisweet chocolate*
1 *cup cocoa powder*

2 *cups heavy cream, well chilled*
3 *tbsp. confectioners' sugar*
1 *tbsp. vanilla extract*

1. Preheat oven to 375°.

2. Lightly butter an 18-inch jelly roll pan. Line it with wax paper, making sure the paper overlaps the narrow ends by about 1 inch.

3. Beat the egg yolks in a mixing bowl with the sugar, using an electric mixer or an egg beater, until eggs are pale yellow, about 5 minutes.

4. In a saucepan melt the chocolate with about ¼ cup of water over low heat, stirring constantly and not allowing it to burn.

5. When chocolate is melted, remove from heat and allow it to cool to room temperature. Then mix the chocolate into the egg yolk mixture.

6. In a separate bowl beat the egg whites until they form soft peaks. The best way is to use a large whisk in a copper bowl, but an electric mixer can be used.

7. Fold the egg yolk and chocolate mixture very carefully into the egg whites, doing your best not to crush the air bubbles out of the whites.

8. Pour the cake mixture onto the wax paper in the jelly roll pan. Bake in the preheated oven for 15 minutes, reducing the temperature to 350° for the last 5 minutes.

9. Remove the cake from the oven and allow it to cool to room temperature.

10. When cool, sprinkle the top of the cake with about half the cocoa powder run through a sifter.

11. Lay out a sheet of wax paper on the counter or table, and quickly flip the cake pan over onto the paper. Lift off the pan, then peel off the wax paper that was on the bottom.

12. Beat the heavy cream mixed with the confectioners' sugar and vanilla extract until it is fairly stiff. Spread it evenly over the top of the cake.

13. Roll up the cake, the long way, like a jelly roll. If it cracks, don't worry, the cocoa powder will hide it.

14. Slide the roll onto a serving platter or plain wooden bread board, sprinkle the top with the remaining cocoa powder, and refrigerate until ready to serve.

15. To serve, cut thin slices with a very sharp knife to avoid crushing.

Pound Cake

This recipe makes 2 loaves, each 9 by 5 by 3 inches.

1 lb. butter (4 sticks)
4 cups sifted cake flour
12 eggs, separated
2 cups superfine granulated sugar
2 tsp. vanilla extract

1. Put the butter in a mixing bowl and cream it with an electric mixer until it is very light. Continue beating, adding the sifted cake flour, a little at a time, until all of it is added.

2. In a separate bowl beat together the egg yolks and the sugar until the mixture is pale yellow and thick. Beat the vanilla into this mixture.

3. Beat the butter and flour mixture into the egg yolk mixture until well blended.

4. Separately, using either the electric mixer (clean the blades) or a wire whisk, beat the egg whites until they form stiff peaks. Fold the whites into the other mixture carefully, trying not to crush too many of the air bubbles out of the whites.

5. Butter 2 loaf pans, 9 by 5 by 3 inches, and turn half the batter into each.

6. Preheat oven to 325°.

7. Bake the pound cakes for 1 hour and 20 minutes. Test with a cake needle for doneness; it should be plunged into the center of a cake and come out clean.

8. Remove the cakes from the oven and let them cool in the pans and shrink away from the sides a little before turning them out. Cool them on wire racks before slicing.

Variations:

Using the basic recipe above, you can vary the flavors of the pound cake by substituting almond or orange extract for the vanilla extract. You can add grated lemon or orange rind to the batter. You can add raisins (not too many), or you can add cocoa powder to produce a chocolate pound cake.

For serving you can slice and toast the cake, or serve it with ice cream, or with fruit compotes.

Christmas Fruitcake

3 cups chopped mixed candied fruits
1 cup dark raisins
1 cup light raisins
1 cup dried red currants
1 cup strawberry jam
1 tsp. vanilla extract
¾ cup brandy
¾ cup chopped walnuts
¾ cup chopped pecans
1½ cups all-purpose flour
12 tbsp. butter (1½ sticks)
½ tsp. grated nutmeg
1 tsp. ground cinnamon
¼ tsp. ground allspice
4 eggs
¾ cup brown sugar

1. In a large mixing bowl combine the candied fruits, raisins, currants, jam, vanilla and brandy. Let this mixture soak for 3 or 4 hours, turning occasionally.

2. Preheat oven to 325°.

3. Butter 2 standard 9-inch loaf pans.

4. Mix the chopped walnuts and pecans into the fruit mixture.

5. Using an electric mixer, combine the flour, butter, nutmeg, cinnamon and allspice into a smooth cream.

6. Separately, beat the eggs and brown sugar together into a thick mixture. Combine the flour and butter mixture with the egg mixture into a batter.

7. Pour the batter into the fruit and nut mixture, and stir well with a wooden spoon.

8. Fill the loaf pans up to about 1 inch below the tops. Cover them with a cookie sheet or a piece of aluminum foil, and bake in the preheated oven for 1½ hours.

9. Uncover and bake for about 1 hour more, until the tops of the cakes are browned.

10. Remove from oven and cool in the pans to room temperature. Remove from pans, wrap tightly in plastic wrap, and store until use. These cakes benefit from aging for a few days before being served, so I advise making them on some rainy day, and having them available for guests.

Strawberry Cheesecake

For this recipe you will need two 9-inch springform cake pans. Each cake should serve 6 people. You can substitute one 12-inch pan, but then the baking time should be increased by 15 or 20 minutes to make sure the center of the cake cooks sufficiently.

FOR THE CRUST:

50 vanilla wafers

2 cups ground walnuts

¾ cup melted butter

¼ cup sugar
   softened butter to coat cake pans

FOR THE CHEESE FILLING:

   2 lbs. cream cheese, softened at room temperature
   1 cup sour cream
1½ cups sugar
   1 tbsp. vanilla extract
   8 eggs, separated
   2 cups heavy cream, whipped to soft peaks
   1 cup cake flour

FOR THE TOPPING:

2 pint boxes medium-size to large strawberries
1 recipe Red-Currant Glaze (p. 267)

1. Preheat oven to 325°.

2. Crush the vanilla wafers into fine crumbs. Combine the crumbs with the ground walnuts, melted butter and sugar. Coat bottom and sides of the cake pans with the softened butter, then divide the crumb mixture into halves and put half in an even layer across the bottom of each pan. Pack down well.

3. In a mixing bowl blend together well the cream cheese, sour cream, ¾ cup of the sugar, the vanilla extract and the egg yolks.

4. Beat the egg whites separately with an electric mixer; as they begin to make soft peaks add to them the remaining ¾ cup sugar, a little at a time, until you have a stiff mixture, like a meringue.

5. Add the cheese mixture and the whipped cream to the egg whites, sprinkle the cake flour on top, and fold the whole thing together carefully to avoid crushing the air bubbles out of the whipped cream and the egg whites.

6. Pour half the mixture over the crust in each cake pan. Bake in the preheated oven for 1 hour and 20 minutes. Treat this like a soufflé and do not open the oven door. The cheesecake is ready when the top has *slightly* browned.

7. When the cake is ready, turn off the oven, open the door, and let the cake cool very slowly to room temperature in the oven. Without removing the springforms, refrigerate the cakes.

8. While the cakes are chilling, hull the strawberries and wash them. Arrange them on top of the cakes, large side down, in an attractive pattern. When the strawberries are on, prepare the glaze according to the recipe.

9. Pour on the warm glaze to cover the strawberries and let the glaze get firm before removing the springforms and serving the cakes.

Golden Cupcakes

	softened butter
2	cups sifted cake flour
1	cup sugar
¾	tsp. salt
2½	tsp. baking powder
3	tbsp. butter
3	tbsp. shortening
1	cup milk
1½	tsp. vanilla extract
5	egg yolks

1. Preheat oven to 375°.

2. Butter 24 cupcake cups, either separate ones or in muffin tins. You can use the inexpensive light-weight aluminum kind. Flour them very lightly after buttering, but do not take the flour for this purpose from the measured 2 cups for the recipe.

3. Combine the sifted flour, sugar, salt and baking powder in a bowl. Melt the butter and shortening together, allow to cool for a few minutes, then add to the bowl along with the milk and vanilla extract.

4. Beat with an electric mixer until well blended. Add egg

yolks and continue beating to a smooth consistency.

5. Fill the cupcake cups or muffin tins half full of the batter. Bake in the preheated oven for about 20 minutes, until the cupcakes rise above the level of the tins.

6. Remove from oven and let them cool in the tins to room temperature. Then remove from the tins. You can spread the tops with any of the icings or frostings you prefer.

Chocolate Brownies

---

    1 *tbsp. softened butter*
    6 *oz. semisweet cooking chocolate*
  12 *tbsp. unsalted butter (1½ sticks)*
    6 *eggs*
    3 *cups superfine granulated sugar*
    1 *tbsp. vanilla extract*
1½ *cups sifted all-purpose flour*
  ¾ *cup chopped walnuts*
  ¾ *cup chopped almonds*

1. Preheat oven to 325°.

2. Butter a standard 18-inch jelly roll pan, and swish a little flour around in it to make a thin coating. Knock out excess flour.

3. Put the chocolate and butter in the top part of a double boiler over simmering water and melt slowly, stirring occasionally. When the chocolate is melted, stir well and remove from heat.

4. Using an electric mixer, beat the eggs and sugar together. Keep the mixer going at slow speed and add all the remaining ingredients, adding the melted chocolate last. Stop as soon as the mixture is an even light-brown color and the nuts are well distributed.

5. Pour the batter into the pan, spreading to the corners with a spatula and leveling the mixture. Bake in preheated oven for 30 minutes.

(cont'd)

6. Remove from oven, and allow to cool in the pan for at least 1 hour. Cut the brownies into pieces 1 by 3 inches and serve.

Puff Paste

1 lb. butter (4 sticks)
4 cups sifted all-purpose flour
2 tsp. salt
1¼ cups ice water

1. Cut the 4 sticks of butter lengthwise into halves so that you have 8 flat pieces each about ½ inch thick.

2. Combine the flour, salt and water in a bowl and knead it into a firm dough. Continue to knead the dough until it has a smooth finish. The ideal implement for this step is an electric mixing machine with a dough hook. Lacking that, you'll have to do it by hand.

3. Cover the dough with a damp towel and let it rest for 15 minutes.

4. On a floured board, roll out the dough into a square about 12 inches on a side, a little more than ¼ inch thick.

5. Arrange the pieces of butter to cover half the square of dough. Fold the other half of the dough over them and press the edges together to seal in the butter. Wrap the whole thing in wax paper and refrigerate it for 30 minutes.

6. Return dough to the floured board, and roll it into a rectangle about ¼ inch thick. Now fold it in thirds, bringing one third over from the left, and then one third over from the right on top. Roll it out again into a long rectangle, and fold in thirds again. Again wrap and refrigerate for 30 minutes.

7. Repeat this folding in thirds, rolling out, folding again, and refrigerating for 30 minutes *four more* times. The dough is now ready for use in any of the puff-paste recipes which follow. The dough can be refrigerated for several days, or frozen indefinitely.

Elephant Ears (or Palmiers)

1 recipe Puff Paste (p. 260)
1 cup granulated sugar

1. Roll out the puff paste into a rectangle half as wide as it is long, about 17 inches by 9 inches, and ¼ inch thick.

2. Preheat oven to 425°.

3. Sprinkle the top of the dough with some of the granulated sugar, a thin coating.

4. Fold the dough from the ends into the center so that the top pieces just meet. Sprinkle the newly exposed surfaces with sugar. Repeat the folding process to the center again, and sprinkle with sugar. Finally bring the two sides together to the center and pat down.

5. Cut the folded dough into slices just under ½ inch thick, and arrange them on a cookie sheet, leaving a little space in between for expansion. Bake them in the preheated oven for about 10 minutes, until golden brown. Be careful not to let them burn, although a few bits of sugar may burn without harming the pastry.

6. This recipe should yield about 20 large elephant ears, providing one per person for 12, with some second helpings.

Napoleons

1 recipe Puff Paste (p. 260)
3 cups heavy cream, well chilled
6 tbsp. superfine granulated sugar
3 tsp. vanilla extract
2 cups confectioners' sugar

1. Roll out the puff paste to a thickness of ⅛ inch. Fit the dough onto 1 very large or 2 smaller cookie sheets. Refrigerate the sheets.

2. Preheat oven to 350°.

3. Bake the dough for about 1 hour, until nicely puffed up and golden brown. When done, remove from the oven and allow to cool to room temperature.

4. While the dough is cooling, whip the cream with the superfine sugar and the vanilla extract until stiff. Be careful not to overbeat and wind up with unwanted butter.

5. When the dough is cool, run a sharp serrated knife through it horizontally, dividing the top half from the bottom half. Now spread the bottom piece(s) with the whipped cream in an even layer. Replace the top half of the dough on top of the whipped cream. Refrigerate the pastry.

6. When the pastry is chilled, using a sharp serrated knife, cut the Napoleons into pieces about 3 inches by 2 inches. Sprinkle the tops with an even layer of confectioners' sugar and serve.

Puff Paste Jam Turnovers

1 recipe Puff Paste (p. 260)
2 cups fruit jam or preserves (strawberry, raspberry, currant, etc.)
2 eggs
2 tbsp. milk

1. Roll out the puff paste to a thickness of ¼ inch.

2. Being careful to cut closely, cut out circles of the paste about 3 to 4 inches in diameter.

3. Put 1 tablespoon of jam in the center of each circle. Moisten your fingers with water, fold the circles of paste in half and press the edges together, using the moisture on your fingers to help seal the edges tightly.

4. Arrange the turnovers on 1 or 2 cookie sheets.

5. Beat the eggs and milk together. Using a pastry brush, brush a coating of the mixture on top of the turnovers. Refrigerate the turnovers until well chilled.

6. Preheat oven to 400°.

7. Remove turnovers from the refrigerator and with a fork prick them once in the center.

8. Bake in the preheated oven for 10 to 12 minutes, or until they are golden brown. Serve at room temperature after cooling. Do not serve them fresh from the oven because the jam inside will be dangerously hot.

Puff Paste Tart Shell

This prebaked tart shell made of puff pastry is prepared first, then filled with pastry cream and whatever fruit you have chosen. If you want the tarts to taste freshly baked, do not prepare them too far in advance of serving.

1 recipe Puff Paste (p. 260)
1 egg
2 tbsp. milk

1. The method of preparing this shell leaves you the choice of shape. The easiest shape to use is the square or rectangle, because of the straight sides. After the dough is formed, before baking, you will need a pan of some kind to weight the center while the sides are allowed to puff up. Therefore, choose a rectangular or square pan of the proper size first.

2. Roll out the dough ⅛ inch thick to a size about 2 inches wider all around than your planned weight pan. Cut a 1-inch strip from all 4 sides. Wet the edges of the central piece, then apply the strip all around the edge, placing it flat on the moistened portion of the bottom piece. This last operation will require some trimming because your 1-inch strip is a little longer than you need.

3. Preheat oven to 425°.

4. Slip the dough onto a baking sheet or cookie sheet. Prick the bottom full of holes with a fork and press down the edges

with the tines of a fork. Butter the bottom of the weight pan you chose and place it on the bottom of the pastry. The space above the strips forming the edges must be unobstructed to allow them to puff up, thus forming the sides of the shell.

5. Beat the egg and milk together, and brush the mixture on the exposed edges, being careful not to let it drip down the sides, which might inhibit puffing in spots.

6. Bake in the preheated oven for about 15 minutes, until the edges have puffed up and are beginning to brown. Remove the weight pan, and bake for a few more minutes, until the center starts to brown just slightly. Remove from oven.

7. The tart shell is now ready for filling.

Short Paste Tart Shell

This prebaked tart shell made of sweet short paste is prepared first, then filled with pastry cream and whatever fruit you have chosen. If you want tarts that taste freshly baked, do not prepare them too far in advance of serving, although they will keep fresh for several hours longer than the Puff Paste Tart Shell.

3 cups all-purpose flour, sifted
¼ tsp. salt
3 tbsp. granulated sugar
6 tbsp. butter
5 tbsp. vegetable shortening
½ cup ice water

1. In a mixing bowl combine the flour, salt and sugar. Cut first the butter, then the shortening, into small pieces into the dry ingredients. Using your hands, knead them together into a mass.

2. Add the ice water, and gather the dough into a ball.

3. Flour a pastry board and knead the ball of dough on it

to further blend the ingredients. Wrap the dough in wax paper or aluminum foil and refrigerate.

4. Before rolling out the dough, prepare a flan ring 12 by 12 inches or 9 by 16 inches, or any other equivalent size, and a baking sheet or cookie sheet. The best sheets are made of heavy-gauge aluminum which will not buckle during baking.

5. Roll out the dough to a thickness of about ⅛ inch, and fit it into the flan ring on the baking sheet. You can patch it easily if it tears, using your fingers to press the dough together. Make sure the dough adheres to the sides of the ring, and patch any thin places. Then trim off the excess and press the edges with the tines of a fork to make a pattern.

6. Preheat oven to 400°.

7. Butter one side of a piece of aluminum foil large enough to fit on top of the dough with some extra foil on the sides.

8. Prick the dough with a fork at 1-inch intervals all over, then fit in the aluminum foil, buttered side down. Fill the aluminum foil with some dried beans, or marbles, or anything oven-proof which will provide some weight to hold down the dough.

9. Bake in the preheated oven for 10 minutes. Remove from oven, remove aluminum foil, and prick the bottom with a fork again. Return to the oven and bake until the shell browns slightly, about 10 more minutes.

10. Remove from oven, but leave the shell in the flan ring on the baking sheet until after filling.

Tarts for Twelve

These tarts require the previous preparation of prebaked pastry shells, using either the Puff Paste Tart Shell (p. 263) or the Short Paste Tart Shell (p. 264). Having prepared the shell, you then make the pastry cream described below, and follow with one of the fruit fillings and glazes.

French Pastry Cream

>   6 egg yolks
> 1 ½ cups granulated sugar
>   ¾ cup sifted all-purpose flour
> 2 ½ cups milk
>   2 tbsp. butter
>   2 tbsp. vanilla extract

1. Beat the egg yolks and sugar together with an electric mixer until the mixture becomes pale yellow. Continue beating while adding the sifted flour, little by little, until it is all absorbed.

2. Bring the milk to just below the boiling point in a saucepan. I advise using a saucepan with a little pouring spout on one side. Pour the hot milk *slowly* into the egg yolk mixture, beating the whole time with the mixer.

3. Transfer the mixture to a saucepan, turn on heat, and stir constantly with a whisk while it comes to a boil. Reduce heat and continue cooking and stirring for 2 more minutes. The cream should thicken appreciably.

4. Off heat, beat in the butter and vanilla extract, stirring until the butter melts.

5. The cream is now ready to put into the tart shell.

Apricot Glaze

>   2 cups apricot preserves
>   ½ cup granulated sugar

1. Rub the preserves through a sieve into a saucepan.

2. Add the sugar and bring the mixture to a boil. Stir for 1 minute at the boil and remove from heat. Keep warm until ready to use.

Red-Currant Glaze

2 cups red-currant jelly
½ cup granulated sugar

1. Combine the jelly and the sugar in a saucepan.
2. Bring to a boil, stir for 1 minute while boiling, and remove from heat. Keep warm until ready to use.

Apple Glaze

2 cups apple jelly
½ cup granulated sugar

1. Combine the jelly and the sugar in a saucepan.
2. Bring to a boil, stir for 1 minute while boiling, and remove from heat. Keep warm until ready to use.

Apricot Tart

1 prebaked tart shell
1 recipe French Pastry Cream (p. 266)
2 dozen canned half-apricots, drained
1 recipe Apricot Glaze (p. 266)

1. Fill the tart shell with the French Pastry Cream, spreading it in an even layer.
2. Arrange the apricot halves, round side up, on top of the cream.
3. Pour warm glaze over the top of the fruit, being careful to coat completely.
4. Let cool and serve.

Peach Tart

Substitute canned peach halves for the apricot halves in the previous recipe. Use apricot glaze.

Apple Tart

6 *firm ripe apples*
¼ *cup lemon juice*
2 *tbsp. sugar*
1 *prebaked tart shell*
1 *recipe French Pastry Cream (p. 266)*
1 *recipe Apple Glaze (p. 267)*

1. Peel, core and quarter the apples and cut into thin slices. Put the slices into a bowl with the lemon juice and sugar, toss well, and let stand in the refrigerator for about 1 hour.

2. Fill the tart shell with the pastry cream, spreading it into an even layer.

3. Arrange the apple slices on top of the pastry cream in a decorative pattern.

4. Pour warm apple glaze over the fruit, making sure to coat the entire surface.

5. Let cool and serve.

Strawberry Tart

2 to 3 *pint boxes ripe, well-shaped strawberries*
1 *prebaked tart shell*
1 *recipe French Pastry Cream (p. 266)*
1 *recipe Red-Currant Glaze (p. 267)*

1. Hull the strawberries and wash them under cold running water.

2. Fill the tart shell with the pastry cream, making an even layer.

3. Arrange the strawberries, large side down, on top of the cream in neat rows.

4. Pour warm currant glaze over the fruit, making sure an even coating is applied to all.

5. Let cool and serve.

Other Fruit Tarts:

You can follow the same procedures as in the preceding recipes, using sliced bananas with any of the glazes, orange sections with apricot glaze, raspberries with currant glaze, pear halves with apple glaze or apricot glaze, blueberries with any of the glazes, etc. You are limited only by your own imagination.

Almond-Orange Tarts

For this recipe, which uses the same sweet short paste as we used for the larger tarts, you will need some barquette molds. These are tin molds, just under 5 inches long, in the shape of little boats. They may be fluted or not. If you have only a dozen molds, you will need to do the baking in 2 shifts because the recipe should produce 24 tarts.

1 *recipe Short Paste Tart Shell (p. 264)*
2 *envelopes unflavored gelatin*
½ *cup fresh orange juice*
10 *eggs*
1 *cup sugar*
½ *tsp. salt*
2 *tbsp. grated orange rind*
1 *tsp. almond extract*
2 *cups chilled heavy cream, whipped*
48 *whole blanched almonds*

1. Roll out the paste according to the directions in the recipe. Using 1 tart mold as a guide to mark the dough, cut out pieces of dough to fit the molds. Fit dough in snugly, and trim the edges.

2. Bake in a 400° oven until golden brown. Remove from oven, and let cool in the molds. When cool, carefully turn out. If you are nervous about breaking the shells, leave the cooked shells in the molds and do not remove them until after they are filled. But to do that you have to have 24 molds.

3. Combine the gelatin with the orange juice and stir well to dissolve. Cook this mixture in the top part of a double boiler over simmering water to melt completely.

4. Put the eggs, sugar and salt in a large metal mixing bowl. Immerse the bowl in a pan or skillet of water on the stove, and bring the water to a simmer. Beat the eggs over the hot water until they increase in bulk substantially and get foamy. Beat in the orange gelatin mixture. Remove the pan from heat and let it cool to room temperature.

5. Stir in the orange rind and almond extract. Whip the cream, and fold the whipped cream into the mixture.

6. Using a pastry bag, pipe the filling into the tart shells. Garnish each with 2 blanched almonds, and refrigerate for at least 2 hours to set. When gelatin sets firm, the tarts are ready to serve.

Piecrust

This basic recipe is the first step in preparing all the various pies that follow. The quantity is designed for making two 10-inch, 1-crust pies—pies without a top crust. Make sure you have 2 pie dishes of this size. I recommend the kind made of ovenproof glass, because you can see the color of the crust on the bottom and sides as it bakes with no guesswork.

    4 cups sifted all-purpose flour
    2 tbsp. sugar
    2 tsp. salt
1½ cups hydrogenated vegetable shortening
  ½ cup ice water

1. Sift the flour, sugar and salt together into a mixing bowl.

2. Cut the shortening into the flour mixture and toss with your fingers until the dough has the appearance of little white balls.

3. Sprinkle the ice water over the dough, a little at a time, and keep mixing the dough, until all the water has been added. Gather the dough into a ball, knead it a little, and gather it again into a ball. Wrap it in wax paper and refrigerate until ready to use.

4. Divide the dough into two portions. Roll out each portion on a lightly floured board to a thickness of about ⅛ inch.

5. Slip one sheet of dough into the pie dish, press it down so that there are no air bubbles between crust and dish, trim off the edges, and press the lip all around with the tines of a fork or the back of a knife blade in a decorative pattern. Prick the bottom of the crust at 1-inch intervals with a fork. Refrigerate until ready to bake pie.

6. Repeat the process with the second half of the dough, filling the second pie dish.

Apple Pie

---

  1 recipe Piecrust (p. 270)
 12 large firm apples
  3 cups sugar
  2 tsp. salt
  7 tbsp. flour
  ¾ cup heavy cream

1. Make piecrust and use it to line two 10-inch pie dishes.

2. Peel and core the apples and cut into chunks into a bowl.

3. Combine the sugar, salt, flour and cream in a bowl and blend well. Pour this mixture over the bowl of apple chunks and toss to mix well.

4. Preheat oven to 375°.

5. Fill each crust-lined pie dish with half the mixture. Cover the pies with aluminum foil, tucking it all around.

6. Bake 45 minutes in the preheated oven. Remove foil, and continue baking for another 15 minutes.

7. Remove from oven and let the pies cool until ready to serve. If you serve them hot from the oven it will be difficult to keep the filling from running.

Apricot Pie

4 cans, 1 lb. each, apricot halves
1¼ cups flour
2 cups sugar
¾ tsp. grated nutmeg
¼ lb. butter (1 stick)
1 recipe Piecrust (p. 270)
3 tbsp. lemon juice

1. Drain the apricot halves.

2. Mix the flour, sugar and nutmeg together. Cut the butter into this mixture in small pieces, and mix with a fork.

3. Prepare the 2 unbaked pie shells as directed.

4. Preheat oven to 400°.

5. Arrange the apricot halves in the unbaked pie shells. Sprinkle half the lemon juice over the apricots in each pie. Spread a thin coating of the sugar and flour mixture over the surfaces of the pies.

6. Bake in the preheated oven for 45 minutes.

7. You can serve these pies hot, or at room temperature, or refrigerated.

Banana Custard Pie

 1 recipe Piecrust (p. 270)
10 eggs
 3 cups heavy cream
 3 cups milk
1½ cups sugar
 1 tsp. salt
 2 tsp. vanilla extract
 4 cups thinly sliced bananas

1. Preheat oven to 450°.

2. Prepare the pie shells as directed. Bake them in the pre-heated oven for 15 minutes. Remove from oven and let stand at room temperature.

3. Beat the eggs in a mixing bowl, just long enough to combine yolks and whites.

4. Combine the cream and milk in a saucepan, and bring almost to the boiling point over medium heat. Remove from heat and let it cool for a few minutes.

5. Add the sugar, salt and vanilla to the mixture, stir, then pour into the beaten eggs, and mix to blend well.

6. Preheat oven to 350°.

7. Prepare 2 pans of warm water large enough to hold the pie dishes with enough water to reach two thirds of the way up the sides of the pie dishes.

8. Divide the sliced bananas into halves and arrange a layer of the slices on the bottom of each piecrust. Use up all the slices. Pour the custard over the banana slices, filling the pies.

9. Set the pies in the pans of water, then into the preheated

oven. Bake for 40 minutes. Test the custard with a cake needle, which should come out clean.

10. Remove pies from the oven, let them cool to room temperature, then chill in the refrigerator until time to serve.

Coconut Custard Pie

1 recipe Piecrust (p. 270)
10 eggs
1½ cups sugar
½ tsp. salt
1 tbsp. vanilla extract
6 cups milk
2 cups shredded coconut

1. Prepare two 10-inch unbaked pie shells as directed.

2. Preheat oven to 450°.

3. Using an electric mixer, beat together the eggs, sugar, salt and vanilla.

4. Scald the milk (almost to the boiling point), then with the mixer running, pour the milk slowly into the egg mixture, beating the whole time.

5. Remove mixer, sprinkle in the shredded coconut, stir it in with a spoon, then pour half the custard into each of the pie shells.

6. Bake the pies in the preheated oven for 15 minutes. When ready, a cake needle inserted into the custard should come out clean.

7. After removing pies from oven, let them cool to room temperature, then refrigerate them. Serve chilled.

Blueberry Pie

1 recipe Piecrust (p. 270)
2 cups sugar
½ cup cornstarch
¼ tsp. salt
½ cup water
8 cups fresh blueberries
2 tbsp. butter
3 tbsp. lemon juice
2 cups heavy cream, chilled

1. Preheat oven to 450°.
2. Prepare piecrust, and bake the pie shells in the preheated oven for 15 minutes until golden brown. Remove from oven and let stand at room temperature.
3. Put the sugar, cornstarch, salt, water, and 6 cups of the blueberries in a saucepan. Bring to a boil over medium heat, stirring until the mixture thickens substantially. Off heat add the butter and lemon juice, then let the filling cool.
4. When filling is cool, stir into it the remaining 2 cups of blueberries.
5. Fill the pie shells with the blueberry mixture.
6. Whip the chilled cream until it forms soft peaks. Pipe the whipped cream through a pastry bag to make a decorative pattern on top of the pies. Refrigerate until ready to serve.

Cherry Pie

10 cups fresh cherries, pitted
2½ cups sugar
¼ tsp. salt
½ cup flour

(cont'd)

2 tbsp. lemon juice
1 recipe Piecrust (p. 270)
5 tbsp. butter
1 recipe Red-Currant Glaze (p. 267)

1. Toss together in a bowl the cherries, sugar, salt, flour and lemon juice.

2. Prepare the piecrust and line the 2 pie dishes as directed.

3. Preheat the oven to 375°.

4. Put half the cherry mixture in each pie shell. Dot the surface of the cherry filling with butter.

5. Bake in the preheated oven for 45 minutes.

6. Remove the pies from the oven and let them cool.

7. While they are cooling, prepare the Red-Currant Glaze and pour half of it over each pie, making sure you get an even coat over the entire surface.

8. You can serve the pies warm, or cool them and serve at room temperature, but do not refrigerate.

Cream Puffs

1 cup milk
¼ lb. butter (1 stick)
1 tsp. salt
1 tbsp. sugar
2 cups all-purpose flour
8 eggs
1 recipe French Pastry Cream (p. 266)

1. Put the milk in a saucepan and melt the butter in it over medium heat, without letting the milk boil. Dissolve the salt and the sugar in the hot milk.

2. When these ingredients are combined, turn up heat; have the flour sifted into a small bowl and ready to add. Just as the milk begins to come to a boil, dump in all the flour.

3. Turn off heat, and mix the flour and liquid together quickly until it forms a smooth paste. Transfer the mixture to a mixing bowl and let it cool to lukewarm.

4. Beat the eggs into the batter, one or two at a time. The result should be a smooth, shiny dough.

5. Preheat the oven to 400°.

6. Using a pastry bag, squeeze the dough through a wide tube onto a greased cookie sheet or sheets into whatever-size cream puffs you desire. They may range from 1 to 2 inches in diameter. Be careful to space them apart so that they do not bake connected to each other.

7. Bake them in the preheated oven for 25 minutes, or until they puff up and turn a light golden color. Turn off the oven, cut a small slit in the side of each puff with a knife, and put them back in the oven to dry the insides. Transfer the cream puffs to a cooling rack to cool before filling.

8. Prepare the French Pastry Cream. Fill the cream puffs with the cream by piping it through a pastry bag into the slit at the side of each puff.

Optional: You can substitute sugar and vanilla-flavored whipped cream for the pastry cream.

Almond Coffee Ring

    1 envelope active dry yeast (check date on package)
    ⅓ cup lukewarm water (105° to 115°)
    1 cup superfine granulated sugar
 1½ cups milk
    ⅜ lb. butter (1½ sticks)
    3 egg yolks, beaten well
    1 tsp. salt
    1 cup white raisins
    6 cups all-purpose flour, sifted
    8 tbsp. melted butter   (cont'd)

1 *cup slivered blanched almonds*
1 *egg white*
2 *tbsp. granulated sugar*

1. Put the yeast in the lukewarm water with 1 teaspoon of the superfine sugar and stir.

2. In a saucepan scald the milk. When it has almost reached the boiling point, put the ⅜ pound butter in it off the heat and let butter melt, stirring occasionally.

3. Combine in a bowl the yeast mixture, the scalded milk and butter, the rest of the superfine sugar, the egg yolks, salt, raisins and 2 cups of the flour. Beat with an electric mixer until very smooth. Continue beating, adding the rest of the flour a little at a time. The mixture will get very thick and require increasing the power setting on the mixer. At one point, the mixer will no longer be powerful enough. Then continue adding the flour, but knead by hand.

4. Form the kneaded dough into a ball, brush the top of it with a little melted butter, and put it in a large bowl. Cover the bowl with a damp towel and put it in a warm place to rise. The dough should double in bulk in about 2 hours.

5. When the dough has risen sufficiently, separate it into halves, and knead each half for a minute or two. Place on a board covered with the damp towel and let stand for 15 minutes.

6. Roll out each half of the dough into a long rectangle, about 8 inches wide and ¼ inch thick. Brush the top with melted butter and sprinkle on an even layer of slivered almonds, using ¼ cup of the almonds for each half.

7. Roll up each section of dough to produce a long, thin cylinder.

8. Butter 1 or 2 baking sheets with the remaining melted butter. Put the 2 rolls of dough on the baking sheets, and curve the ends around to meet and form 2 rings. Slash the tops with a sharp knife at an angle every 2 inches.

9. Beat the egg white in a little bowl with 1 tablespoon water. Brush this mixture over the tops of the rings.

10. Sprinkle the rings with the remaining slivered almonds, using ¼ cup on each. Sprinkle 1 tablespoon of granulated sugar over each ring.

11. Cover the rings with damp towels and allow them to rise again until they double in size.

12. Preheat oven to 375°.

13. When the rings have doubled in size, bake them in the preheated oven for about 30 minutes until they are golden brown. Remove from oven and serve hot, or let them cool to serve later.

Apple Strudel

For this recipe the best kind of work area is a table at least the size of a card table covered with a large pastry cloth. This is needed for the paper-thin strudel dough to be stretched properly.

  5 *eggs*
  ½ *lb. butter (2 sticks), softened*
  ½ *tsp. salt*
2½ *cups all-purpose flour, sifted*
 10 *medium-size apples*
1¼ *cups chopped blanched almonds*
  5 *tbsp. chopped citron*
  ½ *cup dried currants*
1¼ *cups sugar*
  4 *tsp. ground cinnamon*

1. Beat the eggs in a mixing bowl with half the butter until smooth. Continue beating and add the salt, then the flour, little by little, until all the flour is incorporated.

2. Knead the dough vigorously for about 30 minutes. It can be done with a dough hook attachment to an electric mixer, or else by hand. The dough should be smooth, shiny and very elastic.

3. Roll out the dough on the pastry cloth very thin, then

stretch out the dough to the limit of its tension, weighing it down at the corners with whatever is handy.

4. Peel, core and chop the apples.

5. Make a line of chopped apples about 3 inches in from one of the long edges of the dough. Sprinkle the almonds, then the citron, currants, sugar and cinnamon over the line of apples. Distribute 3 tablespoons of the butter over the line of filling.

6. Fold the 2 shorter ends of the dough in about 2 inches, just far enough to cover the ends of the line of filling. Then roll up jelly roll style.

7. Preheat oven to 400°.

8. Spread the remaining softened butter over the top of the rolled-up strudel. Cut the strudel into halves and pinch the cut ends together to avoid loss of filling.

9. Butter a large jelly roll pan, and lay the 2 strudels, side by side, in the pan.

10. Bake in the preheated oven for about 40 minutes, or until the pastry has turned a deep brown. Transfer to a serving platter and serve hot.

Polish Babka

For this recipe you will need two 7-inch Kugelhupf pans. Another consideration is that the recipe requires 18 egg yolks. Instead of wasting the whites of the eggs, I recommend planning to make meringues or soufflés, which require many whites and few yolks.

FOR THE FONDANT ICING:

3 cups granulated sugar
5 tbsp. clear corn syrup
1 cup water

1. Stir the ingredients in a heavy saucepan over medium

heat until fully dissolved. Make sure no sugar crystals are left clinging to the sides of the pan. This can be assured by covering the saucepan tightly and letting the resulting steam inside clean the sides.

2. Insert a candy thermometer and boil the syrup to a temperature of 240°. Remove from heat immediately and allow the bubbling to subside.

3. Pour out the syrup into a shallow jelly roll pan or roasting pan. Let it cool off a few minutes until you can touch it without burning your hand.

4. Stir the mixture vigorously with a wooden spoon. It will turn white and stiff. Gather it into a mass, then knead it thoroughly until it becomes smooth and creamy. When all of it has been kneaded well, wrap it in a moist towel and let it stand for a couple of hours.

5. Unwrap, knead well again, and place in an airtight container at room temperature until ready to use.

FOR THE BABKA:

7 *cups all-purpose flour*
3 *cups milk*
5 *packages active dry yeast*
½ *cup lukewarm water (105° to 115°)*
⅔ *cup sugar*
1 *tsp. salt*
18 *egg yolks*
½ *lb. butter (2 sticks), softened*
¾ *cup white raisins*
¾ *cup dark raisins*
½ *cup rum*
   fondant icing

1. Put 2 cups of flour in a mixing bowl. Heat the milk and add it to the flour. Beat the mixture with an electric mixer until smooth.

2. Combine the yeast with the lukewarm water, the sugar and salt. Stir until the yeast is dissolved and then let it stand until

it foams up and begins to bubble a little, giving off a strong odor of yeast. Beat this yeast mixture into the flour and milk mixture in the mixing bowl.

3. Beat the egg yolks, softened butter and the rest of the flour into the dough.

4. The dough must be kneaded thoroughly, either by hand or with a dough hook attachment to the electric mixer. If you do it by hand, try to get some help, because you should work the dough for at least 30 minutes. If by machine, of course, it's easy. The resulting dough should be smooth, shiny and elastic, and should not stick to your finger.

5. Cover the dough with a damp towel and let it rise in a warm place until it doubles in bulk.

6. Preheat oven to 375°.

7. Punch down the dough and fold in the raisins so that they are well distributed.

8. Butter the Kugelhupf pans. Divide the dough into halves and put each half in one of the pans.

9. Cover the pans and let the dough rise until it fills the pans.

10. Bake in the preheated oven for 45 minutes, until the babkas are golden brown.

11. Remove from oven and turn out onto cooling racks.

12. Add the rum to the fondant icing in a saucepan, heat it over low heat until it is smooth and creamy and will pour, but it should stick to the cakes. Do not try to hurry this step, and don't let the fondant get too hot or too liquid.

13. Pour the fondant over the cakes, being careful to use about half on each. Pour it directly from the pan around onto the top edges of the cakes so that the tops are completely glazed and the icing falls down the sides in random drops. Do not attempt to cover every inch of the cakes. When the icing cools the cakes are ready to serve.

9

Other Desserts

Mixed Fruit Compote

---

   1 *cup sugar*
2½ *cups water*
   2 *tbsp. lemon juice*
   2 *tsp. vanilla extract*
   4 *pears*
   4 *peaches*
   6 *apricots*
 ½ *fresh pineapple*

   1. Combine the sugar, water, lemon juice and vanilla in a large saucepan and bring to a simmer. Cook at a simmer for 5 minutes.

   2. Peel, quarter and core the pears. Dip the peaches into boiling water, then hold them under cold running water, and peel. Cut them into halves and remove the pits. Do the same for the apricots as for the pears. Cut away the prickly skin of the pineapple, then cut out the hard white core; cut the remaining edible portions into chunks.

3. Slip all the fruit into the syrup and cook gently, timing 10 minutes after syrup begins to simmer again.

4. After cooking, let the compote cool to room temperature, then refrigerate until serving time.

Melon Basket

1 whole watermelon
1 recipe Tropical Fruit Salad (below)

1. Wash the watermelon to remove any dirt.

2. Using a sharp knife, cut a thin lengthwise slice from the outside of the rind to create a flat base on which the watermelon can stand without rolling.

3. Set the melon on this flat surface. Cut 2 wedges away from the top half, leaving a "basket handle" running lengthwise on top. Now, scoop out all the melon meat from the inside of the melon, leaving only a basket made of the rind.

4. Using a melon-ball cutter, make watermelon balls out of all the larger pieces of melon you have removed.

5. Mix the watermelon balls into the tropical fruit salad, toss, and then fill the basket with it. If you like, add a sprinkling of sugar over the top before serving. This basket would make a fine centerpiece for a buffet.

Tropical Fruit Salad

1 whole pineapple
2 mangoes
4 papayas
3 bananas
4 oranges

2 grapefruits
2 cups shredded fresh coconut
2 cups sugar

1. Cut the top off the pineapple and trim away the prickly skin with a sharp knife. Cut out the hard white core, then cut the remaining edible portions into 1-inch chunks.

2. Peel the mangoes with a sharp paring knife, and cut into bite-size pieces, working your way down to the pit.

3. Peel the papayas, cut them into halves, scoop out the seeds, then cut into bite-size pieces.

4. Peel and slice the bananas.

5. Peel and section the oranges; cut each section into halves.

6. Do the same for the grapefruits as for the oranges.

7. Combine all the fruits with the shredded coconut and sugar, toss well, and refrigerate for several hours. Serve cold.

Poached Peaches

---

12 large fresh peaches
1½ cups sugar
4 cups water
1 tbsp. lemon juice
1 tsp. vanilla extract

1. Bring about 3 quarts of water to a boil in a saucepan. One by one, spear the peaches on a fork, dip them into the boiling water, then hold them under running water for a moment. Peel them with a small sharp paring knife, cut them into halves, and remove the pits.

2. Combine the sugar, water, lemon juice and vanilla extract in a large saucepan. Bring mixture to a boil, and simmer for 5 minutes to reduce volume.

3. Add the peach halves to the syrup and simmer them un-

til they are tender, about 10 minutes. When they are ready, remove them from the syrup with a slotted spoon and transfer them to a serving bowl.

4. Serve hot, with raspberry sauce (below).

Raspberry Sauce

    4 cups fresh raspberries (or substitute frozen ones)
    ¼ cup sugar
    2 tsp. lemon juice
    2 tbsp. kirsch

Combine half the ingredients in a blender and run at medium speed for 15 seconds, then do the same with the other half. Serve the sauce with the hot poached peaches.

Pears Poached in Wine

    ¾ cup water
    2 tbsp. lemon juice
    12 firm ripe pears
    3 cups dry red wine
    1 cup sugar

1. Mix the water and lemon juice and have it ready.

2. Peel the pears very carefully, quarter and core them, and slip the quarters into the lemon juice and water mixture.

3. In a large saucepan bring the wine and sugar to a simmer. Add the pears and liquid to the wine, reduce heat, and cook slowly for 10 to 12 minutes, until pears are tender but not falling apart.

4. Remove the pear quarters with a slotted spoon and put them in a serving bowl.

5. Continue cooking the poaching liquid until it has been reduced by half and thickened slightly. If it is still too liquid, combine a tablespoon of arrowroot with a little water, dissolve the arrowroot completely in the water, then add it to the wine mixture.

6. Chill the pears and the wine syrup and pour the syrup over them in the serving bowl just before serving.

Baked Apples with Currant Jelly

12 large tart apples
 3 cups red-currant jelly
¼ lb. butter (1 stick), softened
 2 cups boiling water
½ cup granulated sugar

1. Preheat oven to 375°.

2. Wash the apples well. Using a cylindrical apple corer, cut out the cores to within ¼ inch of the bottom, but do not cut through all the way. Cut away 1 strip of skin about ½ inch wide from the apples at the top, all the way around.

3. Fill the core holes with currant jelly. Spread the upper parts of the apples with the softened butter. Arrange the apples in an ovenproof baking dish. Combine the boiling water with the sugar. Pour this into the pan around (not upon) the apples.

4. Bake in preheated oven for about 45 minutes, until the apples are tender but have not lost their shape and collapsed. Baste with the pan liquid once or twice during the baking.

5. Remove from oven and either serve hot or chill in the refrigerator until serving time.

Optional: Serve with whipped cream or with Vanilla Sauce (p. 304).

Baked Bananas with Cinnamon

12 large firm bananas
 2 tbsp. lemon juice
¼ lb. butter (1 stick)
 2 tbsp. rum
⅔ cup light brown sugar
 2 tbsp. ground cinnamon

1. Preheat oven to 375°.

2. Peel the bananas, and carefully cut them lengthwise into halves.

3. Arrange the bananas, flat side down, in an ovenproof baking dish. Sprinkle the banana halves with lemon juice.

4. Melt the butter with the rum, and pour the mixture over the bananas. Mix the sugar with the cinnamon and sprinkle it over the bananas.

5. Bake the bananas in the preheated oven for 15 minutes, basting with the pan liquid once or twice.

6. Remove from oven and serve hot, spooning some pan liquid over each serving.

Fresh Fruit Gelatins

It's easy to make fruit gelatin by using powdered, chemically flavored, artificially colored products from the market, but the taste does not compare to the taste of gelatin made with fresh fruit.

The recipes below require either one 12-cup mold or two 6-cup molds. You may even use 12 small molds or cups if you wish. I have not attempted to enumerate all the possible combinations, but slices of fruit can always be added to the gelatin before chilling it, and different flavors of gelatin can be combined in one mold by first allowing one flavor to jell solid in the half-filled mold, then adding a layer of a different flavor which has also chilled somewhat, but can still be poured. Do not pour hot gelatin into a cold one of a different flavor because then the bottom one will melt and mix and you will lose the clear line between the two.

Orange Gelatin

 5 envelopes unflavored gelatin
10 cups strained fresh orange juice
 1 cup sugar
 3 tbsp. grated orange rind
 4 oranges, peeled, pitted and cut into slices or sections

1. Dissolve the gelatin in 1 cup of the orange juice.

2. Cook the remaining orange juice with the sugar and grated rind in a saucepan until the sugar is completely melted. Add the softened gelatin and bring to a boil for a moment, then immediately remove from heat.

3. Pour hot mixture into molds and refrigerate.

4. When the gelatin is quite cold and has begun to thicken but is not set, insert the orange pieces in a decorative pattern. Allow to set completely before unmolding to serve.

Lemon Gelatin

Follow instructions for Orange Gelatin (preceding recipe), with the following changes: instead of 10 cups of juice, use 3 cups lemon juice and 9 cups water, and add 1 cup sugar; substitute banana slices for the orange slices; substitute 1 tablespoon grated lemon rind for the orange rind.

Raspberry Gelatin

Follow instructions for Orange Gelatin with the following changes: for the orange juice substitute the liquid resulting from boiling 4 cups of raspberries with 8 cups water and straining out the pulp and seeds; omit orange rind, and substitute fresh raspberries for the orange slices.

Vanilla Custard

4½ cups milk
  6 whole eggs
  6 additional egg yolks
  1 cup sugar
⅛ tsp. salt
  1 tbsp. vanilla extract
     softened butter for custard cups

1. Preheat oven to 325°.

2. Bring the milk to just below the boiling point in a saucepan.

3. Beat the whole eggs, extra egg yolks, sugar and salt together in a mixing bowl with an electric mixer. Continue beating, adding the vanilla, then the hot milk, a little at a time.

4. Butter 12 custard cups each holding 1 cup. Strain the custard into the cups.

5. Set the cups in a pan (or two) of hot water reaching at least halfway up the sides of the cups after they are all immersed. Bake in the preheated oven for 1 hour, until a cake needle inserted in the center of the cup comes out clean.

6. Remove from oven and from hot water, and let the custard cool to room temperature. You can serve them at room temperature or refrigerated.

Chocolate Custard

Follow the directions for Vanilla Custard (preceding recipe), reducing recipe by 2 egg yolks and adding 4 ounces of melted semisweet cooking chocolate to step 3.

Coffee Custard

Follow the instructions for Vanilla Custard, substituting 1 cup of very strong coffee for 1 cup of the milk in the recipe.

Caramel Custard

Follow directions for Vanilla Custard, with the following addition: make a syrup of 1½ cups sugar and ¾ cup water and cook until it has a light brown tint; pour this syrup to the depth of ⅛ inch into each custard cup before straining in the custard. Reserve remaining syrup to pour over custard when served.

Chocolate Mousse

8 oz. semisweet chocolate
¼ tsp. salt
¼ cup water
5 eggs, separated
2 tsp. vanilla extract
1 cup heavy cream, chilled
1 tbsp. sugar

1. In the top part of a double boiler, break the chocolate into small pieces, add the salt and ¼ cup water to it, and cook it over simmering water, stirring until the chocolate melts.

2. Separately in a bowl, beat the egg yolks until they are pale yellow, then add the vanilla extract to them. Continue beating the yolks, and slowly pour into them the melted chocolate mixture. Blend well.

3. In another bowl, beat the egg whites until they form soft peaks.

4. Whip the heavy cream with the sugar in another bowl until it is stiff.

5. Fold into the chocolate mixture first the egg whites, then the cream. Fold only enough to combine and create an even light brown color.

6. Transfer mousse to a large decorative dessert bowl and chill until serving time, or spoon into individual stemmed glasses and chill before serving.

Strawberry Mousse

> 2 *quarts strawberries*
> 1½ *cups sugar*
> 6 *egg whites*
> ⅛ *tsp. salt*
> 1 *tsp. vanilla extract*
> 1 *cup heavy cream, chilled*
> 12 *maraschino or candied cherries*

1. Wash and hull the strawberries. Run them through a blender or food mill to make a purée, then mix the purée with about half the sugar.

2. Beat the egg whites with the salt to soft peaks. Beat into them all but 2 tablespoons of the remaining sugar.

3. Add the vanilla extract and the remaining sugar to the

chilled heavy cream, and whip it to soft peaks.

4. Fold the strawberry purée into the egg whites, then fold the whipped cream into that mixture. Spoon the mousse into individual stemmed glasses, top each with a cherry for decoration, and chill until serving time.

Chocolate Bavarian Cream

For this and the following Bavarian Cream recipes you will require either one 12-cup mold or two 6-cup molds. If you use a tall mold, there is always a little risk that the center of the cream may sink when you unmold it. It is safer to use less-deep decorative molds or ring molds, which do not require as much gelatin to hold their shape when unmolded. You can also use 12 individual molds if you prefer.

    4 envelopes unflavored gelatin
    ¾ cup lukewarm water
    1 tbsp. vanilla extract
    8 eggs, separated
 1½ cups plus 1½ tbsp. sugar
    1 tbsp. cornstarch
    5 oz. semisweet cooking chocolate
 2½ cups milk
    ¼ tsp. salt
    ¾ cup heavy cream, chilled
    ¼ cup Cognac

1. Dissolve the gelatin in the lukewarm water and vanilla extract.

2. Using an electric mixer beat the egg yolks and 1½ cups sugar together until they are pale yellow and stiffened. Beat in the cornstarch. Leave the mixer in place.

3. Break the chocolate into small pieces, or grate it. Bring

the milk almost to a boil in a saucepan with the pieces of chocolate, stirring to melt the chocolate as the milk heats up. Turn off heat just before the boiling point is reached.

4. Start up the electric mixer in the egg yolks again, and pour in the hot milk and chocolate slowly, beating the whole time.

5. Pour the whole mixture into a saucepan, and stir it over medium heat until it gets very thick. Mix in the softened gelatin and vanilla, then remove from heat.

6. Separately beat the egg whites with 1½ tablespoons sugar and the salt until they form stiff peaks. Fold the egg whites into the chocolate custard, gently, then refrigerate this mixture until cool.

7. Beat the chilled heavy cream until it forms soft peaks, adding the Cognac to it at the very end.

8. Fold the whipped cream into the cooled chocolate mixture, then pour into the mold or molds. Refrigerate the molds for at least 4 hours, until set and firm. You can store the Bavarian cream for up to 2 days before serving.

9. To serve, dip the mold very briefly into very hot water, just long enough to loosen. Cover the top of the mold with your upside-down serving plate, reverse it quickly, and shake slightly to unmold.

Strawberry Bavarian Cream

Follow the instructions for Chocolate Bavarian Cream, with the following changes: use orange juice to dissolve the gelatin instead of water; omit chocolate; run enough hulled strawberries through a blender to make 1½ cups of fresh strawberry purée; fold the purée into the whipped cream before adding it to the custard. Serve the dessert with strawberry syrup and garnish with a few sliced fresh strawberries.

Vanilla Bavarian Cream

Follow the instructions for Chocolate Bavarian Cream, with the following changes: use 10 egg yolks instead of 8; use 2 tablespoons vanilla extract or add 1 scraped-out vanilla bean; omit the chocolate.

Orange Bavarian Cream

Follow the instructions for Chocolate Bavarian Cream, with the following changes: use 10 egg yolks instead of 8; use 1 cup orange juice instead of water to dissolve gelatin; add 2 tablespoons of grated orange rind to the egg yolks, and omit chocolate and vanilla; substitute orange liqueur for the Cognac.

Coffee Bavarian Cream

Follow the instructions for Chocolate Bavarian Cream, with the following changes: use 10 egg yolks instead of 8; use 1 cup of very strong coffee instead of water to dissolve the gelatin; add 1 tablespoon of instant coffee powder to the egg yolks, and omit the chocolate.

Ice Cream Molds

There are many ways of serving ice cream, often requiring additional ingredients and sauces which tend to smother the taste of the ice cream itself, but one way which makes this popular dessert look special for parties or entertaining needs no extra ingredients at all. The trick is simply to combine two or more flavors, preferably of contrasting colors, in attractive molds to make a festive dessert. For 12 people you should use a 3-quart mold, or smaller molds whose capacity adds up to at least 3 quarts of ice cream.

1. For a 2-flavor mold, you need 1 3-quart mold and 1 smaller mold of about half that capacity which will fit into the large one without touching the inside edges anywhere. Fill the large mold with 3 pints of one flavor of ice cream. Let it soften in the mold at room temperature.

2. Force the second, smaller mold into the ice cream until it occupies enough space to make the ice cream rise in level to the top of the large mold. Fill the small mold with any objects heavy enough to hold it down in the softened ice cream, then refreeze the whole assembly.

3. When the outside layer is frozen, remove the weights, pour some hot water into the small mold, thus loosening it, and take it out. Fill the remaining cavity with the contrasting colored and flavored ice cream. Freeze again.

4. When you unmold the ice cream and cut into it you will reveal the inside flavor.

Variations: Another technique is to arrange a way of tilting a mold in the freezer. Then alternate layers of 2 or 3 or more flavors of ice cream in it, placing the mold on a slant in the freezer to harden each time before adding the next layer.

When the last layer is put in, set the mold upright for the last freezing to make the bottom level. The effect is a slanted, striped sculpture of ice cream, very effective. You can devise your own methods to prepare variations of this idea without fear of error because even if something slips a little, it will taste good!

Meringues with Ice Cream

     softened butter for greasing cookie sheets
     flour for dusting greased cookie sheets
 10 *egg whites*
 ½ *tsp. salt*
 ½ *tsp. cream of tartar*
2½ *cups superfine granulated sugar*
 2 *quarts ice cream, your favorite*

1. Grease 2 cookie sheets and dust them with flour.
2. Preheat oven to 250°.
3. Using an electric mixer beat the egg whites with the salt and cream of tartar. When they begin to stiffen slightly, continue beating, adding the sugar a little at a time, until it is all beaten in.
4. Using a pastry bag and a plain tube or nozzle, pipe rounds of meringue about 2½ inches in diameter onto the cookie sheets, keeping the rounds at least 1 inch apart from each other. There should be enough for 24 rounds.
5. Turn off the oven heat, and put the cookie sheets in the oven. Leave in oven for 4 hours without opening the door. After 4 hours, touch a meringue to see if it's firm.
6. To serve, remove rounds from cookie sheets with a spatula. Place each on a dessert plate, top with a scoop of ice cream, and top with second meringue.

Meringue Torte

Follow the instructions for Meringues with Ice Cream (preceding recipe) with the following changes: pipe 4 large rounds of the meringue, two on each cookie sheet, each using a quarter of the mixture; prepare Chocolate Buttercream Filling (following recipe); when cool, spread on the layers, making a 4-layer meringue cake. Keep cake refrigerated until serving time.

Chocolate Buttercream Filling

½ cup superfine granulated sugar
2 tbsp. strong coffee
⅛ tsp. cream of tartar
2 egg yolks
¼ lb. unsalted butter (1 stick), softened
2 oz. semisweet cooking chocolate
2 tsp. vanilla extract

1. Heat the sugar with the coffee and cream of tartar until it thickens into a syrup. Temperature of a candy thermometer inserted in the syrup should read 240°. Remove from heat immediately when it reaches this temperature.

2. Using an electric mixer, beat the egg yolks until they thicken, then beat in the syrup, a little at a time, until it is all absorbed. Beat in the soft butter, a little at a time.

3. Separately, break the chocolate into pieces, and combine with the vanilla extract and about 1 tablespoon of water. Melt in a saucepan over low heat, stirring constantly to prevent burning.

4. Beat melted chocolate into the previous mixture, then refrigerate.

Rice Pudding with Raisins

2½ cups milk
¼ tsp. salt
¾ cup granulated sugar

2 tbsp. softened butter
2 tsp. vanilla extract
6 eggs
1 tsp. grated lemon rind
1 tbsp. lemon juice
1 cup white raisins
4 cups cooked rice
  softened butter for baking dish
1 cup graham cracker crumbs

1. In a large mixing bowl beat together the milk, salt, sugar, butter, vanilla and eggs. Stir in the lemon rind, lemon juice and raisins.

2. Add the cooked rice to the mixture and mix well.

3. Preheat oven to 325°.

4. Butter a large deep baking dish, and coat bottom and sides with graham cracker crumbs.

5. Pour the pudding into the dish and bake in a preheated oven for 1 hour and 10 minutes.

6. Serve hot, or allow to cool to room temperature, then refrigerate until serving time.

7. Serve with a bottled fruit syrup, such as boysenberry or raspberry syrup.

Tapioca Pudding

6 cups milk
1 tbsp. vanilla extract
4 eggs, separated
1 cup plus 2 tbsp. sugar
½ tsp. salt
½ cup quick-cooking tapioca
¾ cup heavy cream, chilled

1. In a saucepan combine 5 cups of the milk with the vanilla

extract, and heat over medium heat without boiling.

2. Beat the egg yolks in a bowl with the other cup of milk, ½ cup of the sugar and the salt. Add the egg yolk mixture to the hot milk, then add in the tapioca.

3. Reduce heat to low, and continue stirring and cooking until the mixture thickens considerably. This should take about 15 minutes. Turn off heat.

4. In a separate bowl beat the egg whites with another ½ cup of sugar until they form soft peaks. Fold the soft egg whites into the hot tapioca mixture.

5. Serve warm, garnished with the heavy cream, whipped with remaining 2 tablespoons sugar.

Optional: Omit the whipped cream and serve the pudding with canned stewed fruits or berries.

Dessert Crêpes Surprise

---

  2 cups flour
  1 tbsp. superfine granulated sugar
⅛ tsp. salt
  4 eggs
  2 cups milk
  3 tbsp. melted butter, cooled
    softened butter for frying crêpes
  2 cups apricot jam, rubbed through a sieve
¼ cup water
  2 quarts vanilla ice cream
  1 cup slivered blanched almonds

Note: For this recipe you must have a 7- or 8-inch crêpe pan.

1. Using a mixing bowl and an electric mixer, beat together the flour, sugar, salt, eggs, milk and cooled melted butter. Let

this batter stand for 30 minutes and mix again for a few seconds before using.

2. Heat oven to about 200°, and place an ovenproof pie dish in it. As each crêpe is made you will put it into this dish to keep warm until all are done.

3. Heat the crêpe pan over medium heat. To make each crêpe, put about ½ tablespoon of softened butter in the pan and swirl it around to coat entire surface. Spoon in about 2 tablespoons batter, or a little more, and swirl it around to make a thin coating over the entire cooking surface. This step must be done quickly; you can add a little more batter if necessary. Be prepared to experiment the first time and waste 1 or 2 crêpes.

4. Cook the crêpe until the edges start to brown. Flip it over quickly with a spatula and cook the other side for 30 seconds to 1 minute, depending on the thickness. Reverse into the warm dish in the oven. Continue this process until all the batter has been used. The recipe should yield about 24 crêpes.

5. Heat the sieved apricot jam with the water in a saucepan and mix well. Turn off heat when syrup is hot and runny.

6. After the main course is cleared from the table, assemble the dessert. Put each warm crêpe down on a working surface, place a small scoop of ice cream on it, and fold over the flaps of the crêpe to cover the ice cream. Slip the crêpe onto a dessert plate. Repeat to make 1 portion of 2 crêpes. Pour a little hot apricot syrup over the crêpes and sprinkle with some slivered almonds. You will need someone to help serve each portion as soon as assembled until everyone is served. This is not the kind of dessert you can serve on a large platter for everyone to help himself.

Crêpes Suzette

1 recipe Dessert Crêpes Surprise (p. 300) (omitting ice cream, almonds and apricot jam)

2 oranges
(cont'd)

10 pieces of lump sugar
¼ lb. unsalted butter (1 stick)
1 tbsp. lemon juice
½ cup Cointreau
½ cup Grand Marnier
½ cup Cognac

1. Prepare the crêpes and keep warm according to the recipe instructions.

2. Rub the oranges with the lumps of sugar to impregnate the sugar with the oil of the orange skin. Mash the lumps of sugar.

3. Squeeze the oranges and strain the juice.

4. Combine the butter, orange sugar, orange juice and lemon juice in a small saucepan and cook for long enough to melt sugar. Add the Cointreau and Grand Marnier and heat almost to boiling, stirring well.

5. Brush the warm crêpes with the hot sauce, roll them, and place them in a large ovenproof serving dish or chafing dish.

6. In the dining room, pour the Cognac over the crêpes, ignite it, and serve quickly, 2 crêpes per person for twelve.

Dessert Waffles

These waffles are heavier and richer than the normal breakfast-type waffles. They can be used as a dessert combined with whipped cream, various syrups or various berries, or they can be topped with a scoop of ice cream.

6 eggs, separated
3 cups sifted cake flour
¼ cup sugar
1 tbsp. baking powder
2 tsp. salt
3 cups heavy cream

1. Preheat the waffle iron and have a platter ready to receive the completed waffles in a warm oven.

2. Beat all the ingredients except the egg whites together in a bowl with an electric mixer or a wire whisk until a smooth batter results.

3. Whip the egg whites in a separate bowl until they make soft peaks.

4. Fold the egg whites carefully into the batter, being careful not to crush too many air bubbles out of them.

5. Bake the waffles in the electric waffle iron according to the directions for your appliance. When they are golden brown and ready, transfer to the warm platter and continue. The recipe should yield 12 large waffles, depending on the size of your waffle iron.

Batter for Fruit Fritters

    2 cups all-purpose flour
    ¼ cup superfine granulated sugar
    ½ tsp. salt
    2 tsp. baking powder
    2 eggs
 1½ cups milk
    2 tbsp. melted butter

1. Sift the flour, sugar, salt and baking powder together.

2. Beat the eggs and milk together, then add the melted butter to the mixture.

3. Mix the liquid into the flour mixture and beat to a smooth batter.

4. Batter is ready for use for fritters. Refrigerate if you are not going to use it right away, then beat again before using.

Orange Sauce for Fritters

2 tbsp. cornstarch
1 cup sugar
2 cups orange juice, strained
1 cup orange marmalade, rubbed through a sieve or lique-
    fied in a blender
5 tbsp. butter
1 tsp. vanilla extract

1. Mix the cornstarch with the sugar in a saucepan, then add the orange juice, and cook over medium heat, stirring until sugar is dissolved and syrup is clear.

2. Stir in the sieved marmalade, butter and vanilla, and continue heating until butter melts. Remove from heat and serve.

Vanilla Sauce for Fritters

¼ cup sugar
1 tbsp. cornstarch
2 egg yolks
2 cups milk
2 tsp. vanilla extract

1. In a saucepan mix the sugar and cornstarch. Beat in the egg yolks with a wire whisk. Heat over low heat, beating constantly, then add the milk and the vanilla.

2. Continue beating until the sauce thickens. Remove from heat and cool. When cool, strain before serving.

Apple Fritters

1 tsp. ground cinnamon
½ cup sugar.
8 large apples
¼ cup lemon juice
oil for deep frying
1 recipe Batter for Fruit Fritters (p. 303)

1. Mix the cinnamon and sugar.

2. Peel the apples carefully and then core them with a round corer that cuts a cylinder out of the middle of the apple.

3. Cut the apples into doughnut-shaped slices, about ¼ inch thick. Sprinkle them with half the cinnamon sugar, then with the lemon juice. Let stand for about 1 hour, turning occasionally without breaking the slices.

4. Heat the oil or shortening in your deep fryer to 375°. Use a fat thermometer if the fryer does not have a thermostat.

5. Preheat oven to 450°.

6. Dip the apple slices, a few at a time, into the batter until well coated. Fry them in the hot oil until they are golden brown, turning them once.

7. Transfer them to a baking pan, sprinkle them with the remaining cinnamon sugar, and bake them for just long enough for the sugar to turn into a glaze.

8. Remove and serve hot, with Vanilla or Orange Sauce (see recipes, p. 304).

Banana Fritters

6 bananas
2 tbsp. plus ½ cup sugar
2 tbsp. lemon juice

(cont'd)

    2 tbsp. kirsch
      oil for deep frying
  1 recipe Batter for Fruit Fritters (p. 303)

1. Peel the bananas and cut each into 4 pieces.

2. Sprinkle them with 2 tablespoons sugar, the lemon juice and kirsch.

3. Heat the oil in the deep fryer to 375°, using a fat thermometer if the fryer has no thermostat.

4. Dip the banana pieces, a few at a time, into the batter until they are well coated. Fry them in the hot oil until golden brown.

5. Drain on paper towels, then roll in remaining ½ cup granulated sugar.

6. Serve hot with Vanilla or Orange Sauce (see recipes, p. 304).

Jelly Doughnuts

    1 envelope active dry yeast
    ¼ cup lukewarm water (105° to 115°)
    ¾ cup milk
    4 tbsp. butter
    4 tbsp. sugar
    ½ tsp. salt
    2 eggs
  3½ cups sifted all-purpose flour
    2 cups jelly or jam (your favorite flavor)
     oil or shortening for deep frying
    1 cup plain granulated sugar, or sugar mixed with 1 tbsp.
     ground cinnamon

1. Dissolve the yeast in the lukewarm water. Scald the milk and melt the butter in the milk. Remove from heat and let the milk cool to room temperature.

2. Using an electric mixer or egg beater, mix the yeast with the milk, sugar, salt and eggs. Beat in the flour, a little at a time.

3. Cover the batter with a damp towel, and let it rise in a warm place until doubled in bulk. This should take 1½ to 2 hours.

4. Transfer the dough to a floured board. Roll it out to a thickness of about ¼ inch or a little more, then cut into 2-inch rounds with a cookie cutter. Don't forget to gather up all the scraps after the first cutting, roll them into a ball, roll out the ball, and cut the last few rounds from it.

5. Divide the cut rounds into equal halves. Put 2 or 3 teaspoons of jam or jelly in the center of half the rounds. Moisten the edges of a round with jelly, then top with another round. Pinch the two together, thus enclosing the jelly and forming the doughnuts. Continue until all are filled and paired. Cover the prepared doughnuts with a towel, and let them rise again until they double in size.

6. When they are almost doubled, preheat the oil in your deep fryer to 375°.

7. Fry the doughnuts, only a few at a time, without crowding. Fry until the bottoms are golden brown, then turn them over with tongs or a slotted spoon, and do the other side. Remove them to paper towels to drain. Continue until all are done.

8. Roll the finished doughnuts in the sugar or cinnamon sugar. If you do not serve them right away, store them in an airtight container to stay fresh. Do not refrigerate them. This recipe should yield about 2 dozen.

Index